Modern Data Architectures with Python

A practical guide to building and deploying data pipelines, data warehouses, and data lakes with Python

Brian Lipp

BIRMINGHAM—MUMBAI

Modern Data Architectures with Python

Copyright © 2023 Packt Publishing

All rights reserved. No part of this book may be reproduced, stored in a retrieval system, or transmitted in any form or by any means, without the prior written permission of the publisher, except in the case of brief quotations embedded in critical articles or reviews.

Every effort has been made in the preparation of this book to ensure the accuracy of the information presented. However, the information contained in this book is sold without warranty, either express or implied. Neither the author, nor Packt Publishing or its dealers and distributors, will be held liable for any damages caused or alleged to have been caused directly or indirectly by this book.

Packt Publishing has endeavored to provide trademark information about all of the companies and products mentioned in this book by the appropriate use of capitals. However, Packt Publishing cannot guarantee the accuracy of this information.

Publishing Product Manager: Sanjana Gupta

Book Project Manager: Kirti Pisat

Content Development Editor: Joseph Sunil

Technical Editor: Devanshi Ayare

Copy Editor: Safis Editing

Proofreader: Safis Editing

Indexer: Subalakshmi Govindhan

Production Designer: Jyoti Kadam

DevRel Marketing Coordinator: Vinishka Kalra

First published: September 2023

Production reference: 1300823

Published by Packt Publishing Ltd.

Grosvenor House

11 St Paul's Square

Birmingham

B3 1RB, UK.

ISBN 978-1-80107-049-2

www.packtpub.com

I would like to thank everyone for the project. It's been a long journey, and it's finally done.

– Brian

Joy is wonderful. Through it, one can escape the worst of circumstances.

– The Rebbe of Lubavitch

Contributors

About the author

Brian Lipp is a technology polyglot, engineer, and solution architect with a wide skillset in many technology domains. His programming background has ranged from R, Python, and Scala to Go and Rust development. He has worked on big data systems, data lakes, data warehouses, and backend software engineering. Brian earned a master of science from the Seidenberg School of **Computer Science of Information Systems** (**CSIS**), Pace University, in 2009. He is currently a senior data engineer, working with large tech firms building out data ecosystems.

About the reviewers

Parwaz J Dalvi is a seasoned, accomplished, and Hands-On Engineering and Technology Leader for Data, AI-ML, and Cloud. He has worked as a Chief Enterprise Data Architect, Solutions Architect, Consultant, Teacher, Speaker, and Mentor with more than two decades of experience. He has expertise in working on enterprise-wide business transformation solutions for Data and Cloud, Machine Learning, Artificial Intelligence, Data Science, and Analytics across multiple domains.

Parwaz has architected more than 25 large data warehouse projects. He has previously been associated with companies like Oracle, IBM, and TCS. Parwaz is a TOGAF-certified professional. He has a passion for teaching, course-content design, and research in data and information management.

Anirban Datta is an accomplished Senior Data Engineering Consultant with 18+ years of experience, known for his skills in architecting data domains and crafting solutions using the Azure Databricks platform. With expertise spanning Data Fabric, Data Mesh, and Data Lake architectures, and proficiency in Python, Pyspark, and a multitude of Azure services, Anirban has been instrumental in creating scalable, resilient, and meticulously designed data ecosystems. His expertise ranges from Retail and Oil & Gas to Healthcare, Telecom, and Travel & Tourism industries.

Table of Contents

Preface xv

Part 1: Fundamental Data Knowledge

1

Modern Data Processing Architecture 3

Technical requirements 3
Databases, data warehouses, and data lakes 4
OLTP 4
OLAP 4
Data lakes 4
Event stores 6
File formats 6
Data platform architecture at a high level 8

Comparing the Lambda and Kappa architectures 10
Lambda architecture 10
Kappa architecture 11
Lakehouse and Delta architectures 12
Lakehouses 13
The seven central tenets 13
The medallion data pattern and the Delta architecture 14
Data mesh theory and practice 16
Defining terms 18
The four principles of data mesh 18
Summary 19
Practical lab 19
Solution 20

2

Understanding Data Analytics 21

Technical requirements 21
Setting up your environment 22
Python 22
venv 22
Graphviz 22
Workflow initialization 22
Cleaning and preparing your data 23
Duplicate values 23

Working with nulls	24	**Data modeling patterns**	**35**
Using RegEx	26	Relational	35
Outlier identification	27	**Dimensional modeling**	**38**
Casting columns	28	Key terms	38
Fixing column names	29		
Complex data types	29	**OBT**	**40**
Data documentation	**32**	**Practical lab**	**40**
diagrams	32	Loading the problem data	40
Data lineage graphs	33	Solution	41
		Summary	**41**

Part 2: Data Engineering Toolset

3

Apache Spark Deep Dive 45

Technical requirements	**45**	Job creation pipeline	51
Setting up your environment	**45**	**Delta Lake**	**52**
Python, AWS, and Databricks	46	Transaction log	52
Databricks CLI	46	Grouping tables with databases	53
Cloud data storage	**47**	Table	54
Object storage	47	**Adding speed with Z-ordering**	**62**
Relational	47	Bloom filters	62
NoSQL	47	**Practical lab**	**62**
Spark architecture	**48**	Problem 1	63
Introduction to Apache Spark	48	Problem 2	63
Key components	48	Problem 3	63
Working with partitions	49	**Solution**	**63**
Shuffling partitions	49	**Summary**	**65**
Caching	50		
Broadcasting	51		

4

Batch and Stream Data Processing Using PySpark   67

Technical requirements	67	Debugging	79
Setting up your environment	68	Writing to disk	79
Python, AWS, and Databricks	68	Batch stream hybrid	80
Databricks CLI	68	Delta streaming	80
		Batch processing in a stream	80
Batch processing	69	Practical lab	81
Partitioning	70	Setup	81
Data skew	70	Creating fake data	81
Reading data	71	Problem 1	81
Spark schemas	72	Problem 2	82
Making decisions	74	Problem 3	82
Removing unwanted columns	74		
Working with data in groups	74	Solution	82
		Solution 1	82
The UDF	75	Solution 2	83
Stream processing	77	Solution 3	84
Reading from disk	78	Summary	85

5

Streaming Data with Kafka   87

Technical requirements	87	Brokers	93
Setting up your environment	87	Producers	93
Python, AWS, and Databricks	88	Consumers	95
Databricks CLI	88	Schema Registry	96
Confluent Kafka	89	Kafka Connect	101
Signing up	89	Spark and Kafka	106
Kafka architecture	91	Practical lab	107
Topics	92	Solution	107
Partitions	92	Summary	114

Part 3: Modernizing the Data Platform

6
MLOps 117

Technical requirements	117	Training our model	123
Setting up your environment	117	Working together	123
Python, AWS, and Databricks	118	**AutoML**	**124**
Databricks CLI	118	**MLflow**	**125**
Introduction to machine learning	119	MLOps benefits	125
Understanding data	119	**Feature stores**	**127**
The basics of feature engineering	120	Hyperopt	129
Splitting up your data	120	**Practical lab**	**130**
Fitting your data	121	Create an MLflow project	132
Cross-validation	121		
Understanding hyperparameters and parameters	**123**	**Summary**	**135**

7
Data and Information Visualization 137

Technical requirements	137	A multiple line chart	142
Setting up your environment	138	A bar chart	142
Principles of data visualization	**139**	A scatter plot	143
Understanding your user	139	A histogram	144
Validating your data	140	A bubble chart	144
Data visualization using notebooks	**140**	GUI data visualizations	145
Line charts	140	**Tips and tricks with Databricks notebooks**	**147**
Bar charts	140	Magic	147
Histograms	140	Markdown	147
Scatter plots	140	Other languages	148
Pie charts	140	Terminal	148
Bubble charts	141	Filesystem	148
A single line chart	141	Running other notebooks	148

Widgets	148	Connecting BI tools	154
Databricks SQL analytics	**149**	**Practical lab**	**157**
Accessing SQL analytics	149	Loading problem data	158
SQL Warehouses	149	Problem 1	159
SQL editors	150	Solution	159
Queries	151	Problem 2	161
Dashboards	152	Solution	162
Alerts	152	**Summary**	**165**
Query history	153		

8

Integrating Continous Integration into Your Workflow   167

Technical requirements	**167**	Anatomy of a package	178
Setting up your environment	**168**	**DBX**	**179**
Databricks	168	Important commands	179
Databricks CLI	168	**Testing code**	**180**
The DBX CLI	169	**Terraform – IaC**	**181**
Docker	169	IaC	181
Git	170	The CLI	182
GitHub	170	HCL	182
Pre-commit	172	**Jenkins**	**183**
Terraform	172	Jenkinsfile	184
Docker	173	**Practical lab**	**186**
Install Jenkins, container setup, and compose	173	Problem 1	186
CI tooling	**176**	Problem 2	190
Git and GitHub	176	**Summary**	**195**
Pre-commit	177		
Python wheels and packages	**178**		

9

Orchestrating Your Data Workflows   197

Technical requirements	**197**	Databricks	198
Setting up your environment	**198**	Databricks CLI	198
		The DBX CLI	199

Orchestrating data workloads	199	REST APIs	207
Making life easier with Autoloader	199	The Databricks API	207
Reading	199	Python code	207
Writing	200	Logging	208
Two modes	200	Practical lab	211
Useful options	200	Solution	211
Databricks Workflows	202	Lambda code	212
Terraform	206	Notebook code	213
Failed runs	206	Summary	213

Part 4: Hands-on Project

10

Data Governance — 217

Technical requirements	217	Data context	223
Setting up your environment	217	Data source	223
Python, AWS, and Databricks	217	Batch request	224
The Databricks CLI	218	Validator	224
What is data governance?	219	Adding tests	225
Data standards	219	Saving the suite	225
Data catalogs	219	Creating a checkpoint	225
Data lineage	220	Datadocs	226
Data security and privacy	221	Testing new data	226
Data quality	221	Profiler	227
Great Expectations	222	Databricks Unity	227
Creating test data	222	Practical lab	231
		Summary	237

11

Building out the Groundwork — 239

Technical requirements	239	Git	240
Setting up your environment	240	GitHub	241
The Databricks CLI	240	pre-commit	243

Terraform	243	Schema repository	247
PyPI	244	Schema repository	248
Creating GitHub repos	**246**	ML repository	249
Terraform setup	**247**	Infrastructure repository	252
Initial file setup	247	**Summary**	**258**

12

Completing Our Project 259

Technical requirements	259	Building our data pipeline application	274
Documentation	260	Creating our machine learning application	279
Schema diagram	260		
C4 System Context diagram	263	Displaying our data with dashboards	282
Faking data with Mockaroo	265	Summary	283
Managing our schemas with code	267		

Index 285

Other Books You May Enjoy 294

Preface

Hello! Data platforms are popping up everywhere, but only some cars in the shop are the same. We are at the dawn of seeing most data stored not in company-owned data centers but, instead, in the cloud. Cloud storage is exceptionally cheap, and this abundance of cheap storage drives our choices. Cloud storage is cheap, and cloud processing is often significantly more affordable than adequately housing computers in a data center. With this increase in cheap, flexible cloud capability comes the flexibility to have elasticity – the ability to grow and shrink as needed. Virtual compute engines do not run directly on physical machines but, instead, run in abstractions called containers, allowing for temporary use. You no longer need to pay for expensive deep-learning hardware. The cloud can give you quick access at a fraction of the cost.

The next step in this evolution was putting together stacks of technology that played well into what was called a data platform. This was often riddled with incompatible technologies being forced to work together, many times requiring duct tape to get everything to work together. As time went on, a better choice appeared.

With the advent of open technologies to process data such as Apache Spark, we started to see a different path altogether. People began to ask fundamental questions.

What types of data does your platform fully support? It became increasingly important that your data platform equally supports semi-structured and structured data. What kinds of analysis and ML does your platform support? We started wanting to create, train, and deploy AI and ML on our data platforms using modern tooling stacks. The analysis must be available in various languages and tooling options, not just a traditional JDBC SQL path. How well does it support streaming? Streaming data has become more and more the norm in many companies. With it comes a significant jump in complexity. A system built to process, store, and work with streaming platforms is critical for many. Is your platform using only open standards? Open standards might seem like an afterthought, but being able to swap out aged technologies without the forced lift and shift migrations can be a significant cost saver. Open standards allow for various technologies to work together without any effort, which is a stark contrast to many closed data systems. This book will serve as a guide into all the questions and show you have to work with data platforms efficiently.

Who this book is for

Data is present in every business and working environment. People are constantly trying to understand and use data better.

This book has three different intended readerships:

- **Engineers**: Engineers building data products and infrastructure can benefit from understanding how to build modern open data platforms
- **Analysts**: Analysts who want to understand data better and use it to make critical decisions will benefit from understanding how to better interact with it
- **Managers**: Decision makers who write the checks and consume data often need to understand data platforms from a high level better, which is incredibly important

What this book covers

Chapter 1, Modern Data Processing Architecture, provides a significant introduction to designing data architecture and understanding the types of data processing engines.

Chapter 2, Understanding Data Analytics, provides an overview of the world of data analytics and modeling for various data types.

Chapter 3, Apache Spark Deep Dive, provides a thorough understanding of how Apache Spark works and the background knowledge needed to write Spark code.

Chapter 4, Batch and Stream Processing with Apache Spark, provides a solid foundation to work with Spark for batch workloads and structured streaming data pipelines.

Chapter 5, Streaming Data with Kafka, provides a hands-on introduction to Kafka and its uses in data pipelines, including Kafka Connect and Apache Spark.

Chapter 6, MLOps, provides an engineer with all the needed background and hands-on knowledge to develop, train, and deploy ML/AI models using the latest tooling.

Chapter 7, Data and Information Visualization, explains how to develop ad hoc data visualization and common dashboards in your data platform.

Chapter 8, Integrating Continuous Integration into Your Workflow, delves deep into how to build Python applications in a CI workflow using GitHub, Jenkins, and Databricks.

Chapter 9, Orchestrating Your Data Workflows, gives practical hands-on experience with Databricks workflows that transfer to other orchestration tools.

Chapter 10, Data Governance, explores controlling access to data and dealing with data quality issues.

Chapter 11, *Building Out the Ground Work*, establishes a foundation for our project using GitHub, Python, Terraform, and PyPi among others.

Chapter 12, *Completing Our Project*, completes our project, building out GitHub actions, Pre-commit, design diagrams, and lots of Python.

To get the most out of this book

A fundamental knowledge of Python is strongly suggested.

Software/hardware covered in the book	OS requirements
Databricks	Windows, macOS, or Linux
Kafka	
Apache Spark	

If you are using the digital version of this book, we advise you to type the code yourself or access the code via the GitHub repository (link available in the next section). Doing so will help you avoid any potential errors related to the copying and pasting of code.

Download the example code files

You can download the example code files for this book from GitHub at `https://github.com/PacktPublishing/Modern-Data-Architectures-with-Python`. If there's an update to the code, it will be updated in the existing GitHub repository.

We also have other code bundles from our rich catalog of books and videos available at `https://github.com/PacktPublishing/`. Check them out!

Conventions used

There are a number of text conventions used throughout this book.

Code in text: Indicates code words in text, database table names, folder names, filenames, file extensions, pathnames, dummy URLs, user input, and Twitter handles. Here is an example: "Mount the downloaded WebStorm-10*.dmg disk image file as another disk in your system."

A block of code is set as follows:

```
validator.expect_column_values_to_not_be_null(column="name")
validator.expect_column_values_to_be_between(
    column="age", min_value=0, max_value=100
)
```

When we wish to draw your attention to a particular part of a code block, the relevant lines or items are set in bold:

```
adapter = HTTPAdapter(max_retries=restries)
```

Any command-line input or output is written as follows:

```
databricks fs ls
```

Bold: Indicates a new term, an important word, or words that you see on screen. For example, words in menus or dialog boxes appear in the text like this. Here is an example: "Here we have the main page for workflows; to create a new workflow, there is a **Create job** button at the top left."

> **Tips or important notes**
> Appear like this.

Get in touch

Feedback from our readers is always welcome.

General feedback: If you have questions about any aspect of this book, mention the book title in the subject of your message and email us at customercare@packtpub.com.

Errata: Although we have taken every care to ensure the accuracy of our content, mistakes do happen. If you have found a mistake in this book, we would be grateful if you would report this to us. Please visit www.packtpub.com/support/errata, select your book, click on the Errata Submission Form link, and enter the details.

Piracy: If you come across any illegal copies of our works in any form on the Internet, we would be grateful if you would provide us with the location address or website name. Please contact us at copyright@packtpub.com with a link to the material.

If you are interested in becoming an author: If there is a topic that you have expertise in and you are interested in either writing or contributing to a book, please visit authors.packtpub.com.

Share Your Thoughts

Once you've read *Modern Data Architectures with Python*, we'd love to hear your thoughts! Scan the QR code below to go straight to the Amazon review page for this book and share your feedback.

https://packt.link/r/1-801-07049-0

Your review is important to us and the tech community and will help us make sure we're delivering excellent quality content.

Download a free PDF copy of this book

Thanks for purchasing this book!

Do you like to read on the go but are unable to carry your print books everywhere?

Is your eBook purchase not compatible with the device of your choice?

Don't worry, now with every Packt book you get a DRM-free PDF version of that book at no cost.

Read anywhere, any place, on any device. Search, copy, and paste code from your favorite technical books directly into your application.

The perks don't stop there, you can get exclusive access to discounts, newsletters, and great free content in your inbox daily

Follow these simple steps to get the benefits:

1. Scan the QR code or visit the link below

https://packt.link/free-ebook/9781801070492

2. Submit your proof of purchase
3. That's it! We'll send your free PDF and other benefits to your email directly

Part 1: Fundamental Data Knowledge

In this part, we will introduce data and the theory behind working with data. We will look at ways of organizing and conceptualizing data processing and storage. We will also look at common data philosophies like Data Mesh and Delta Lake. We will then check how we can model and shape data to meet the needs of data products.

This part has the following chapters:

- *Chapter 1, Modern Data Processing Architecture*
- *Chapter 2, Understanding Data Analytics*

1
Modern Data Processing Architecture

Data architecture has become one of the most discussed topics. This chapter will introduce data architecture and the methodologies for designing a data ecosystem. Architecting a data solution is tricky and often riddled with traps. We will go through the theories for creating a data ecosystem and give some insight into how and why you would apply those theories.

To do so, we will cover the essential concepts, why they are helpful, and when to apply them.

By the end of this chapter, you will have built the foundation of your data solution, and once completed, you should be comfortable with architecture data solutions at a high level.

In this chapter, we're going to cover the following main topics:

- Databases, data warehouses, and data lakes
- Data platform architecture at a high level
- Lambda versus Kappa architecture
- Lakehouse and Delta architectures
- Data mesh theory and practice

Technical requirements

You can use many tools to create the diagrams and technical documentation for this chapter.

I suggest the following:

- Lucid Chart
- Draw.io
- OmniGraffle

Databases, data warehouses, and data lakes

The history of data processing is long and has had several unique innovations. As a result, we can look around today and see several patterns in our offices – everything from data stored as a file on a network drive, local hard drive, or technology such as S3 to **relational database management systems** (**RDBMSes**) and data warehouses. We will now go through the major types of data storage systems and see some of the benefits and disadvantages of each.

OLTP

When people think of storing data, the first thing that always comes to mind is the traditional relational database. These databases are designed to process and store short data interactions reliably and consistently. On the other hand, **online transaction processing** (**OLTP**) systems are very good at handling small interactions, called **create, read, update, and delete** (**CRUD**). OLTP systems come in two primary flavors: relational and NoSQL. We will cover the details of each type later, but for now, we should simply understand that within these two types of data stores, we can use any data that has some amount of structure to it. A classic example of a use case for OLTP would be a web application for a grocery store. These types of data actions are small and quick. Therefore, we would typically not see a much-extended workload on an OLTP system in typical data processing usage. Some examples of OLTP systems are MongoDB, Microsoft SQL, PostgreSQL, and CockroachDB, among others. In other words, a data storage system that is used to run a business on a day-to-day basis is an OLTP system. These have frequent insert, update, and delete operations and we are more interested in the throughput of these systems compared to their response time from a performance perspective. Most of these OLTP systems will be **ACID**-compliant (that is, **atomicity, consistency, isolation, and duration**).

OLAP

On the other side of the spectrum, we have **online analytical processing** (**OLAP**) systems, which are better designed to handle intense data processing workloads. We will avoid being pedantic about what precisely an OLAP is and instead paint a broad picture – two examples are an OLAP data warehouse and a lakehouse. A data warehouse, at its core, is simply an OLAP system that stores and curates data using data warehousing techniques. Data warehouses are trusted sources of data for decision-making. More often than not, a data warehouse will only store structured data. On the other hand, a data lake is a form of storage that stores data in its most native format. Data lakes can also serve as entry points to data warehouses. We will cover lakehouses in more detail later, but they can be understood as hybrids of data warehouses and data lakes.

Data lakes

So, we spoke of data warehouses and databases, which use data that follows a basic structure or schema. Since the cost of disk storage has reduced over time, the desire to keep more and more data has become a reality. This data began to take on less structure, such as audio, video, and text documents.

Our current OLTP and OLAP systems were not the ideal tools for enormous amounts of data or data with a wide variety of structures. The data lake emerged as a way to store all the data in systems such as HDFS and AWS S3. Data lakes typically have schema on read, whereas OLTP and OLAP systems generally are schema on read and write. This wide range of flexibility often leads to a data dumping ground or a data swamp. The conventional data warehouses were monolithic, on-premises systems with the compute and storage combined. With the advent of big data, we saw distributed computing, where data was spilt across multiple machines. However, each machine still had combined compute and storage. With the advent of the cloud, this paradigm of splitting both the compute and storage across machines enabled by distributed computing took effect. This is much more efficient. Moreover, on the cloud, the services we use and therefore this OPEX model worked better than the conventional CAPEX model, which was a dead-cost investment.

With the emergence of data lakes came large-scale data processing engines such as Apache Hadoop, Apache Spark, and Apache Flink, to name a few. The most crucial detail to understand about this type of technology is the separation of the storage layer and the compute layer. This pattern exists in all systems designed to handle big data. You may not even know that a system uses this pattern, as with Snowflake or Big Query. There are both significant benefits and negative considerations regarding this type of data processing.

There is one universal rule when understanding data processing – the costs. Moving data is very expensive. Moving data from processor to disk is expensive but moving it across the network is exponentially costly. This must be a design consideration when you're picking your stack. There are situations where that cost is acceptable, and your application is okay with waiting a few extra seconds. This is one of the reasons you don't typically see decoupled storage and compute patterns with CRUD web applications.

In the following diagram, the left shows a typical data warehouse or database that has everything built into one system – that is, the storage and compute engines are together. The right-hand side of the diagram shows that they are decoupled, meaning they're separate systems:

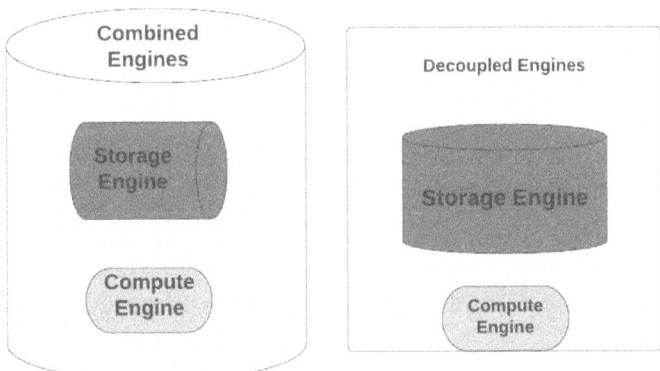

Figure 1.1: Storage and compute

Event stores

Another trend in data storage is using systems such as Kafka, a distributed event store and streaming processing engine. Event stores can be considered data stores with several logs that can be watched or read from start to finish. Event stores are often associated with real-time processing. The term *real-time* is often used to describe data that is flowing in a relatively real-time-like process. Real-time data is used in many data platforms and can come with its own set of complexities and problems. We will provide a whole chapter on streaming data using both Spark and Kafka. For now, it's enough to understand that real-time data attempts to store, process, and access data as soon as it's recorded.

File formats

Whenever you're working with data, you will inevitably want to save it in a file. The question is, which file should you choose? Some formats are ideal for short-term office work. Other formats, on the other hand, are designed for long-term storage. When you're selecting what file format to use, first, consider the use case for the file and how long you will keep it.

CSV

Here is an example of a CSV file. In this case, I am using , for the column delimiter and \\n for the line delimiter:

```
id,first_name,last_name,email\n
1,Alyce,Creeber,acreeber0@hibu.com\n
2,Gladi,Fenney,gfenney1@reference.com\n
3,Mendy,Papen,mpapen2@jalbum.net\n
4,Gerri,Kernan,gkernan3@berkeley.edu\n
5,Luca,Skeen,lskeen4@hostgator.com\n
```

Comma-separated values (**CSV**) files are the most common data files that are found in an office (outside of an Excel file). CSV is a text format that uses a set of characters to identify column cells and end-of-line characters. CSVs are used for structured data. Sometimes, you can create semi-structured scenarios, but it's not very effective. CSVs are text files, so the file's structure can often have varying characteristics such as headers, banners, or free-form text. CSVs are an excellent short-term office file format for doing work. However, CSVs don't provide data types, which, combined with the other issues mentioned previously, makes them a terrible choice for long-term storage.

JSON

Here, we have an example **JavaScript Object Notation** (**JSON**) object with three objects inside the parent object:

```
[{
  "id": 1,
```

```
      "first_name": "Ermanno",
      "last_name": "Marconi",
      "email": "emarconi0@bbb.org"
  }, {
      "id": 2,
      "first_name": "Lory",
      "last_name": "Maskew",
      "email": "lmaskew1@walmart.com"
  }, {
      "id": 3,
      "first_name": "Karee",
      "last_name": "Hubbucke",
      "email": "khubbucke2@pagesperso-orange.fr"
  }]
```

JSON is a plain text-based format that uses strict syntax to define semi-structured or structured data. In the preceding example, we are mimicking structured data, but we could have nested more objects or used an array. JSON format overcomes the issue of the poorly defined syntax of CSVs, which makes it a more ideal choice for most use cases. However, JSON is not my first choice for long-term storage because it lacks data types and contains no compression.

Avro

Here is an example schema file for the Avro format. Notice how we have two "columns" of data called Make and ID in the awesome_startup namespace:

```
{
   "type" : "record",
   "namespace" : "awesome_startup",
   "name" : "cars",
   "fields" : [
      { "name" : "Make" , "type" : "string" },
      { "name" : "ID" , "type" : "int" }
   ]
}
```

Avro is a popular open standard protocol often found in data lakes. Avro serializes data, making it small and compact compared to formats such as JSON. Avro supports both structured and semi-structured data like JSON. Avro has a secondary file that is in JSON format that defines the data types and structure of your data. With this schema file, you can evolve your schema by making changes but keep backward compatibility. This is a huge advantage when it comes to long-term data storage. Avro is designed to be accessed row by row or row storage. Row storage is ideal for cases when you look up a row and read the whole row. Although Avro is a significant step up from JSON, it still lacks in several ways. What happens when the schema file is lost? Typically, the data is unusable, which is less than ideal. Row storage is perfect for CRUD-style workflows, but many data-intense workflows will read a whole column at a time; this can be costly in Avro.

Parquet

Parquet has emerged as the best-of-breed file format in the majority of cases. Parquet supports semi-structured data and structured data like Avro. Parquet is an open standard format that, like Avro, serializes its data for small footprints. On the other hand, Parquet stores the schema within the file, which overcomes several shortcomings of Avro. Parquet, unlike row-oriented formats like Arvo, is column-oriented. This translates into faster data access and writing for most workflows.

Data platform architecture at a high level

What is data architecture, and why do I care? Data architecture is the process of designing and building complex data platforms. This involves taking a comprehensive view, which includes not only moving and storing data but also all aspects of the data platform. Building a well-designed data ecosystem can be transformative to a business.

What goes into architecting a data platform? In picking your solution, you will evaluate the price, cloud vendors, and multi-cloud options, among many other choices. Using a hosted option for a service might make sense, or it may be inappropriate. You might want to stick with one vendor for everything, or you may decide to get the best-of-breed technologies. Will you need streaming data? How will you manage your data? What is the long-term vision for the project? Is vendor and product lock-in something to consider? All these questions and more are answered by the data architect and the platform that gets designed.

I will now introduce a data platform reference architecture that is used to organize and better understand what exists in your data ecosystem.

Here is a data architecture reference diagram. I have put data governance, processing, and storage across all areas since they interact with everything:

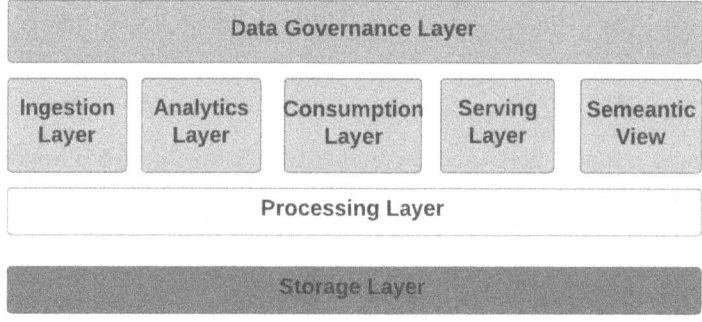

Figure 1.2: Data platform architecture

Let's break this architecture down.

Storage layer

In this layer, we include technologies that persist data in long-term storage, such as OLTP, OLAP, lakehouses, event stores, and data lakes. We also have file types such as Parquet, Avro, and CSV.

Ingestion layer

The ingestion layer focuses on taking your data from whatever source system it may live in, such as a social media site, and moving that data into the storage layer. This layer may include commercial products such as Fivetran or Stich, but often, it will also involve writing code to accomplish this task.

Analytics layer

In the analytics layer, we will see a variety of work that ranges from data science, machine learning, and artificial intelligence to graph analytics and statical analysis. The output from the analysis will be represented in a "view" that the consumption layer can access. You will also see data modeling in this layer. Data modeling is the process of building tables to better understand and represent your data from various perspectives.

Consumption layer

The consumption layer stores the output views created by the analytics layer. The technology chosen for this layer can vary, but one example might be a machine learning model that's recorded and tracked in MLflow and stored in S3.

Serving layer

The serving layer consists of **business intelligence** (**BI**), dashboards, data visualizations, search engines, and other systems that use data products in the consumption layer.

Data governance layer

The data governance layer contains master data management, data quality enforcement, data security, data auditing, and metadata management. We will cover the fundamental concepts of this layer in a separate chapter.

Processing layer

The processing layer is the workhorse that handles moving data between all the other layers. Technologies such as Apache Spark, Flink, Snowflake, DBT, Dataflow, and Azure Data Factory handle this task.

Semantic view

The semantic view, also known as the virtual layer, is an optional abstraction in your data platform that allows you to decouple user access from data storage. In simple terms, users will have a view of the data stored in its "original" source, but without the need to access the source directly. Data could be stored in anything ranging from relational databases and data lakes to REST APIs. This virtual layer is then used to create new modeled data products. Users might access these data products from various sources, such as BI tooling, notebooks, or even internally developed applications using whatever access method is needed. These new data products are curated from different sources and are tailored to the needs of the users and the use cases. Often, standard terms are normalized across data products. In an ideal world, there is no storage in the semantic layer. However, you may need to store copies of the data for faster access, for example, if you're integrating with another corporate application. There are several benefits to this added complexity, including central data governance and future proofing for any data storage solution changes.

Comparing the Lambda and Kappa architectures

In the beginning, we started with batch processing or scheduled data processing jobs. When we run data workloads in batches, we are setting a specific chronological cadence for those workloads to be triggered. For most workloads, this is perfectly fine, but there will always be a more significant time delay in our data. As technology has progressed, the ability to utilize real-time processing has become possible.

At the time of writing, there are two different directions architects are taking in dealing with these two workloads.

Lambda architecture

The following is the Lambda architecture, which has a combined batch and real-time consumption and serving layer:

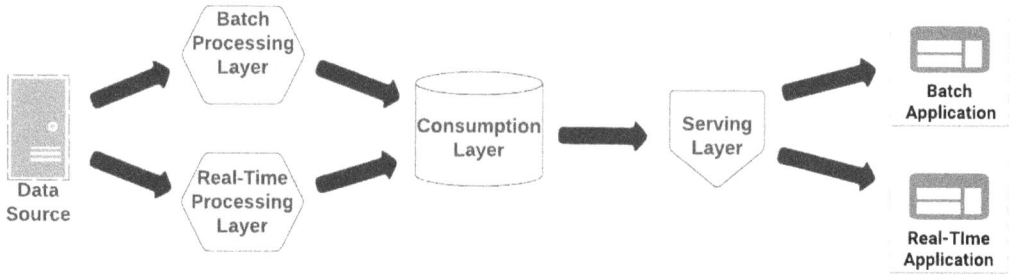

Figure 1.3: Combined Lambda architecture

The following diagram shows a Lambda architecture with separate consumption and serving layers, one for batch and the other for real-time processing:

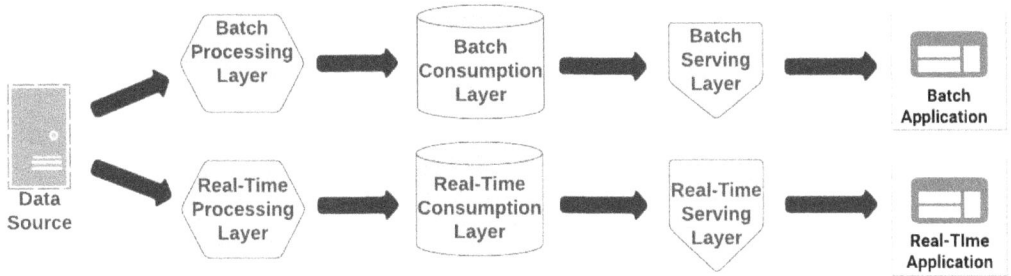

Figure 1.4: Separate combined Lambda architecture

The Lambda architecture was the first attempt to deal with both streaming and batch data. It grew out of systems that started with just traditional batch data. As a result, the Lambda architecture uses two separate layers for processing data. The first layer is the batch layer, which performs data transformations that are harder to accomplish in real-time processing workstreams. The second layer is a real-time layer, which is meant for processing data as soon as its ingested. As data is transformed in each layer, the data should have a unique ID that allows the data to be correlated, no matter the workstream.

Once the data products have been created from each layer, there can be a separate or combined consumption layer. A combined consumption layer is easier to create but given the technology, it can be challenging to accomplish complex models that span both types of data. In the consumption layer, batch and real-time processing can be combined, which will require matching IDs. The consumption layer is a landing zone for data products made in the batch or real-time layer. The storage mechanism for this layer can range from a data lake or a data lakehouse to a relational database. The serving layer is used to take data products in the consumption layer and create views, run AI, and access data through tools such as dashboards, apps, and notebooks.

The Lambda architecture is relatively easy to adopt, given that the technology and patterns are typically known and fit into a typical engineer's comfort zone. Most deployments already have a batch layer, so often, the real-time layer is a bolt-on addition to the platform. What tends to happen over time is that the complexity grows in several ways. Two very complex systems must be maintained and coordinated. Also, two distinct sets of software must be developed and maintained. In most cases, the two layers do not have similar technology, which will translate into a variety of techniques and languages for writing software in and keeping it updated.

Kappa architecture

The following diagram shows the Kappa architecture. The essential details are that there is only one set of layers and batch data is extracted via real-time processing:

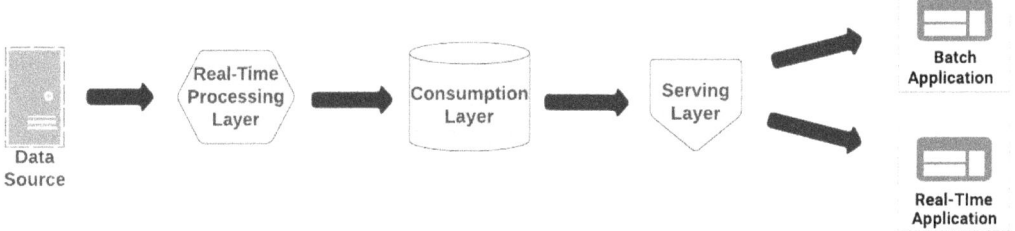

Figure 1.5: Kappa architecture

The Kappa architecture was designed due to frustrations with the Lambda architecture. With the Lambda architecture, we have two layers, one for batch processing and the other for stream processing. The Kappa architecture has only a single real-time layer, which it uses for all data. Now, if we take a step back, there will always be some amount of oddness because batch data isn't real-time data. There is still a consumption layer that's used to store data products and a serving layer for accessing those data products. Again, the caveat is that many batch-based workloads will need to be customized so that they only use streaming data. Kappa is often found in large tech companies that have a wealth of tech talent and the need for fast, real-time data access.

Where Lambda was relatively easy to adopt, Kappa is highly complex in comparison. Often, the minimal use case for a typical company for real-time data does not warrant such a difficult change. As expected, there are considerable benefits to the Kappa architecture. For one, maintenance is reduced significantly, and the code base is also slimmed down. Real-time data can be complex to work with at times. Think of a giant hose that can't ever be turned off. Issues with data in the Kappa architecture can often be very challenging, given the nature of the data storage. In the batch processing layer, it's easy to deploy a change to the data, but in the real-time processing layer, reprocessing the data is no trivial matter. What often happens is secondary storage is adopted for data so that data can be accessed in both places. A straightforward example of why having a copy of data in a secondary system is, for example, when in Kafka, you need to constantly adjust the data. We will discuss Kafka later, but I will just mention that having a way to dump a Kafka topic and quickly repopulate it can be a lifesaver.

Lakehouse and Delta architectures

Introduced by Databricks, the lakehouse and Delta architectures are a significant improvement over previous data platform patterns. They are the next evolution by combining what works from previous modalities and improving them.

Lakehouses

What is a lakehouse? Why is it so important? It's talked about often, but few people can explain the tenets of a lakehouse. The lakehouse is an evolution of the data warehouse and the data lake. A lakehouse takes the lessons learned from both and combines them to avoid the flaws of both. There are seven tenets of the lakehouse, and each is taken from one of the parent technologies.

The seven central tenets

Something that's not always understood when engineers discuss lakehouses is that they're general sets of ideas. Here, we will walk through all seven essential tenets – openness, data diversity, workflow diversity, processing diversity, language-agnostic, decoupled storage and compute, and ACID transactions.

Openness

The openness principle is fundamental to everything in the lakehouse. It influences the preference for open standards over closed-source technology. This choice affects the long-term life of our data and the systems we choose to connect with. When you say a lakehouse is open, you are saying it uses nonproprietary technologies, but it also uses methodologies that allow for easier collaboration, such as decoupled storage and compute engines.

Data diversity

In a lakehouse, all data is welcome and accessible to users. Semi-structured data is given first-class citizenship alongside structured data, including schema enforcement.

Workflow diversity

With workflow diversity, users can access the data in many ways, including via notebooks, custom applications, and BI tools. How the user interacts with the data shouldn't be limited.

Processing diversity

The lakehouse prioritizes both streaming and batch equally. Not only is streaming important but it also uses the Delta architecture to compress streaming and batch into one technology layer.

Language-agnostic

The goal of the lakehouse is to support all methods of accessing the data and all programming languages. However, this goal is not possible practically. When implemented, the list of methods and languages supported in Apache Spark is extensive.

Decoupling storage and compute

In a data warehouse, data storage is combined with the same technology. From a speed perspective, this is ideal, but it creates a lack of flexibility. When a new processing engine is desired, or a combination of many storage engines is required, the data warehouse's model fails to perform. A unique characteristic taken from data lakes is decoupling the storage and compute layers, which creates several benefits. The first is flexibility; you can mix and match technologies. You can have data stored in graph databases, cloud data warehouses, object stores, or even systems such as Kafka. The second benefit is the significant cost reduction. This cost reduction comes when you incorporate technologies such as object stores. Cloud object stores such as AWS's S3, Azure's Blob, and GCP's Object Storage represent cheap, effective, and massively scalable data storage. Lastly, when you follow this design pattern, you can scale at a more manageable rate.

ACID transactions

One significant issue with data lakes is the lack of transactional data processing. Transactions have substantial effects on the quality of your data. They affect anything from writing to the same table at the same time to a log of changes made to your table. With ACID transactions, lakehouses are significantly more reliable and effective compared to data lakes.

The medallion data pattern and the Delta architecture

The medallion data pattern is an approach to storing and serving data that is less based on building a data warehouse and more focused on building your raw data off a single source of truth.

Delta architecture

The following diagram shows the Delta architecture. It looks just like Kappa, but the key difference is that you are not forcing batch processing out of real-time data. Both exist within the same layers and systems:

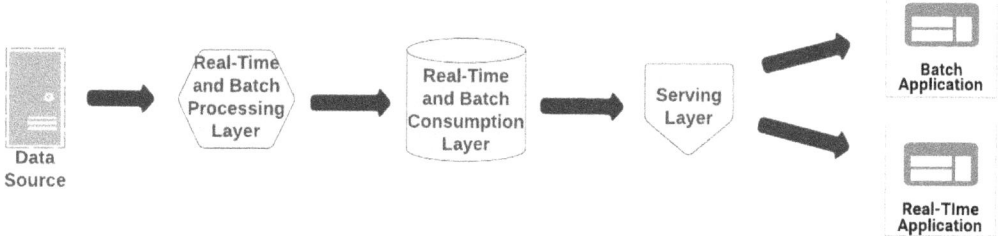

Figure 1.6: Delta architecture

The Delta architecture is a lessons-learned approach to both the Kappa and Lambda architectures. Delta sees that the complexity of trying to use real-time data as the sole data source can be highly complex and, in the majority of companies, overkill. Most companies want workloads in both batch and real-time, not excluding one over the other. Yet, Delta architectures reduce the footprint to one layer. This processing layer can handle batch and real-time with almost identical code. This is a huge step forward from previous architectural patterns.

The medallion data pattern

The medallion data pattern is an organized naming convention that explains the nature of the data being processed. When referencing your tables, labeling them with tags allows for clear visibility into tables.

The following diagram shows the medallion data pattern, which describes the state of each dataset at rest:

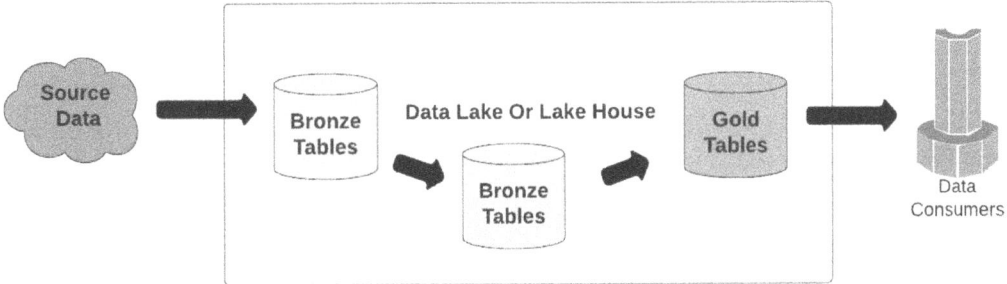

Figure 1.7: Medallion architecture

As you can see, the architecture has different types of tables (data). Let's take a look.

Bronze

Bronze data is raw data that represents source data without modification, other than metadata. Bronze tables can be used as a single source of truth since the data is in its purest form. Bronze tables are incrementally loaded and can be a combination of streaming and batch data. It might be helpful to add metadata such as source data and processed timestamps.

Silver

Once you have bronze data, you will start to clean, mold, transform, and model your data. Silver data represents the final stage before creating data products. Once your data is in a silver table, it is considered validated, enriched, and ready for consumption.

Gold

Gold data represents your final data products. Your data is curated, summarized, and molded to meet your user's needs in terms of BI dashboarding, statistical analysis, or machine learning modeling. Often, golden data is stored in separate buckets to allow for data scaling.

Data mesh theory and practice

Zhamak Dehghani created data mesh to overcome many common data platform issues while working for ThoughtWorks in 2019. I often get asked by seasoned data professionals, why bother with data mesh? Isn't it just data silos all over again? The fundamentals of a data mesh are that it's a decentralized data domain and scaling-focused but with those ideas also comes rethinking how we organize not only our data but also our whole data practice. By learning and adopting data mesh concepts and techniques, we cannot only produce more valuable data but also better enable users to access our data. No longer do we see orphaned data with little interaction from its creators. Users have direct relationships with data producers, and with that comes higher-quality data.

The following diagram shows the typical spaghetti data pipeline complexity that many growing organizations fall into. Imagine trying to maintain this maze of data pipelines. This is a common scenario for spaghetti data pipelines, which are very brittle and hard to maintain and scale:

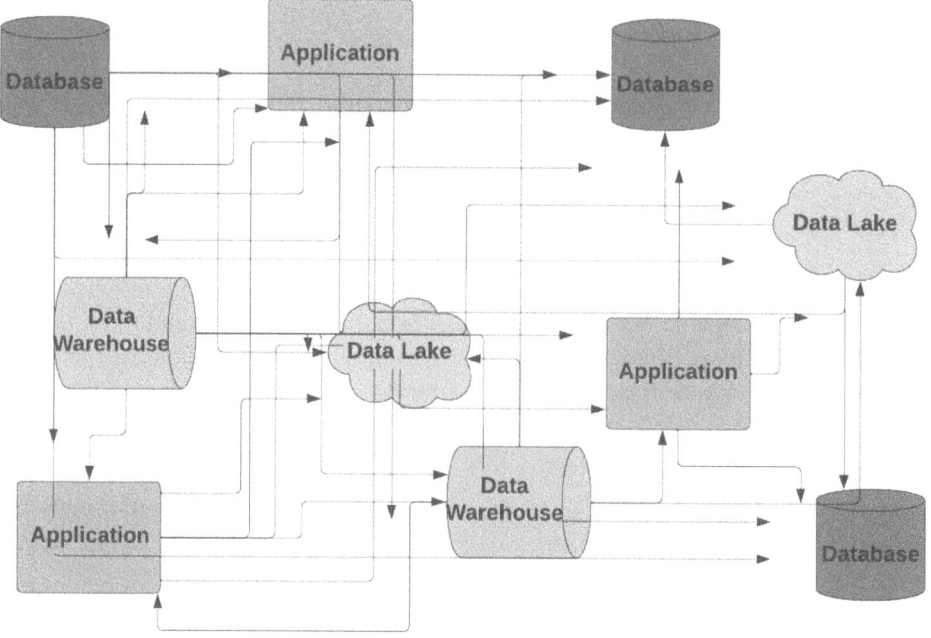

Figure 1.8: Classic data pipeline architecture

The following diagram shows our data platform once it's been decentralized, which means it's free of brittle pipelines and able to scale:

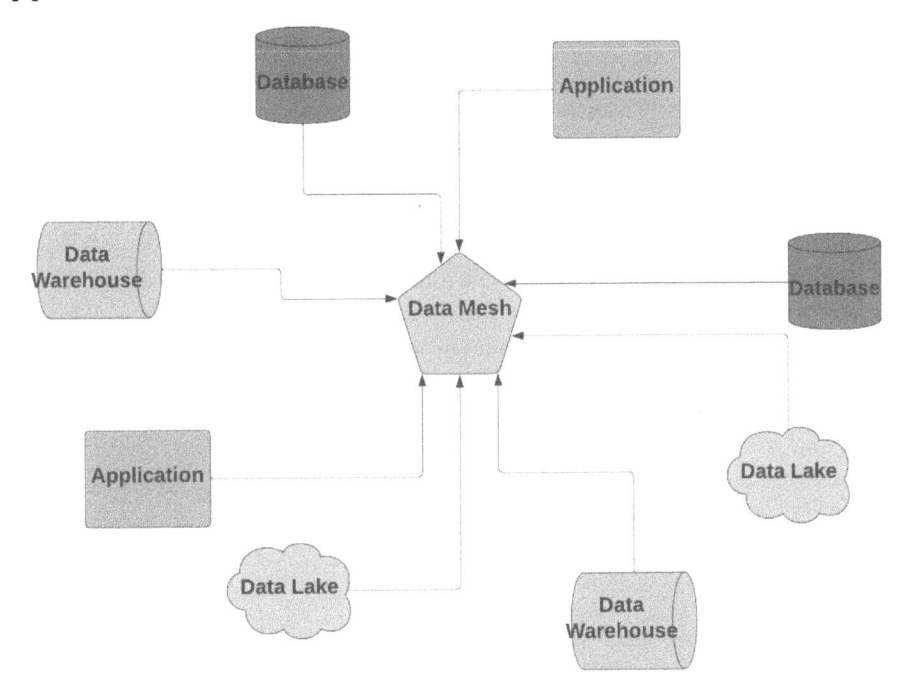

Figure 1.9: Data mesh architecture

Anyone who has worked on a more extensive organization's data team can tell you how complex and challenging things get. You will find a maze of complex data pipelines everywhere. Pipelines are the blood of your data warehouse or data lake. As data is shipped and processed, it's merged into a central warehouse. It's common to have lots of data with very little visibility into who knows about the data and the quality of that data. The data sits there, and people who know about it use it in whatever state it lives in. So, let's say you find that data. What exactly is the data? What is the path or lineage the data has taken to get to its current state? Who should you contact to correct issues with the data? So many questions, and often, the answers are less than ideal.

These were the types of problems Zhamak Dehghani was trying to tackle when she first came up with the idea of a data mesh. Dehghani noticed all the limitations of the current landscape in data organizations and developed a decentralized philosophy heavily influenced by Eric Evans's domain-driven design. A data mesh is arguably a mix of organizational and technological changes. These changes, when adopted, allow your teams to have a better data experience. One thing I want to make very clear is that data mesh does not involve creating data silos. It involves creating an interconnected network of data that isn't focused on the technical process but on the functionality concerning the data. Organizationally, a domain in data mesh will have a cross-functional team of data experts, software experts, data product owners, and infrastructure experts.

Defining terms

A data mesh has several terms that need to be explained for us to understand the philosophy fully. The first term that stands out is the *data product owner*. The data product owner is a member of the business team who takes on the role of the data steward or overseer of the data and is responsible for data governance. If there is an issue with data quality or privacy concerns, the data steward would be the person accountable for that data. Another term that's often used in a data mesh is *domain*, which can be understood as an organizational group of commonly focused entities. Domains publish data for other domains to consume. Data products are the heart of the data mesh philosophy. The data products should be self-service data entities that are offered close to creators. What does it mean to have self-service data? Your data is self-service when other domains can search, find, and access your data without having to have any administrative steps. This should all live on a *data platform*, which isn't one specific technology but a cohesive network of technologies.

The four principles of data mesh

Let's look at these four principles – that is, data ownership, data as a product, data availability, and data governance.

Data ownership

Data ownership is a fundamental concept in a data mesh. Data ownership is a partnership between the cross-functional teams within a domain and other domains that are using the data products in downstream apps and data products. In the traditional model, data producers allow a central group of engineers to send their data to a single repository for consumption. This created a scenario where data warehouse engineers were the responsible parties for data. These engineers tried to be the single source of truth when it came to this data. The source is now intimately involved with the data consumption process. This reduces and improves the data quality and removes the need for a central engineering group to manage data. To accomplish this task, teams within a domain have a wide range of skill sets, including software engineers, product owners, DevOps engineers, data engineers, and analytics engineers. So, who ultimately owns the data? It's very simple – if you produce the data, you own it and are responsible for it.

Data as a product

Data as a product is a fundamental concept that transforms the data that is offered to users. When each domain treats the data that others consume as an essential product, it reinvents our data. We market our data and have a vested interest in that data. Consumers want to know all about the data before they buy our product. So, when we advertise our data, we list the characteristics users need to make that educated decision. These characteristics are things such as lineage, access statistics, data contract, the data product owners, privacy level, and how to access the data. Each product is a uniquely curated creation and versioned to give complete visibility to consumers. Each version of our data product represents a new data contract with downstream users. What is a data contract? It's an agreement between the producers and consumers of the data. Not only is the data expected to be clean and kept in high quality but the schema of the data is also guaranteed. When a new version comes out, any schema changes must be backward-compatible to avoid breaking changes. This is called schema evolution and is a cornerstone to developing a trusted data product.

Data is available

As a consumer of data in an organization, I should be able to find data easily in some type of registry. The data producers should have accurate metadata about the data products within this registry. When I want to access this data, there should be an automated process that is ideally role-based. In an ideal world, this level of self-service exists to create an ecosystem of data. When we build data systems with this level of availability, we see our data practice grow, and we evolve our data usage.

Data governance

Data governance is a very loaded term with various meanings, depending on the person and the context. In the context of a data mesh, data governance is applied within each domain. Each domain will guarantee quality data that fulfills the data contract, all data meets the privacy level advertised, and appropriate access is granted or revoked based on company policies. This concept is often called federated data governance. In a federated model, governance standards are centrally defined but executed within each domain. Like any other area of a data mesh, the infrastructure can be shared but in a distributed manner. This distributed approach allows for standards across the organization but only via domain-specific implementations.

Summary

In this chapter, we covered the data architecture at a very high level, which can be overwhelming. Designing a solution is complex, but we covered many fundamental topics such as data meshes and lakehouses that should help you build data platforms. In the following few chapters, we will walk you through building the components of a data platform, such as BI tooling, MLOps, and data processing.

Practical lab

This isn't an ideal chapter for a lab because it's a chapter on theory. So, let's introduce a common thread in our chapters: *Mega Awesome Toys*. Mega Awesome Toys has hired us to consult on its cloud data transformation. The chief data officer has explained that Mega Awesome Toys has factories across the globe, with lots of IoT data coming in from machinery building toys. It also has substantial financial data from sales and toy production. It is also expanding into online sales and has a growing amount of web-based data coming in large amounts. The company has settled on AWS as its cloud provider. Its websites use MongoDB, and it has several other relational databases. Its data warehouse is on a small Microsoft SQL deployment. It has several data analysts, data scientists, and data engineers who all use Python and SQL. It also has a team of software engineers. Its long-term goal is to leverage machine learning and statistics from its data into all areas of its business. It is desperate for technology leadership as it migrates off on-premises solutions.

Solution

There are several key details to take note of:

- AWS
- MongoDB
- Microsoft SQL and other relational databases
- Python and SQL for data usage
- Data scientists, analysts, and engineers
- A team of software engineers

One possible solution is as follows:

- MongoDB has a hosted cloud offering called Atlas that is 100% compatible with AWS. So, yes, there are AWS-native choices, but given there is no need to choose an AWS product here, I would suggest a best-of-breed solution.

- Relational databases are a dime a dozen, and AWS RDS is perfect. Therefore, I would suggest choosing a flavor. I recommend PostgreSQL on RDS unless global scaling is an essential requirement; then, I would look at CockroachDB or AWS Aurora. Since there isn't much magic in relational databases, using RDS is easy in most cases.

- Given the skills, roles, and long-term goals that have been set, I would recommend the lakehouse architecture combined with a data mesh approach. Since streaming (real-time) was directly mentioned, I would shy away from having that over Kafka and instead use Databricks as a component for the data platform. For a long time, Databricks has set itself as the front-runner for machine learning, artificial intelligence, statistics, data lakes, data warehouses, and more. It is compatible with all major cloud vendors.

2
Understanding Data Analytics

A new discipline called analytics engineering has emerged. An analytics engineer is primarily focused on taking the data once it's been delivered and crafting it into consumable data products. An analytics engineer is expected to document, clean, and manipulate whatever users need, whether they are data scientists or business executives. The process of curating and shaping this data can abstractly be understood as data modeling.

In this chapter, we will go over several approaches to data modeling and documentation. We will, at the same time, start looking into PySpark APIs, as well as working with tools for code-based documentation.

By the end of the chapter, you will have built the fundamental skills to start any data analytics project.

In this chapter, we're going to cover the following main topics:

- Graphviz and `diagrams`
- Covering critical PySpark APIs for data cleaning and preparation
- Data modeling for SQL and NoSQL
- Dimensional data modeling

Technical requirements

I suggest the following:

- PyCharm
- A Databricks notebook
- A Python environment with the following packages installed:
  - PySpark
  - `diagrams`
- Graphviz

Setting up your environment

In this chapter, we will mostly work locally in an IDE; I would like to help walk you through setting that environment up.

Python

You have several options for installing Python. Some directions are the following:

- `https://github.com/pyenv/pyenv` or `https://github.com/pyenv-win/pyenv-win` for Windows
- Using the system Python tool

Type the following:

```
python --version
```

You will be presented with a version of Python 3.5 or above, ideally.

venv

We can install and set up our virtual environment using the following:

```
python3 -m pip install virtualenv
python3 -m venv chapter2
chapter2\Scripts\activate
pip install <package>
deactivate
```

Graphviz

Graphviz is a very common and widely used graphic drawing tool. Its commonly used to create programmatically generated charts and diagrams.

Installations are available for every major OS here: `https://graphviz.org/`.

Workflow initialization

For this chapter, all Python code assumes you have run the following code.

First, enable the virtual environment and start the Python interpreter or put your code into a Python module and run it with the following:

```
 python [file name]:
chapter2\Scripts\activate
python
```

Let's first import our libraries:

```
from functools import partial
from pyspark.sql import SparkSession
from pyspark.sql.functions import col, when, regexp_replace, flatten, explode, struct, create_map, array
from pyspark.sql.types import StructType,StructField, StringType, IntegerType, ArrayType, TimestampType
```

Then, let's set up a local `spark` instance:

```
spark = SparkSession.builder.appName('chap_2').master("local[*]").getOrCreate()
```

Cleaning and preparing your data

The history of data processing is long and has had several unique innovations. When you pull up data in Excel or any other data processing tool, you often see issues with the data that require fixes and changes. Data issues are extremely common, even with robust data practices. We will now go through several fundamental techniques using Apache Spark for cleansing and wrangling your data.

Duplicate values

Here, we set up our example DataFrame:

```
data_frame = spark.createDataFrame(data = [("Brian," "Engr," 1),
    ("Nechama", "Engr", 2),
    ("Naava", "Engr", 3),
    ("Miri", "Engr", 4),
    ("Brian", "Engr", 1),
    ("Miri", "Engr", 3),
  ], schema = ["name", "div", "ID"])
```

The first method we can use is the `distinct` method. It will filter and show only unique rows:

```
data_frame.distinct().show(truncate=False)
+-----+----+---+
|name |div |ID |
+-----+----+---+
|Brian|Engr|1  |
|Jill |Engr|2  |
|James|Engr|3  |
|Miri |Engr|4  |
|Miri |Engr|3  |
+-----+----+---+
```

An alternative to `distinct` is `dropDuplicates`, which gives you the option to look at an entire row:

```
data_frame.dropDuplicates().show(truncate=False)
+-----+----+---+
|name |div |ID |
+-----+----+---+
|Brian|Engr|1  |
|Jill |Engr|2  |
|James|Engr|3  |
|Miri |Engr|4  |
|Miri |Engr|3  |
+-----+----+---+
```

You can also look at a subset of a row using a list of columns:

```
data_frame.dropDuplicates(["ID"]).show(truncate=False)
+-----+----+---+
|name |div |ID |
+-----+----+---+
|Brian|Engr|1  |
|Jill |Engr|2  |
|James|Engr|3  |
|Miri |Engr|4  |
+-----+----+---+
```

Working with nulls

It can be extremely common to receive data with null values.

Here, we set up our example DataFrames:

```
data_frame_2 = spark.createDataFrame(data = [("Brian," "Engr", 1),
    ("Nechama", "", None),
    ("Naava", "Engr", 3),
    ("Miri", "", 4),
    ("Brian", "Engr", None),
    ("Miri", "", 3),
  ], schema = ["name", "div", "ID"])
data_frame = spark.createDataFrame(data = [("Brian", "Engr", 1),
    ("Nechama", "Engr", None),
    ("Naava", "Engr", 3),
    ("Miri", "Engr", 4),
    ("Brian", "Engr", None),
    ("Miri", "Engr", 3),
  ], schema = ["name", "div", "ID"])
```

Using `isNull` and `isNotNull` is a very useful way to handle null values. In these examples, we are filtering rows based on the existence or the lack of nulls in the ID column:

```
data_frame.filter(col("ID").isNull()).show()
+-------+----+----+
|   name| div|  ID|
+-------+----+----+
|Nechama|Engr|null|
|  Brian|Engr|null|
+-------+----+----+

data_frame.filter(col("ID").isNotNull()).show()
+-----+----+---+
| name| div| ID|
+-----+----+---+
|Brian|Engr|  1|
|Naava|Engr|  3|
| Miri|Engr|  4|
| Miri|Engr|  3|
+-----+----+---+
```

In this example, we are checking that both the ID and the name columns are not null:

```
data_frame.filter(col("ID").isNotNull() &  (col("name").isNotNull())).show()
+-----+----+---+
| name| div| ID|
+-----+----+---+
|Brian|Engr|  1|
|Naava|Engr|  3|
| Miri|Engr|  4|
| Miri|Engr|  3|
+-----+----+---+
```

We also have the option of using the `select` method and creating a null label column. Using a label can be beneficial at times. One example could be to use that column as a feature for a machine learning model:

```
data_frame.select(col("*"), col("ID").isNull().alias("null")).show()
```

```
+-------+----+----+----------+
|   name| div|  ID| null     |
+-------+----+----+----------+
|  Brian|Engr|   1|     false|
```

```
|Nechama|Engr|null|      true|
|  Naava|Engr|   3|     false|
|   Miri|Engr|   4|     false|
|  Brian|Engr|null|      true|
|   Miri|Engr|   3|     false|
+-------+----+----+----------+
```

Here is an example of using the `select` method to build a cleaned version of a column that incorrectly defined nulls as empty strings. It is very common to find cases where nulls are set to alternative values:

```
data_frame_2.select(col("*"), when(col("div") == "" ,None).
otherwise(col("div")).alias("cleaned_div")).show()
+-------+----+----+-----------+
|   name| div|  ID|cleaned_div|
+-------+----+----+-----------+
|  Brian|Engr|   1|       Engr|
|Nechama|    |null|       null|
|  Naava|Engr|   3|       Engr|
|   Miri|    |   4|       null|
|  Brian|Engr|null|       Engr|
|   Miri|    |   3|       null|
+-------+----+----+-----------+
```

Using RegEx

RegEx is an amazing tool when cleaning and working with data. Going into extensive details on RegEx is outside the scope of our discussion, but let's go through how to use it to clean data.

Here, we replace the one value in the `ID` column with an alternative value. Yes, we could have handled this using the same method we used to replace null values. The difference is here we have a very complex language (RegEx) to pattern-match with:

```
data_frame.select(col("*"), regexp_replace('ID', '1', '10').
alias("fixed_ID")).show()
+-------+----+----+----------------------------+
|   name| div|  ID|Fixed_ID                    |
+-------+----+----+----------------------------+
|  Brian|Engr|   1|                          10|
|Nechama|Engr|null|                        null|
|  Naava|Engr|   3|                           3|
|   Miri|Engr|   4|                           4|
|  Brian|Engr|null|                        null|
|   Miri|Engr|   3|                           3|
+-------+----+----+----------------------------+
```

Here, we are replacing all values in the name column that start with Mi to start with mi instead:

```
data_frame.select(col("*"), regexp_replace('name', '^Mi', 'mi').
alias("cleaned_name")).show()
+-------+----+----+-------------------------------+
|   name| div|  ID|cleaned_name                   |
+-------+----+----+-------------------------------+
|  Brian|Engr|   1|                          Brian|
|Nechama|Engr|null|                        Nechama|
|  Naava|Engr|   3|                          Naava|
|   Miri|Engr|   4|                           miri|
|  Brian|Engr|null|                          Brian|
|   Miri|Engr|   3|                           miri|
+-------+----+----+-------------------------------+
```

Outlier identification

It can be common to look for outliers in columns, and this is often used in analysis and data science workflows.

We set up our example DataFrame here:

```
data_frame_3 = spark.createDataFrame(data = [("Brian", "Engr", 1),
    ("Nechama", "Engr", 1),
    ("Naava", "Engr", 3),
    ("Miri", "Engr", 5),
    ("Brian", "Engr", 7),
    ("Miri", "Engr", 9),
], schema = ["name", "div", "ID"])
```

Here, we are using * to unpack a list and pass each element into the select method individually. This can be a very useful technique to use. We are also using the binary not operator to reverse the range identification and pass it to the when method:

```
data_frame_3.select(col("name"),
        *[
            when(
                ~col("ID").between(3, 10),
                "yes"
            ).otherwise("no").alias('outlier')
        ]
    ).show()
+-------+-------+
|   name|outlier|
+-------+-------+
```

```
|  Brian|    yes|
|Nechama|    yes|
|  Naava|     no|
|   Miri|     no|
|  Brian|     no|
|   Miri|     no|
+-------+-------+
```

Casting columns

Data columns can sometimes be set to the wrong data type when dealing with raw tables. This type of error ideally should be fixed as far upstream as possible.

First, let's create our example DataFrame:

```
data_frame_4 = spark.createDataFrame(data = [("Brian", "Engr", "1"),
    ("Nechama", "Engr", "1"),
    ("Naava", "Engr", "3"),
    ("Miri", "Engr", "5"),
    ("Brian", "Engr", "7"),
    ("Miri", "Engr", "9"),
  ], schema = ["name", "div", "ID"])
```

We will first look at the schema of the DataFrame to see what the data types are. We will notice that the ID column is string, not int:

```
data_frame_4.schema
StructType([StructField('name', StringType(), True),
StructField('div', StringType(), True), StructField('ID',
StringType(), True)])
```

Here, we cast the ID column from string to int:

```
data_frame_4.select(col("*"),col("ID").cast('int').alias("cleaned_ID")).show()
+-------+----+---+----------+
|   name| div| ID|cleaned_ID|
+-------+----+---+----------+
|  Brian|Engr|  1|         1|
|Nechama|Engr|  1|         1|
|  Naava|Engr|  3|         3|
|   Miri|Engr|  5|         5|
|  Brian|Engr|  7|         7|
|   Miri|Engr|  9|         9|
+-------+----+---+----------+
```

Fixing column names

It's very common to have columns come from data sources with odd naming conventions. When passing data between teams, one team often has norms that won't match another team's coding practices.

Here we are using the `alias` method on the `column` object to rename the name column:

```
data_frame_4.select(col("ID"),col("name").alias("user_name")).show()
+---+---------+
| ID|user_name|
+---+---------+
|  1|    Brian|
|  1|  Nechama|
|  3|    Naava|
|  5|     Miri|
|  7|    Brian|
|  9|     Miri|
+---+---------+
```

Complex data types

We are now going to set up DataFrames for these examples. Keep in mind that Spark always has a strongly enforced schema on all columns, so every row has the same schema, no matter whether the dataframe is structured or semi-structured when working with DataFrames:

```
schema_5 = StructType([
        StructField('user', StructType([
            StructField('name', StringType(), True),
            StructField('age', IntegerType(), True),
            StructField('id', IntegerType(), True)
            ])),
        StructField('codes', ArrayType(StringType()), True),
        StructField('location_id', IntegerType(), True),
        ])
data_5 =   [(("Bruce Lee", 21, 1), [5,6,7,8],9)]
data_frame_5 = spark.createDataFrame(data=data_5,schema=schema_5)
```

Now we will select the name element of the `user` array:

```
data_frame_5.select("user.name").show()
+---------+
|     name|
+---------+
|Bruce Lee|
+---------+
```

In the `codes` column, we have an array of values. We can access them manually using the bracket notation:

```
data_frame_5.select(col("codes")[0]).show()
+--------+
|codes[0]|
+--------+
|       5|
+--------+
```

Now we will set up another DataFrame for a different example. Take note that the array has two secondary arrays, and then within each of them, there are small arrays:

```
data_frame_6 = spark.createDataFrame([([[9, 7], [56, 12], [23,43]],),
([ [400, 500]],)],["random_stuff"])
data_frame_6.show(truncate=False)
+---------------------------+
|random_stuff               |
+---------------------------+
|[[9, 7], [56, 12], [23, 43]]|
|[[400, 500]]               |
+---------------------------+
```

We will now use the `flatten` function to turn the preceding structure into a simplified two-element array:

```
data_frame_6.select(flatten("random_stuff")).show(truncate=False)
+----------------------+
|flatten(random_stuff) |
+----------------------+
|[9, 7, 56, 12, 23, 43]|
|[400, 500]            |
+----------------------+
```

Another very useful function is the `explode` function. It will take a column with an array and transform the whole DataFrame by extracting the array into several unique rows of the DataFrame:

```
data_frame_5.select(col("location_id"), explode("codes").
alias("new")).show()
+-----------+---+
|location_id|new|
+-----------+---+
|          9|  5|
|          9|  6|
|          9|  7|
|          9|  8|
+-----------+---+
```

Here is another example of using the `explode` function, this time on a hash structure:

```
data_frame_7 = spark.createDataFrame([ ({"apple": "red"},
1), ({"orange": "orange"}, 2)], ["fruit", "id"])
data_frame_7.show(truncate=False)
+------------------+---+
|             fruit| id|
+------------------+---+
|     {apple -> red}|  1|
|{orange -> orange}|  2|
+------------------+---+
```

Notice that now we have `key` and `value` columns:

```
data_frame_7.select(col("id"), explode("fruit")).show()
+---+------+------+
| id|   key| value|
+---+------+------+
|  1| apple|   red|
|  2|orange|orange|
+---+------+------+
```

Lastly, we will create a complex semi-structured DataFrame. We are using the `create_map` and `array` functions to create this structure:

```
test = \ data_frame_4.select(col("id"),create_
map("id",struct(["name","div"])).alias("complex_map"),
array(["name","div"]).alias("complex_array"))
test.show(truncate=False)
+---+----------------------+---------------+
|id |complex_map           |complex_array  |
+---+----------------------+---------------+
|1  |{1 -> {Brian, Engr}}  |[Brian, Engr]  |
|1  |{1 -> {Nechama, Engr}}|[Nechama, Engr]|
|3  |{3 -> {Naava, Engr}}  |[Naava, Engr]  |
|5  |{5 -> {Miri, Engr}}   |[Miri, Engr]   |
|7  |{7 -> {Brian, Engr}}  |[Brian, Engr]  |
|9  |{9 -> {Miri, Engr}}   |[Miri, Engr]   |
+---+----------------------+---------------+
```

Let's take a look at the final schema:

```
test.schema
StructType([StructField('id', StringType(), True),
StructField('complex_map', MapType(StringType(),
StructType([StructField('name', StringType(), True),
```

```
StructField('div', StringType(), True)]), False), False),
StructField('complex_array', ArrayType(StringType(), True), False)])
```

Here, we have worked with complex semi-structured data, often found in web data. It's accustomed to working with well-processed data structured into rows and columns. The reality is that most data in its raw form will not be structured, and knowing the basics of how to deal with that data is very useful. We will now look at documenting our data, which is essential and a very handy skill to acquire.

Data documentation

Data can get complex and often documentation is non-existent. We will look into two areas that can be documented with code. Using code to document GUI tools allows for code to be stored and reviewed effectively like any other code written.

diagrams

The `diagrams` library is very useful for creating solution diagrams. A solution diagram is often a broad picture of the architecture and key components. It can be organized in a way that explains key interactions.

Here, we are creating a small example document using the `diagrams` package:

```
from diagrams import Cluster, Diagram
from diagrams.aws.analytics import Quicksight, EMR
with Diagram("Data Platform", show=False):
    with Cluster("Dev"):
        dashboards = Quicksight("Tableau")
        spark_clusters = [EMR("Notebook_cluster"), EMR("Jobs_cluster")]
        dashboards >> spark_clusters
```

Here is a second example using custom icons to better represent your current tech stack:

```
from diagrams import Cluster, Diagram
from diagrams import Diagram, Cluster
from diagrams.custom import Custom
with Diagram("Dataplatform", show=False, filename="dataplatform_custom"):
    with Cluster("Prod - VPC"):
        compute = [Custom("Tiny", "./db_cluster.png") , Custom("Med", "./db_cluster.png")]
        dashboards = Custom("Tiny", "./tabl.png")
        dashboards << compute
```

Here, we can see an example output of the preceding code:

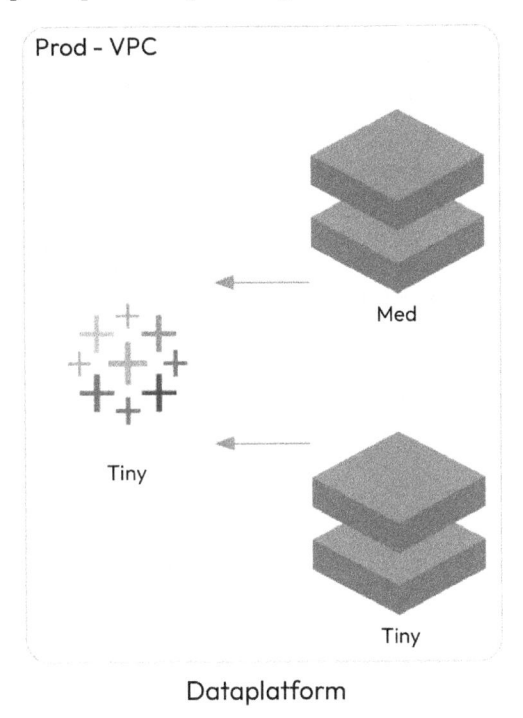

Figure 2.1: Sample output for the diagrams library

Data lineage graphs

Data lineage is often a complex process to map out and requires a great deal of effort using complex tooling. Graphviz works extremely well for this task and any other schema-related graphing tasks. Graphviz has the added benefit of being code, so it goes through the normal software development life cycle. Here, we are using the DOT language, but Python is also supported by Graphviz.

The basic components of the following graph are the setup, table schema, and then the lineage DAG. There is no reason this can't be turned into an automated process.

```
sales.gv file:
```

First, we will create a basic pre-table defining the settings for the graph:

```
digraph {
    graph [pad="1.1", nodesep="1.7", ranksep="2.7"];
    node [shape=plain]
    rankdir=LR;
```

We will now define the `Books` table:

```
Books [label=<
<table border="0.1" cellborder="1.2" cellspacing="0.5">
  <tr><td><i>Books Table</i></td></tr>
  <tr><td port="1">ID</td></tr>
  <tr><td port="2">Sales_Assistant</td></tr>
  <tr><td port="3">Name</td></tr>
  <tr><td port="4">ISBN</td></tr>
  <tr><td port="5">Purchase_Date</td></tr>
</table>>];
```

Next, we will define the `Computers` table:

```
Computers [label=<
<table border="0.1" cellborder="1.2" cellspacing="0.5">
  <tr><td><i>Computers Table</i></td></tr>
  <tr><td port="6">ID</td></tr>
  <tr><td port="7">Sales_Assistant</td></tr>
  <tr><td port="8">Model</td></tr>
  <tr><td port="9">Purchase_Date</td></tr>
</table>>];
```

Lastly, we will define the `Sales` table:

```
Sales [label=<
<table border="0.1" cellborder="1.2" cellspacing="0.5">
  <tr><td><i>Sales Table</i></td></tr>
  <tr><td port="10">ID</td></tr>
  <tr><td port="8">Sales_Assistant</td></tr>
  <tr><td port="9">Purchase_Date</td></tr>
</table>>];
```

We now define our relationships between table columns. Make sure to get the number correct or the graph will look off:

```
Books:1 -> Sales:10
Books:2 -> Sales:8
Books:5 -> Sales:9
Computers:6 -> Sales:10
Computers:7 -> Sales:8
Computers:9 -> Sales:9
}
```

Now, let's create a .png file:

```
dot sales.gv -Tpng -o sales.png
```

This results in the following output:

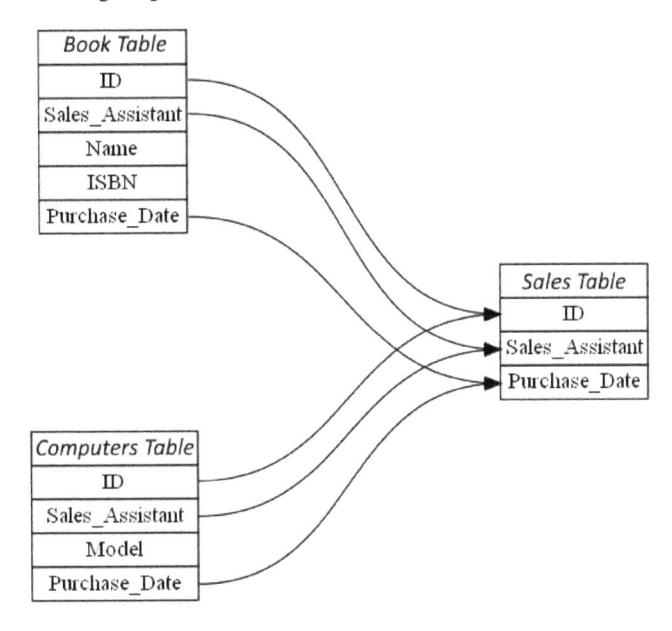

Figure 2.2: Relationship output between our tables

We have a few tools to do some documentation of our data and data applications. It's crucial when onboarding or working with a data team to have useful documents that allow you fully understand the intent and application of what the team is trying to do. Next, we will look at data modeling patterns, focusing on traditional techniques you might find.

Data modeling patterns

Data modeling is simply defining the shapes and forms in which our data will be persisted or accessed via. Modeling can work for structured data and semi-structured data. Modeling typically starts with understanding what the user wants and finding an appropriate shape or form to meet that need.

Relational

Relational modeling for transactional databases is a common set of techniques for making your data reliable, fast to write, and not duplicated.

First normal form

The first normal form is the process of making sure each column has only atomic values. That translates into conforming arrays and other types of semi-structured data.

An example of something not in first normal form is as follows:

```
|               fruit| id|
+--------------------+---+
|     {apple -> red}|  1|
```

Here is the result of it being in first normal form:

```
| fruit| id|color|
+------+---+-----+
|apple |  1|  red|
```

Second normal form

The second normal form is the processing of taking something in the first normal form and removing partial dependencies. The second normal form is a way to better organize your data and reduce the space used by deduplication. Partial dependency can be understood as when a column depends on some of the primary keys but not all.

Consider the following:

```
| Student_ID |  Book_ID | Book_Price|
```

`Book_Price` can't be used to determine `Book_ID` or `Student_ID`, and it can't be combined with `Student_ID` or `Book_ID` to determine the other column. `Book_Price` is what is called a non-prime attribute since it's isolated from the other two columns. The `Candidate` key is a combination of `Book_ID` and `Student_ID`. `Book_Price` can identify `Book_Price`, so `Book_Price` relies on `Book_ID`. This is a case of a non-prime attribute dependency. `Book_Price` is the non-prime attribute, and it depends on only part of the candidate key. This is not in second normal form.

A solution is to create two tables:

```
Students:
|Student_ID| Book_ID|
Books:
|Book_ID| Book_Price|
```

Third normal form

The third normal form starts with one or more tables that are in second normal form and then removes any transitive dependencies. A transitive dependency can be understood as a column that relies on something other than the key. This type of relationship creates instability in your table; fixing this type of situation usually involves splitting the table.

Consider the following:

```
|customer_id| state|country| name| ssn|
```

`state` relies on `ID`, and `country` relies on `state`. So, this is a transitive relationship, and it doesn't directly rely on the key.

The solution is as follows.

Create two tables:

```
|customer_id| state|country| name| ssn|
| state|country|
```

According to Codd's rule of normalization, there are seven rules, but data in the third normal form can be considered suitable for OLTP systems. The more normalized the database, the more consistency there is, but this can also lead to database-locking issues.

NoSQL

There are four types of NoSQL data models and technologies, as follows:

- Key-value pair (for example, Redis)
- Columnar (for example, Cassandra)
- General-purpose (for example, MongoDB)
- Graph (for example, Neo4j)

They differ significantly as a group from the traditional structure of data models and technologies, which normally relies on flat data structures.

NoSQL is a broad range of technologies, but in this case, we will talk about columnar and general document stores. Columnar and general document data stores do not typically allow you to join tables, so denormalization is required. Many architects will recommend you first bring your schema into the third normal form before you start looking at deformalizing your data; this creates a well-organized plan for your data. The two main types of denormalization are creating useful copies of columns and creating pre-calculated aggregate values in tables.

Creating copies of a column in multiple tables has several benefits, including being able to read and process data faster; the reason for this is that we are removing the need to join data. Keep in mind that joins are expensive, and the larger your data is, the more expensive those joins will be. This also allows for queries to your tables to be less complex. This comes as a cost, though; you will have more complex procedures for writing data. These complex procedures may produce errors and will take longer to complete. There is a potential that you will have inconsistent columns if your writing process has any bugs in it. Lastly, this will increase data storage costs, but given our current environment, that isn't a worry. This style of denormalization is perfect for NoSQL but also for any OLAP scenario.

The second style of denormalization is to create pre-calculated aggregate fields. Like the first style of denormalization, this creates faster reads since the calculations are already completed. The downside to this approach is that again your writing process now includes creating these premade calculations. You will find this type of denormalization heavily used in dimensional modeling, which will explore in the next section.

Dimensional modeling

A dimensional model is traditionally seen in OLAP techniques such as data warehouses and data lakes using Apache Spark. The goal of dimensional modeling is to reduce duplication and create a central source of truth. One reason for the reduction of data duplication is to save on storage costs, which isn't as much of a factor in modern cloud storage. This data model consists of dimensions and facts. The dimension is the entity that we are trying to model in the real world, such as CUSTOMER, PRODUCT, DATE, or LOCATION, and the fact holds the numerical data such as REVENUE, PROFIT, SALES $ VALUE, and so on. The primary key of the dimensions flows to the fact table as a foreign key but more often than not, it is not hardcoded into the database. Rather, it is managed through the process that manages loading and maintaining data, such as **Extract, Transform, and Load** (ETL). This data model is business-user-friendly and is used for analytical reporting and analysis.

Ralph Kimball created the dimensional modeling warehouse, which is largely documented in his book *The Data Warehouse Toolkit*. Kimball designed a bottom-up approach, which basically means Kimball suggests first defining business needs and then creating your data warehouse. Since we are dealing with denormalized models, they're fast to create and modify. Dimensional modeling is heavily focused on reading data fast. Dimensional modeling classically is in a star schema, in which facts point to dimensions and dimensions do not point to other dimensions. Dimensions will then sit in the middle of the schema, resembling a star.

Key terms

We will explore some of the key terms used in dimensional modeling here:

- **Dimensions**: Dimensions are the who, what, and where you would record in your model. Dimensions will be the context of the values you see in the facts table.

- **Conformed dimensions**: A conformed dimension is a dimension that means the same thing to all the facts it relates to.
- **Facts**: Facts are values that are used to better understand a business goal/problem tied to dimensions. Facts are given in a certain level of detail or grain.
- **Slowly Changing Dimensions (SCDs)**: SCDs are used to record change over time, and in general, any SCD beyond type 1 should have a reasonable business use case:
  - **Type 1**: A Type 1 SCD is a table that records no change; any update to the table replaces an entry if there is a match for that key. This is the default behavior of many tables.
  - **Type 2**: Type 2 SCD is the application of taking the table, adding a current column, and, as new versions come in, changing the current flag so that the old data is set to `false`, and the new row is set to `true`. Type 2 SCD tables can hold an unlimited amount of historical data.
  - **Type 3**: Type 3 SCD is very similar to Type 2 but with a few differences. First, the current column is replaced with an `effective_date` column. Secondly, the table will hold a limited period of data.
  - **Type 4**: Type 4 SCD is the practice of keeping the original table up to date like Type 1 but creating a history table with past values and creation dates. This will allow for faster changes to be handled and faster reads from the table.
- **Dimensional workflows**: The first step in creating a dimensional model is to research the business goals and needs and what problems they are looking to solve. With that in mind, you are then able to understand what the data needs are. This can also include working with the BI team to see what data is needed for your dashboards. Once you have mapped out your goals, problems, and needs, you will need to understand the level of detail the data needs to be stored in; this is often called the grain. The grain defines the lowest level of detail your data must be stored in. This can be extremely important when considering different ways a business might aggregate data, and in many cases, you will not be able to derive a lower grain. Once our grain is clear, we can start defining our dimensions. We define our dimensions first so that we understand what data should be stored in our facts tables. Once our dimensions are created, our facts are now possible to define. Facts are the last needed information before creating our star schema.

We have discussed the basics of traditional data warehousing, and how data can be organized into facts and dimensions. This style is very good for creating a single source of truth, with very little data duplication. It is debated whether this style is needed in modern computing. I can't say if it is or isn't but an alternative is to use the **One Big Table** (**OBT**) approach when creating data products. This approach is more focused on finding the optimal data product for the specific use case, and will often create data duplication in multiple tables.

OBT

There has been some discussion in the community about storing information in one large table. Essentially, this is a denormalized table with all the benefits and issues mentioned before with denormalization. Personally, I believe there can be huge benefits to the OBT approach, but with the increase in complexity as your needs grow, storing everything in one table can become very problematic. The more columns that grow in your table, the more likely you will have inserts in your table, and this can grow to the point where it's impossible to maintain. An alternative approach might be to create data products once your OBT is becoming too much to handle. That data product would be a single table based on specific use cases that are pulled from a dimensional model. This allows for the best of both worlds and will negate all the negatives of each option. The only downside to this approach is you have increased complexity and storage.

Practical lab

We have a bronze table being loaded into our data lake using a third-party tool. There has been a request to clean up the data and resolve known issues. Your task is to write the needed Python code that will address each of the following issues.

The following are the issues present:

- **Wrong column name**: The `date` column is spelled wrong
- **Nulls not correctly identified**: The `sales_id` column has null values as `NA` strings
- **Data with missing values is unwanted**: Any data with a null in `sales_id` should be dropped
- **Duplicate sales_id**: Take the first value of any duplicate rows
- **Date column not DateType**: The `date` column is not a DateType

Loading the problem data

The following code will create our bronze table:

```
bronze_sales = spark.createDataFrame(data = [
    ("1", "LA", "2000-01-01",5, 1400),
    ("2", "LA", "1998-2-01",4, 1500),
    ("2", "LA", "1998-2-01",4, 1500),
    ("3", "LA", "1997-4-01",6, 1300),
    ("4", "LA", "2005-5-01",2, 1100),
    ("NA", "LA", "2013-6-01",1, 1200),
], schema = ["sales_id", "city", "dat"," clerk_id", "total_sales"])
```

Solution

We will explore the solution to our problem here:

1. Here, we are using the `select` method, choosing all columns, renaming the `dat` column `date`, and dropping the original:

   ```
   one = bronze_sales.select(col("*"), col("dat").alias("date")).
   drop("dat")
   ```

2. Now, we are selecting all columns. Then, we use the `when otherwise` logic flow to define and identify the null values and correct them:

   ```
   two = bronze_sales\
       .select(col("*"),
           when(col("sales_id") == "NA" ,None)
           .otherwise(col("sales_id")).alias("cleaned_sales_id"))\
       .drop("sales_id")\
       .select(col("*"), col("cleaned_sales_id").alias("sales_id"))\
       .drop("cleaned_sales_id")
   ```

3. We are now using the `drop na` method on the DataFrame and giving it the `sales_id` column:

   ```
   three = two.na.drop(subset=["sales_id"])
   ```

4. This time, we will use the `dropduplicates` method on our DataFrame on `sales_id`:

   ```
   four = two.dropDuplicates(subset=["sales_id"])
   ```

5. Lastly, we use the `select` method, add all columns, then use the `to_data` function on the `date` column. We replace the `date` column with the corrected date:

   ```
   five = one\
       .select(col("*"), to_date("date").alias("date_fixed"))\
       .drop("date")\
       .select(col("*"), col("date_fixed").alias("date"))\
       .drop("date_fixed")
   ```

Summary

Wow, we have gone through so many concepts in this chapter! First, we reviewed the basics of data modeling in SQL and NoSQL. We then looked at the fundamental Spark APIs for data cleansing and various data documentation tooling. Lastly, we looked at dimensional modeling for data warehousing. We have set up the building blocks for the data analytics engineer role with these techniques and tools. Once you understand the needs of your users, you can now model and cleanse your data.

In the next chapter, we will explore Spark further, as well as some cloud computing techniques.

Part 2: Data Engineering Toolset

In this part, we will go through the bread-and-butter tools found in most companies. We will explore and deeply understand Apache Spark, Delta Lake, Batch processing, and Streaming. We will then look at how to work with Kafka, the most popular dedicated Streaming tool.

This part has the following chapters:

- *Chapter 3, Apache Spark Deep Dive*
- *Chapter 4, Batch and Stream Data Processing using PySpark*
- *Chapter 5, Streaming Data with Kafka*

3
Apache Spark Deep Dive

One of the most fundamental questions for an architect is how they should store their data and what methodology they should use. For example, should they use a relational database, or should they use object storage? This chapter attempts to explain which storage pattern is best for your scenario. Then, we will go through how to set up Delta Lake, a hybrid approach to data storage in an object store. In most cases, we will stick to the Python API, but in some cases, we will have to use SQL. Lastly, we will cover the most important Apache Spark theory you need to know to build a data platform effectively.

In this chapter, we're going to cover the following main topics:

- Understand how Spark manages its cluster
- How Spark processes data
- How cloud storage varies and what options are available
- How to create and manage Delta Lake tables and databases

Technical requirements

The tooling that will be used in this chapter is tied to the tech stack that's been chosen for this book. All vendors should offer a free trial account.

I will be using the following:

- Databricks
- AWS or Azure

Setting up your environment

Before we begin this chapter, let's take some time to set up our working environment.

Python, AWS, and Databricks

As in previous chapters, this chapter assumes you have a working version of Python 3.6 or higher installed in your development environment. It also assumes you have set up an AWS account and have set up Databricks with that AWS account.

If you do not have a working Databricks setup, please refer to the following guide to get started: https://docs.databricks.com/en/getting-started/index.html.

Databricks CLI

The first step is to install the `databricks-cli` tool using the `pip` Python package manager:

```
pip install databricks-cli
```

Let's validate that everything has been installed correctly. If the following command produces the tool's version, then everything is working correctly:

```
Databricks -v
```

Now, let's set up authentication. First, go into the Databricks UI and generate a personal access token. The following command will ask for the host that was created for your Databricks instance and the created token:

```
databricks configure -token
```

We can determine whether the CLI has been set up correctly by running the following command. If no error is returned, then you have a working setup:

```
databricks fs ls
```

Lastly, let's set up our `workspace`, `clusters`, and `dbfs` folders:

```
databricks   fs mkdirs   dbfs:/chapter_3
databricks   workspace mkdirs   /chapter_3
databricks   clusters create -json-file   <file_path to tiny.json>
```

The following is the content of the `tiny.json` file:

```
{   "num_workers":0, "cluster_name":"tiny",   "spark_version":"10.4.x-scala2.12",
    "spark_conf":{
        "spark.master":"local[*, 4]",    "spark.databricks.cluster.profile":"singleNode"
    },  "aws_attributes":{
        "first_on_demand":1,   "availability":"SPOT_WITH_
```

```
FALLBACK",   "zone_id":"us-west-2b",
      "instance_profile_arn":null, "spot_bid_price_percent":100,
      "ebs_volume_type":"GENERAL_PURPOSE_SSD",
      "ebs_volume_count":3, "ebs_volume_size":100
   },   "node_type_id":"m4.large",   "driver_node_type_id":"m4.large",
   "ssh_public_keys":[ ],"custom_
tags":{   "ResourceClass":"SingleNode"}, "spark_env_vars":{   "PYSPARK_
PYTHON":"/databricks/python3/bin/python3"},
    "autotermination_minutes":10, "enable_elastic_
disk":false,   "cluster_source":"UI",   "init_scripts":[ ], "data_
security_mode":"NONE",  "runtime_engine":"STANDARD"}
```

Cloud data storage

Modern data storage in the cloud comes in many flavors. The main flavors are in three general areas: object storage, NoSQL, and relational data storage. Each type of data storage has its pros and cons and should be thoroughly evaluated when you're making decisions.

Object storage

Object storage has become one of the most used storage methods. It comes with plenty of benefits and some significant concerns. The advantages are its filesystem-like nature, its ability to integrate common file types, its massively scalable possibilities, and its relatively low cost. Moreover, object stores can store both structured and semi-structured data and files such as audio and videos. However, object storage does have some characteristics that should always be considered. How do you govern access to your object storage? This can be a significant task. Do you limit what technologies have access to? What files can you store, and how do you store them? How are things maintained, cleaned, and organized? Lastly, how are you creating redundancy? These questions often have layers of answers for each scenario, but in contrast to a traditional database, they can be very complex.

Relational

Relational data storage is a classic choice for storing structured data. Generally, it makes a very good first choice for most data storage projects. SQL is the language that's used to access data from relational databases. Relational data is very limited, though, and typically makes a poor choice for data such as semi-structured data, graph data, and text data.

NoSQL

NoSQL is a general term for data storage that operates outside the traditional relational storage rules. NoSQL can include general document storage such as MongoDB, document search engines such as Elasticsearch, and graph databases such as Neo4j. There is another category that I should mention, but that I shy away from lumping in with other data storage engines. Message queues such as Kafka are often used to store data but contain lots of rough edges to deal with. One example is that data is stored but never deleted, and changes are stored. As a result, making a simple update to a field can become very complex.

Cloud storage is a complex topic. Now that we have introduced the core topics, let's cover Apache Spark and the core concepts needed to work with Spark.

Spark architecture

The Apache Spark architecture is complex, to say the least, and requires in-depth knowledge. However, you only need some background knowledge to be reasonably productive with Spark. So, first, let's go through the basics of Apache Spark.

Introduction to Apache Spark

Spark is a popular parallel data processing framework built from the lessons learned after the Apache Hadoop project. Spark is written in Scala, a JVM language, but supports other languages, including Python, R, and Java, to name a few. Spark can be used as the central processing component in any data platform, but others may be a better fit for your problem. The key thing to understand is that Spark is separated from your storage layer, which allows you to connect Spark to any storage technology you need. Similar tools include Flink, AWS Glue, and Snowflake (Snowflake uses a decoupled storage and compute layer pattern behind the scenes).

Key components

Spark is a cluster-based in-memory processing engine that uses a master/slave approach for coordination. The master is called the driver node, and all other computers in the clusters are worker nodes. If you want to create a single-node cluster, the driver and worker nodes must be combined into one machine. This setup will have issues with larger data, but there are applications where this can be useful.

A driver node will have a driver application, which coordinates the processing of your data job. Each worker node will have an executor application. The driver and the executors will work with each other in the parallel processing workflow, but the executor's process data and the driver will give directions. Each worker node/executor application has several parallelism elements that are created by counting the number of slots. Typically, a slot can be thought of as a core or a thread. If a worker node/executor has 10 slots, then it has 10 parallelism elements. The more you have, the more processing can be done in parallel. There is a trade-off for everything, including cost.

The driver application will have one or more jobs for the cluster to work on. To understand a job, you must first understand lazy evaluation. How Spark works is that all transformations are documented, but nothing is done until an action or the driver application requests an I/O task. Actions range from writing something to a disk to sending a message on a message system such as Kafka. This action is called a job, and the driver will coordinate job executions. Jobs are composed of stages, and stages are groups of tasks that can be done in parallel without the need to move data from one worker node to another. This movement of data is called a shuffle. Again, moving data from one worker node to another is a very expensive cost, so Spark tries to avoid it. A task is the smallest unit of work and is done using a data partition. A partition is a parallel data unit that lives in memory on a single worker node. Partitions are organized into a **resilient distributed dataset** (**RDD**), which is the building block of a DataFrame.

Simply put, an RDD is a representation of data that's not organized into any structure. Any changes that are made to that representation are organized into tasks that get distributed across nodes. DataFrames, on the other hand, are structured and semi-structured representations of data, but they use RDDs behind the scene. One fundamental concept is **partitions**, which we will cover next.

Working with partitions

When working with DataFrames, you must be mindful of how your data is partitioned across the cluster. Some questions you might want to ask are, How many partitions is my data split into at any given time in the job workflow? Can I have control over the number of partitions that get created? How is my data distributed across my partitions? For example, is column X evenly distributed across the network, or is it clumped into a small group of worker nodes? Should I increase or reduce my partitions? Do I have control over which data gets split over which partitions?

Having your partitions closely match your number of parallelism elements is ideal. You don't want to have any executors not processing data, and you don't want too many partitions, which could cause many more of your partitions to have too little data or no data at all.

You can change the number of partitions with shuffling by using the following API:

```
my_data_frame.repartition(10)
```

Alternatively, to reduce partitioning without a shuffle, you can use the following API:

```
my_data_frame.coalesce(5)
```

Shuffling partitions

Shuffling is an important concept when it comes to parallel data processing. When working with multiple nodes to process data, the data is split across each node. When an operation is required that moves that data from one node to another, that movement is called shuffling. In terms of data movement, the slowest process is to move data across the network, which is why it's often avoided.

Spark will automatically set the size of partitions to 200 after any shuffle; adjusting this number used to be a major way to optimize your Spark job. Apache Spark introduced **Adaptive Query Engine (AQE)** in version 3.2.0, which uses runtime statistics to optimize your Spark instructions. Now that AQE is available, this setting should not be adjusted as it won't matter. However, for historical value, here is the code to set the default shuffle partition size:

```
spark.conf.set("spark.sql.shuffle.partitions",100)
```

Caching

Caching is the process of saving your data into memory or on the disk of the worker node for faster retrieval. The general rule of thumb is that reusing the same DataFrame caching *may* be a good idea.

The code for caching a DataFrame is as follows:

```
my_data_frame.persist()
or
my_data_frame.persist(<cache level>)
```

The levels of caching are as follows:

- **Memory only**: Used for storing the DataFrame in memory if the data isn't too large:

    ```
    StorageLevel.MEMORY_ONLY
    ```

- **Memory-only sterilized**: A serialized version of memory only, which translates into smaller data in memory but that is not as fast:

    ```
    StorageLevel.MEMORY_ONLY_SER
    ```

- **Memory with two other nodes**: This is a final addition to the previous level, where the data is also stored in memory on two other nodes. This can be serialized:

    ```
    StorageLevel.MEMORY_ONLY_2
    ```

    You can also use the following code to do this:

    ```
    StorageLevel.MEMORY_ONLY_SER_2
    ```

Spark also offers a version of the preceding level in memory and disk or just disk modes. Data is stored in memory when using memory and disk modes, but if needed, disk mode is also used. It should be noted that retrieving data from memory is always significantly faster than on disk.

The code for each of these levels is as follows:

```
StorageLevel.MEMORY_AND_DISK
StorageLevel.MEMORY_AND_DISK_SER
StorageLevel.MEMORY_AND_DISK_SER_2
```

```
StorageLevel.DISK_ONLY
StorageLevel.DISK_ONLY_2
```

The default is to use memory and disk, so you should look at this first when you're caching data.

The following three code samples can be used to validate that your data has been cached and stored correctly. Each will return a `True` or `False` value:

```
my_data_frame.storageLevel.useMemory
my_data_frame.storageLevel.useDisk
my_data_frame.is_cached
```

Broadcasting

The broadcasting process allows one DataFrame to be sent to all nodes and stored in memory for fast retrieval. This technique's most common use case is joining a small dataset with a large dataset. However, this process is very slow and will require too much data movement across the cluster. Instead, we can broadcast a small dataset and then join using a broadcast join. A broadcast join takes a small dataset and sends it across all nodes, and then joins each node's portion of the larger dataset. This drastically improves performance in those scenarios. AQE will try to automatically change joins to broadcast joins if it feels it's possible. I have seen cases where AQE doesn't set the join to broadcast, but manually doing it worked very well, so keep that in mind.

The code for a broadcast join is as follows:

```
from pyspark.sql.functions import broadcast
my_data_frame.join(broadcast(my_data_frame_2), my_data_frame.id ==
my_data_frame_2.id)
```

Job creation pipeline

When a job is executed on the driver program, it will go through several stages, as of Spark 3.3.0, the latest version at the time of writing this book. Before we go through each of the main stages, let's explain what a plan is. A plan is a list of transformations (not related to master or worker nodes) that must be taken for a given job.

Now, let's go through the main stages of a job:

- **Unresolved logic plan**: We know the syntax has no issues at this point, but our plan might still have issues. One example of issues might be references to columns with wrong names.

- **Analyzed logical plan and an analyzed logical plan with a cache**: Here, our unresolved logical plan is checked against the catalog that Spark manages to see that things such as table names, column names, and data types of columns, among others, are correct.

- **Optimized logical plan**: The plan is sent to the catalyst optimizer, which will take the plan and convert it. The catalyst optimizer will look at several ways it can optimize your code, including what goes in what stage, for example, or what order could be more effective. The most important thing to understand is that the catalyst optimizer will take DataFrame code written in any Spark-compatible language and output an optimized plan. One major reason why using RDDs directly is almost always slower than DataFrames is that they will never go through the catalyst optimizer. As a result, you're not likely to write better RDD code.

- **Spark plan**: The next major step is for AQE to come in and look at our physical plan (created from the optimized logical plan) and make drastic performance improvements. These improvements are performed on non-streaming jobs. The five improvements are adjusting sort merges to broadcast hash joins, adjusting partitions to an optimized state after shuffling, adjusting empty relations, handling skew from sort merges, and shuffling hash joins.

  AQE is a very useful feature to enable most of the time, but there are outlier cases where you might want to disable it. You can do this using the following code:

  ```
  spark.conf.set("spark.sql.adaptive.enabled",false)
  ```

  Setting it to `true` will enable it again:

  ```
  spark.conf.set("spark.sql.adaptive.enabled",true)
  ```

- **Selected physical plan**: The most optical plan is sent to the Tungsten execution engine, which will output even more optimized RDD code in a **directed acyclic graph** (**DAG**). This is a process that goes from start to finish and doesn't loop.

Now that we have gone through the key points of the Apache Spark architecture, looking at and troubleshooting issues should be easier. Understanding what Spark is doing behind the scenes allows you to delve deeper with more research.

Delta Lake

Delta Lake is an evolution in file storage for data tables and merges techniques from data lakes and data warehouse technology. Delta Lake takes the current Parquet technology but adds a transaction log that creates ACID transactions, similar to a database. The key detail to understand is that with transactions, you gain parallelism and reliability, among other features.

Transaction log

One massive adaption Delta Lake gives the traditional data lake is the concept of transactions. A transaction is a small chunk of work that's accomplished in full. In layman's terms, when you send data to a Delta table, you can guarantee that data is written as intended without another user creating anything that hinders that process. This avoids dirty reads and writes and inconsistent data. The main component of this feature is the transaction log, which is an ordered log of every transaction that's made on the table. The transaction log has six actions: adding the file, removing the file, updating metadata, setting a transaction, changing protocol, and committing information. As a reminder, adding a new file is the same as appending new data to the table. The transaction log is stored in the `_delta_log` folder, which contains JSON commit files. The starting JSON filename is `000000.json`.

Now that we have gone through the basic anatomy of a transaction log and what goes on inside them, we will organize objects in the megastore into databases and tables.

Grouping tables with databases

You can organize your tables and other objects into groups using databases/schemas in Spark. Spark uses these terms interchangeably, but we will consistently try to use the term database. You typically have your context set to the default database when you start. It's the best practice to organize your objects into groups and purposefully choose how it's stored.

Tables can be set to two major flavors in Spark: managed and unmanaged. When something is unmanaged, it will exist in the metadata database, but the metadata database will not control the data. One positive to this is that you can't accidentally drop a table. The negative side of using unmanaged tables is losing control and management. I recommend using managed tables and setting the location in the database. I also suggest using permissions on access to mitigate any concern of losing data. To create an unmanaged table, simply define a path for the location of the table. The path can be local, dbfs, or even a cloud storage location such as S3. If you set the location in the database, you do not need to set anything at the table, and you can still use the DROP SQL command.

Default location database

Here, we are creating a database and using the default location for it. Remember that all tables created in that database will be in that location:

```
database_name = "simple_database"
spark.sql(f" CREATE DATABASE IF NOT EXISTS {database_name} COMMENT
'Lets create a managed database';")
spark.sql(f"DESCRIBE DATABASE {database_name}").show()
spark.sql(f"DROP DATABASE IF EXISTS {database_name} CASCADE;")
```

Here, we have the output of the preceding command. We can see several important details, such as its location, comments, and owner:

```
+------------------------+------------------------+
|database_description_item|database_description_value|
+------------------------+------------------------+
|            Catalog Name|           spark_catalog|
|          Namespace Name|         simple_database|
|                 Comment|       Lets create a man...|
|                Location|       dbfs:/user/hive/w...|
```

```
|                        Owner|                        root|
+----------------------------+----------------------------+
```

Specified location database

We can also tell Spark where to put the data in our database. Here, we are using the `dbfs:/tmp/test` location. Using a non-default location can be very useful, for example, in cases where you need to migrate to alternative storage solutions:

```
spark.sql(f" CREATE DATABASE IF NOT EXISTS {database_name} LOCATION
'dbfs:/tmp/test' COMMENT 'Lets create a un-managed database located in
/tmp/';")
spark.sql(f DROP DATABASE IF EXISTS {database_name} CASCADE;")
```

Setting the current database

It can be convenient to tell Spark to use a specific database for the current session. The first command uses the current database, while the second sets the current database:

```
spark.catalog.currentDatabase()
spark.catalog.setCurrentDatabase(database_name)
```

Helper database utilities

When writing utilities around pipelines, validating databases is very useful; the following command can do just that:

```
spark.catalog.databaseExists(database_name)
Output: True
```

Another useful method is the `listDatabase` method, which will let you see any database registered to the metadata database:

```
spark.catalog.listDatabases()
[Database(name='default', catalog='spark_catalog',
'description.....'),
 Database(name='simple_database', catalog='spark_catalog',
description='....')]
```

Table

We will now go over some Delta Lake table functionality using the Python API. Databases always organize tables, so I will include database creations with our examples:

```
database_name = "simple_database"
spark.sql(f" CREATE SCHEMA IF NOT EXISTS {database_name} COMMENT 'Lets
create a managed database using schema';")
```

Here, we are creating an example DataFrame to use:

```
data_frame = spark.createDataFrame(data = [("Brian", 1, 1),
    ("John", 2, 2),
    ("Sam", 3, 3),
    ("Nechama Dina", 4, 4),
    ("Mary", 5, 5)
  ], schema = ["name", "age", "SSN"])
```

Managed table

In this first example, we will create a managed table. Notice that we do not define a location for the table; we simply give it a name. We are setting `overwrite` as the mode, which will tell Spark if a table currently exists and replace it. The key detail here is that we are using the `delta` method and the `saveAsTable` method. Delta has been moved to the default format for tables in Spark, but I prefer to be explicit normally:

```
table_name = "chapter_2"
full_table_name = database_name + "."+ table_name
data_frame.write.format("delta").mode("overwrite").saveAsTable(full_table_name)
```

There is a useful method for listing all tables:

```
spark.catalog.listTables()
```

Here, we can see the output of all the tables I created. Your output may vary:

```
[Table(name='simple_databasechapter_2', catalog='spark_catalog',
namespace=['default'], description=None, tableType='MANAGED',
isTemporary=False)]
```

Here, we are using the SQL `describe` function on a table and then the extended option for that method. There is a Python API version I will show you soon, but the key detail to see is that the extended description will list very useful information, such as the database, location, and provider:

```
spark.sql(f"describe table {full_table_name}").show()
+--------+---------+-------+
|col_name|data_type|comment|
+--------+---------+-------+
|    name|   string|   null|
|     age|   bigint|   null|
|     SSN|   bigint|   null|
+--------+---------+-------+
spark.sql(f"describe extended {full_table_name}").show()
+--------------------+--------------------+-------+
```

```
|          col_name|            data_type|comment|
+------------------+---------------------+-------+
|              name|               string|   null|
|               age|               bigint|   null|
|               SSN|               bigint|   null|
|                  |                     |       |
|# Detailed Table..|                     |       |
|           Catalog|        spark_catalog|       |
|          Database|      simple_database|       |
|             Table|            chapter_2|       |
|              Type|              MANAGED|       |
|          Location|  dbfs:/user/hive/w...|      |
|          Provider|                delta|       |
|             Owner|                 root|       |
|Is_managed_location|                true|       |
|   Table Properties|  [delta.minReaderV...|    |
```

Here, we are using the `delta.tables` library to interact with our Delta tables. The Python version of describing tables uses the detailed method, which returns a DataFrame. To see the DataFrame, you can use the `.show()` method:

```
from delta.tables import DeltaTable
deltaTable = DeltaTable.forName(spark, full_table_name)
deltaTable.detail().show()
```

Unmanaged table

You can create an unmanaged table in two ways. The first way is to create an entry in the metadata database, but this will not allow you to drop the table. The second will not create an entry in the metadata database.

Here, we are using the `option` method and defining a path. This will create an entry for the table in the metadata database:

```
location_unmanaged = "/tmp/delta-table"
data_frame.write.mode("overwrite").option("path", location_unmanaged).
saveAsTable("unmanaged_table")
```

We can also create a standalone Delta table with no metadata. However, I don't recommend this technique simply because managing paths in your code can be a pain:

```
data_frame.write.format("delta").mode("overwrite").save(location_
unmanaged)
```

Reading tables

The Spark API has several ways to read a Delta table. The first way we will explore is to use the path to the unmanaged table that doesn't have an entry in the metadata database. The key detail is that we must set the format to `delta` and use the `load` method:

```
spark.read.format("delta").load(location_unmanaged).show()
+-------+----+---+
|   name| div| ID|
+-------+----+---+
|   Miri|Engr|  4|
|  Brian|Engr|  1|
|   Miri|Engr|  3|
|  Brian|Engr|  1|
|Nechama|Engr|  2|
|  Naava|Engr|  3|
+-------+----+---+
```

We can also use the `delta` library to load the table, providing the path to the `forPath` method:

```
deltaTable = DeltaTable.forPath(spark, location_unmanaged)
deltaTable.toDF().show()
```

In terms of tables that have entries in the metadata database, we have a few choices of APIs to use.

Here, we are using the `DeltaTable` library and providing the table's name to `forName`:

```
deltaTable = DeltaTable.forName(spark, full_table_name)
deltaTable.toDF().show()
```

Lastly, we can use the Spark context to load the table, providing the table name to the `table` method:

```
spark.table(full_table_name).show()
```

Between all these options, I have not seen any performance differences, so it's 100% based on preference only.

Updating a table schema

Delta Lake tables use schema evolution, which will avoid creating breaking changes for our schema. This setting must be enabled first, and if it's not set, you will get a schema error thrown by Spark. Schema evolution will add new columns but will not allow you to remove columns. Also, any data type changes will require the full table to be read and then written again.

Here, we are taking the original DataFrame that was used to create our table, extracting the schema, and adding a column to it. Then, we are creating an empty DataFrame with the updated schema. Finally, we are appending the empty DataFrame with the updated schema to the original table. This case should throw an error because we have not turned on schema evolution:

```
schema = data_frame.schema
schema.add("height", "string", True)
data_frame_2 = spark.createDataFrame(data = [], schema = schema)
data_frame_2.write.format("delta").mode("append").saveAsTable(full_
table_name)
error
AnalysisException: A schema mismatch detected when writing t
```

When we use `mergeSchema` and set it to `True`, it will evolve the table schema:

```
data_frame_2.write.format("delta").mode("append").
option("mergeSchema", "true").saveAsTable(full_table_name)
```

If you have data you want to append to your table, you can use the same command, but instead of using an empty DataFrame, you will use the DataFrame with the new data.

Deleting data

With the `DeltaTable` library, we can do SQL-like data deletions and avoid full table loading, saving us time and resources:

```
deltaTable.delete("age < 2")
```

Updating data

Here, we are updating the data within our table by defining a condition and the data to be changed. This should result in minimal data read as the table was deleted:

```
from pyspark.sql.functions import col, lit
deltaTable.update(
  condition = col('ssn') == 2,
  set = { 'name': lit('Yitzy') }
  set = { 'age': lit(100) }
)
```

Merging into Delta tables

Merge provides the same capabilities as the classic `merge` function in SQL but for the Python API. It is a very compact and efficient way to deal with cases where conditions match and don't match for updates.

Here, we are creating an updated DataFrame for our managed table:

```
update = spark.createDataFrame(data = [("Brian", 1, 1, 299),
    ("John", 2, 2, 400),
    ("Sam", 3, 3, 300),
    ("Nechama Dina", 4, 4, 500),
    ("Mary", 5, 5, 1000),
    ("Monster", 7, 7, 1000)
], schema = ["name", "age", "SSN", "height"])
```

Next, we will use the `merge` method and define the source table and the condition to match. After, we will look at what to do when the condition matches and when it doesn't match:

```
  deltaTable = DeltaTable.forName(spark, full_table_name)
deltaTable.alias("current").merge(
    source = update.alias("update"),
    condition = "current.SSN = update.SSN"
).whenMatchedUpdate(set =
    {
      "height": col("update.height"),
      "age": col("current.age")+ 10
    }
).whenNotMatchedInsert(values =
    {
      "name": col("update.name"),
      "SSN": col("update.SSN"),
      "height": col("update.height")
    }
).execute()
```

The API is very flexible and allows us to use `whenNotMatchedInsertAll` and `when MatchedUpdateAll`. You are not required to have an action for matched and not matched.

Cloning tables

Table cloning is a very useful feature of Delta Lake. Clones are simply a copy of the table but with several useful features. Clones come in two flavors: shallow and deep. Shallow clones copy the transaction log to the new table, and any changes to the clone are stored in the clone's location, but no data is copied to the clone. This allows for efficient data storage. You can write to your shallow clone without worrying about affecting the original.

On the other hand, deep clones copy the transaction log and the data fully. Again, all changes are kept in the clone and do not affect the original table. Deep clones can be resynced from the master using the same code that created it. This resync process is very efficient and will only adjust the clone as minimally as possible to bring it to the latest state. Clones are ideal for backup and disaster recovery. It should also be noted that although Delta Lake has a time travel capability, it should not be used as a backup or disaster solution. Moving too far back into the transaction log becomes very tough, and it's not recommended.

Here, we are creating a shallow clone of the managed table we created previously using the `clone` method and setting the `shallow` argument to `True`:

```
isShallow = True
  deltaTable.clone(target, isShallow, "full_table_name" + "shallow_clone")
```

We can create and resync deep clones by using the same code but setting the `isShallow` argument to `false`:

```
isShallow = False
  deltaTable.clone(target, isShallow, "full_table_name" + "deep_clone")
```

Change data feed

Change data feed (CFD) is Delta Lake's version of **change data capture** (CDC). It is a way of building a table-like log of changes made to the original table. Once enabled, the new changes will be present in the `_change_data` folder. Some changes will not be present, so be aware of this, particularly when it comes to insert-only operations and full table partition deletes. Also, since this is a secondary data storage, be mindful of disk usage on large tables. Lastly, the `vacuum` function will affect CDF.

To enable CDF on a table, you must use SQL and alter the table as follows, setting the `table` property:

```
spark.sql(f"ALTER TABLE {full_table_name} SET TBLPROPERTIES (delta.enableChangeDataFeed = true)")
```

Once enabled, it's very simple to query changes that have been made to a table:

```
spark.read.format("delta") \
.option("readChangeFeed", "true") \
.option("startingVersion", 0) \ ???
.option("endingVersion", 10) \ ???
.table(full_table_name)
```

Time travel

Delta Lake allows time travel through the transaction log for short-term change visits. This can be a powerful tool for resolving issues between data backups.

To get the full history of a table, use the `history` method:

```
fullHistoryDF = deltaTable.history()
```

Here, we are choosing to read a specific version of our table – in this case, version 5238.

We have two possible ways to accomplish this:

```
df = spark.read \
  .format("delta") \
  .option("versionAsOf", "5238") \
  .load("/path/to/my/table")
df = spark.read \
  .format("delta") \
  .load("/path/to/my/table@v5238")
```

Here, we are loading a version of the table based on `date`:

```
deltaTable.optimize().where("date='2021-11-18'").executeCompaction()
```

Managing table files

When working with Delta Lake, utilizing two important functionalities is important – that is, `vacuum` and `optimize`.

`vacuum` will look at the retention period and remove all historical data that is outside that retention period. It will also remove all files in the directory that Delta does not manage. This process is important for reducing excess data; if historical data is needed, using a Delta clone is better than time travel.

Here, we are running `vacuum` against the default, which is 7 days. It's not recommended to have a retention period of fewer than 7 days:

```
deltaTable.vacuum()
```

We can also manually set the retention period when calling `vacuum`:

```
deltaTable.vacuum(9)
```

`optimize` takes small files and optimizes the file size for faster reads.

Here, we are executing an `optimize` function call on a full table:

```
deltaTable.optimize().executeCompaction()
```

On the other hand, we can choose a slice of our table to run optimization on. This can be a better solution for large tables:

```
deltaTable.optimize().where("date='YYYY-MM-DD'").executeCompaction()
```

Now that we've finished working with our databases and table objects, I would like to cover performance enhancements we can make to Delta tables.

Adding speed with Z-ordering

Z-ordering is the process of collocating data related to common files. This can allow for data skipping and a significant reduction in processing time. Z-order is applied per column and should be used like partitions on columns when you're filtering your table.

Here, we are applying Z-order to the whole table for a given column:

```
deltaTable.optimize().executeZOrderBy(COLUMN NAME)
```

We can also use the `where` method to apply Z-ordering to a table slice:

```
deltaTable.optimize().where("date=' YYYY-MM-DD'").
executeZOrderBy(COLUMUN NAME)
```

With that, we have looked at one type of performance enhancement with Delta tables: Z-ordering. Next, we will look at another critical performance enhancement, known as bloom filtering. What makes bloom filtering is that it's a data structure that saves space and allows for data skipping.

Bloom filters

One way to increase read speed is to use bloom filters. A bloom filter is an index that uses the probability of data being in the file to reduce the processing speed. I recommend using bloom filters but remember that they will increase your processing time when you write to the table. If you use a bloom index, it's suggested that you also use Z-ordering on that column.

Here, we are writing a SQL statement that adds a bloom filter to our table for the `SSN` column. The key details to pay attention to are `fpp` and `numItems`. Fpp or the false positive rate determines how many bits are added for a single element. `numItems`, on the other hand, is the number of unique items in a file. These values should be tested and adjusted through experimentation:

```
spark.sql(f"
CREATE BLOOMFILTER INDEX
ON TABLE {full_table_name}
FOR COLUMNS(SSN OPTIONS (fpp=0.01, numItems=60000000))")"
```

Practical lab

Now, let's implement everything we've learned by going through some practical exercises.

Problem 1

Our teams have been requested to create a new database and table for the accounting departments' BI tooling. The database should be called `accounting_alpha` and its location should be set to `dbfs:/tmp/accounting_alpha`. The table should be called `returns_bronze`. The schema of the table should be `Date: Date, Account: String, Debit: Float`, and `Credit:Float`.

Problem 2

Our team is now receiving data to be populated into the table. Perform an append using the new data provided:

```
[(datetime.strptime("1981-11-21", '%Y-%m-%d'), "Banking",
1000.0, 0.1), (datetime.strptime("1776-08-02", '%Y-%m-%d') ,
"Cash",0.1, 3000.2), (datetime.strptime("1948-05-14", '%Y-%m-%d'),
"Land",0.5,10000.5)]
```

Problem 3

There has been a forced change to the table. Using Python, add the `Country: String` column to the table.

Solution

The solution to *Problem 1* is as follows:

1. Here, we are dropping any residual database, then creating a DataFrame and writing the DataFrame as a table:

    ```
    spark.sql(f"DROP DATABASE IF EXISTS {database_name} CASCADE;")
    ```

2. Now, we must import our libraries:

    ```
    from pyspark.sql.types import StructField, DateType, StringType,
    FloatType, StructType
    ```

3. Next, we will create our database. We are defining the location of the database; all tables will be in that location:

    ```
    database_name = "chapter_2_lab"
    spark.sql(f" CREATE DATABASE IF NOT EXISTS {database_name}
    LOCATION 'dbfs:/tmp/accounting_alpha' ;")
    ```

4. Now, we can write our table. First, we will define our table's name and the schema of the table:

```
table_name = "returns_bronze"
schema = StructType([StructField("Date", DateType(), True),
                     StructField("Account", StringType(), True),
                     StructField("Debit", FloatType(), True),
                     StructField("Credit", FloatType(), True)
                     ])
```

5. Finally, we must define an empty DataFrame with our schema and create the table with the empty DataFrame:

```
data_frame = spark.createDataFrame(data = [], schema = schema)
full_table_name = database_name + "."+ table_name
data_frame.write.format("delta").mode("overwrite").
saveAsTable(full_table_name)
```

The solution to *Problem 2* is as follows:

1. First, we must create a schema and a DataFrame from the new data. Then, we can append the new data to the table.

2. Next, we must import our libraries and define our schema:

```
from datetime import datetime
schema = StructType([StructField("Date", DateType(), True),
                     StructField("Account", StringType(), True),
                     StructField("Debit", FloatType(), True),
                     StructField("Credit", FloatType(), True)
                     ])
```

3. Here, we're creating some fake data, creating a DataFrame, and appending that data to the table:

```
data = [(datetime.strptime("1981-11-21", '%Y-%m-%d'), "Banking",
1000.0, 0.1), (datetime.strptime("1776-08-02", '%Y-%m-%d') ,
"Cash",0.1, 3000.2), (datetime.strptime("1948-05-14", '%Y-%m-
%d'), "Land",0.5,10000.5)]
data_frame = spark.createDataFrame(data = data, schema = schema)
data_frame.write.format("delta").mode("append").
saveAsTable(full_table_name)
```

The solution to *Problem 3* is as follows:

1. First, we must create a schema with the added field, then create a DataFrame with that schema. Then, we must append it to the table while turning on mergeSchema.

2. Now, we can define our schema:

   ```
   schema = StructType([StructField("Date", DateType(), True),
                        StructField("Account", StringType(), True),
                        StructField("Debit", FloatType(), True),
                        StructField("Credit", FloatType(), True),
                         StructField("Country", StringType(),
   True),
                       ])
   ```

3. Next, we must create an empty DataFrame and then append the table that contains the empty but updated schema DataFrame. By doing this, the table schema will be updated:

   ```
   data_frame = spark.createDataFrame(data = [], schema = schema)
   data_frame.write.format("delta").mode("append").
   option("mergeSchema", "true").saveAsTable(full_table_name)
   ```

Summary

As we come to the end of this chapter, let's reflect on some of the topics we have covered. We went through some of the fundamentals of cloud storage, and dived deep into Delta tables, a very important technology when it comes to handling data. Finally, we learned how to improve the performance of our tables. In the next chapter, we will become familiar with batch and stream processing using Apache Spark.

4
Batch and Stream Data Processing Using PySpark

When setting up your architecture, you decided whether to support batch or streaming, or both. This chapter will go through the ins and outs of batches and streaming with Apache Spark using Python. Spark can be your go-to tool for moving and processing data at scale. We will also discuss the ins and outs of DataFrames and how to use them in both types of data processing.

In this chapter, we're going to cover the following main topics:

- Batch processing
- Working with schemas
- User Defined Function
- Stream processing

Technical requirements

The tooling that will be used in this chapter is tied to the tech stack that was chosen for the book. All vendors should offer a free trial account.

I will be using the following:

- Databricks
- AWS or Azure

Setting up your environment

Before we begin this chapter, let's take some time to set up our working environment.

Python, AWS, and Databricks

As in the previous chapters, this chapter assumes you have a working version of Python 3.6+ installed in your development environment. We will also assume you have set up an AWS account and have set up Databricks with that AWS account.

Databricks CLI

The first step is to install the `databricks-cli` tool using the `pip` Python package manager:

```
pip install databricks-cli
```

Let's validate that everything has been installed correctly. If the following command produces the tool version, then everything is working correctly:

```
Databricks -v
```

Now, let's set up authentication. First, go into the Databricks UI and generate a personal access token. The following command will ask for the host that was created for your Databricks instance and the created token:

```
databricks configure -token
```

We can determine whether the CLI has been set up correctly by running the following command. If no error is returned, then you have a working setup:

```
databricks fs ls
```

Lastly, let's set up our `workspace`, `clusters`, and `dbfs` folders:

```
databricks   fs mkdirs    dbfs:/chapter_4
databricks   workspace mkdirs   /chapter_4
databricks   clusters create -json-file    <file_path to tiny.json>
```

The `tiny.json` file should contain the following:

```
{    "num_workers":0, "cluster_name":"tiny",   "spark_version":"10.4.x-scala2.12",
   "spark_conf":{
      "spark.master":"local[*, 4]",     "spark.databricks.cluster.profile":"singleNode"
   },   "aws_attributes":{
```

```
        "first_on_demand":1,  "availability":"SPOT_WITH_
FALLBACK",  "zone_id":"us-west-2b",
      "instance_profile_arn":null, "spot_bid_price_percent":100,
      "ebs_volume_type":"GENERAL_PURPOSE_SSD",
      "ebs_volume_count":3, "ebs_volume_size":100
    }, "node_type_id":"m4.large",  "driver_node_type_id":"m4.large",
    "ssh_public_keys":[ ],"custom_
tags":{  "ResourceClass":"SingleNode"}, "spark_env_vars":{ "PYSPARK_
PYTHON":"/databricks/python3/bin/python3"},
      "autotermination_minutes":10, "enable_elastic_
disk":false,  "cluster_source":"UI", "init_scripts":[ ], "data_
security_mode":"NONE", "runtime_engine":"STANDARD"}
```

Batch processing

Batch-processing data is the most common form of data processing, and for most companies, it is their bread-and-butter approach to data. Batch processing is the method of data processing that is done at a "triggered" pace. This trigger may be manual or based on a schedule. Streaming, on the other hand, involves attempting to trigger something very quickly. This is also known as micro-batch processing. Streaming can exist in different ways on different systems. In Spark, streaming is designed to look and work like batch processing but without the need to constantly trigger the job.

In this section, we will set up some fake data for our examples using the Faker Python library. Faker will only be used for example purposes since it's very important to the learning process. If you prefer an alternative way to generate data, please feel free to use that instead:

```
from faker import Faker
import pandas as pd
import random
fake = Faker()
def generate_data(num):
    row = [{"name":fake.name(),
            "address":fake.address(),
            "city":fake.city(),
            "state":fake.state(),
            "date_time":fake.date_time(),
            "friend":fake.catch_phrase()} for x in range(num)]
    return row
panda = pd.DataFrame(generate_data(10000))
fake_data = spark.createDataFrame(panda)
```

Once we have our fake data, we will ensure no data is already in our output folders:

```
%sh
rm -rf /dbfs/tmp/csv_fake_data
```

```
rm -rf /dbfs/tmp/json_fake_data
rm -rf /dbfs/tmp/parquet_fake_data
```

Now that we have cleaned our output folders, we will write our test data using batch processing. The key detail is that I have chosen to use the `format` method to define the type. I prefer this approach to others because it is clear and consistent for all applications. What makes this a batch write is simply the use of the `write` method. We will cover the stream `write` method later in this chapter:

```
fake_data.write.format("csv").save("dbfs:/tmp/csv_fake_data")
fake_data.write.format("json").save("dbfs:/tmp/json_fake_data")
fake_data.write.format("parquet").save("dbfs:/tmp/parquet_fake_data")
```

Partitioning

When we write our data, we can use partitioning to coordinate how it's stored. When we choose a partition column, Spark stores data in a folder structure that resembles `<column_name>=<column_value>`. The goal is that if you use a `where` clause on that column, Spark will only read data located in folders matching the where clause. A simple example might be a folder called `name=brian`. This can create significant speed improvements when reading if you plan on filtering by the partition column.

This feature works with file-based writing, weather streaming, batch, delta, or Parquet.

To add a partition, you can use the `.mode("overwrite")` method. Here is an example of adding a partition for the `state` column for a Delta table:

```
database_name = "chapter4"
spark.sql(f"DROP DATABASE IF EXISTS {database_name} CASCADE ;")
spark.sql(f" CREATE SCHEMA IF NOT EXISTS {database_name};")
df.write.partition("state").mode("overwrite").format("delta").
saveAsTable(f"{database_name}.delta_fake__bucket_data")
```

Data skew

Our data is processed in a cluster, and it's represented as a partition (not to be confused with writing partitions) that exists on workers across the cluster. Data can exist in an uneven representation. This might be hard to envision, but let's create a simplified example. Let's assume you have a column state and 100 states, but all that data exists in only one worker. When another work needs to process information using that state, column data must be passed across the network via shuffling. Fixing data skew is the process of leveling out the data so that it's mostly evenly spread across all workers for maximum parallel processing.

The first technique to resolve data skew is to repartition your data by the suspected data skew column. It is recommended to always repartition to the number of total cores:

```
df = df.repartition(10, "state")
```

Salting can be a very good approach too. In this case, we are creating a column and filling it with data. Then, we're making sure the data is distributed evenly. Salting is useful if you are unsure what column you want to repartition by:

```
from pyspark.sql.functions rand()
df = df.withColumn('salt', rand())
df = df.repartition(100, 'salt')
```

Reading data

We covered writing data first for practical reasons, but in reality, you're going to do a ton of data reading. Spark allows a wide range of sources for reading data, but we will limit our discussion to file-based data storage in this chapter.

You will likely see the core data file types: CSV, Avro, JSON, and Parquet. For some of these formats, Spark will need help figuring out the schema (such as for CSV and JSON). However, whichever format you need to read, the basic syntax is pretty much the same.

Here, I am using an alternative way to specify the format by putting it in the `load` method. I prefer to use the `format` method, as mentioned earlier. This is considered a batch read because we are using the `read` method and not a streaming read, as will be covered later in this chapter. Lastly, this isn't a table, so we must give a path to the `parquet` folder. Spark expects files of a similar type to be grouped in the same folder and files of a different type to be in separate folders. Simply put, if you have a process that delivers data about weather and election results daily, they are stored in separate folders. Also, the schema is expected to match exactly if grouped in the same folder:

```
df = spark.read.load("dbfs:/tmp/parquet_fake_data", format="parquet")
```

For formats such as CSV and JSON, where there is no schema stored for the data, it's necessary to supply Spark with the schema or let it attempt to figure the schema out. I strongly recommend never using schema inference in production. The schema should be managed, and using schema inference, although it might seem very useful in the long run, only allows for errors to creep into your data platform. I have spent many hours trying to resolve schema issues that could have only been avoided if someone had architected with schema enforcement in mind. We can supply the schema as follows:

```
.schema(df.schema)
```

Alternatively, we can do the following:

```
.options("inferSchema" , "true")
```

With that, we have covered the process of reading data with Spark while working with data skew and partitioning. An important topic we need to cover next is working with Spark schemas. Schemas are the structure of our data and are often required in many situations.

Spark schemas

Spark only supports schema on read and write, so you will likely find it necessary to define your schema manually. Spark has many data types. Once you know how to represent schemas, it becomes rather easy to create data structures.

One thing to keep in mind is that when you define a schema in Spark, you must also set its nullability. When a column is allowed to have nulls, then we can set it to True; by doing this, when a Null or empty field is present, no errors will be thrown by Spark. When we define a Struct field, we set three main components: the name, the data type, and the nullibility. When we set the nullability to False, Spark will throw an error when data is added to the DataFrame. It can be useful to limit nulls when defining the schema but keep in mind that throwing an error isn't always the ideal reaction at every stage of a data pipeline.

When working with data pipelines, the discussion about dynamic schema and static schema will often come up. It might seem very useful to just let your schemas change dynamically using some type of programmatic method or using technologies such as schema evolution. The downside to this path is that you will never know what columns you have and the data types they represent. In small cases, this isn't a huge factor, but it has been a massive area of wasted time and money in many of my projects. Columns magically switch data types or add columns when code works in unexpected ways. There is something to be said for schema evolution allowing only new columns, but this should be deeply thought about first before you use this technology. I strongly recommend setting schemas statically by default and managing them in your code. This doesn't need to be very robust, but it allows for a clear central view of what the data should look like for all of your code at all times.

Here, we're importing the needed Python modules:

```
from pyspark.sql.types import StringType,DoubleType, StructField
```

In this example, we are creating two semi-structured schemas with three columns – my_string, my_double, and sub_field – and one column within sub_field called my_name:

```
from pyspark.sql.types import StringType,DoubleType, StructField,
StructType,IntegerType, ArrayType,MapType, LongType


schema_1 = StructType([StructField("my_string", StringType(), True),
                       StructField("my_double", DoubleType(), True),
                       StructField("sub_field", StructType([
                             StructField("my_name", StringType(), True)
                       ]), True)])


schema_2 = StructType([StructField("my_string", StringType(), True),
                       StructField("my_double", DoubleType(), True),
```

```
                    StructField("sub_field", StructType([
                        StructField("my_name", StringType(), True)
                    ]), True)])
```

We can check what our schema will look like using the `fields` method:

```
schema_1.fields
[StructField('my_string', StringType(), True),
 StructField('my_double', DoubleType(), True),
 StructField('sub_field', StructType([StructField('my_name',
StringType(), True)]), True)]
```

Here, we are comparing the two schemas:

```
schema_1 == schema_2
```

Since schemas are objects, they can be compared to each other for validation. My only warning is that you must ensure column order when comparing schemas. Column order is not guaranteed in Spark.

Here, we are getting the list of column names within the schema:

```
schema_1.fieldNames()y
```

I have often found it necessary to build schemas dynamically. Spark makes it rather easy to do; all you need to do is add your new column to the `add` method, as shown here:

```
schema_1.add("my_second_string", StringType(), True)
```

In this example, we are creating a schema with an array for one column. This can be extremely useful for representing groups of values, such as filenames associated with a single row:

```
schema_array = StructType([
  StructField("id", IntegerType()),
  StructField("users", ArrayType(
      StructType([
          StructField("name", StringType()),
          StructField("address", StringType())
      ])
    )
])
```

Here, we're creating a `map` structure, which is very similar to a Python dictionary:

```
schema_map = StructType([
        StructField('address', StringType(), True),
        StructField('id', LongType(), True),
        StructField('my_map', MapType(StringType(),
```

```
                    StructType([
                    StructField('age', DoubleType(), True),
                    StructField('height', DoubleType(), True)])
                                                , True)])
```

Making decisions

PySpark DataFrames support SQL-like functionality, and one very important feature is the use of the IF/ELSE logic. In PySpark DataFrames, the when method is used to create a logical test and define the result, and the otherwise method is used as a catch-all.

In the following code, I'm checking the state column for specific values and creating a new relative location column. Then, I'm using an otherwise guard and a null check with our if-then logic:

```
from pyspark.sql.functions import col, when
streaming_random = stream_df.select(
when(col("state") == "Virginia","Home")\
.when(col("state") == "West Virginia","Vacation")\
.when(col("state").isNull() ,"Nothing")\
.otherwise(col("state")\
.alias("relative_location"))
```

Removing unwanted columns

A very common step in processing data is removing unwanted columns. The drop method can be used to drop multiple or single columns. Here, we are passing a list to the method but using * to have drop receive them as single values, not a list:

```
drop_columns = ["relative_location", "friend"]
update_dataframe.drop(*drop_columns)
```

Working with data in groups

Grouping data is a core task for building gold tables for your data products. First, we must define how we want to group our data and then the mathematical calculations we want to perform, keeping the group in mind. A simple example would be wanting to get the average income per state, which groups income into the state column.

Here, we are adding an age column to our DataFrame for the test data:

```
from pyspark.sql.functions import rand,when
df_random = df.withColumn('age', when(rand() > 0.2, 1).otherwise(0))
```

We are now looking at the average per state using two different syntaxes. My preference is the first since I feel it is more readable in larger code:

```
df_random.groupBy("state").agg(avg("age"))
df_random.groupBy("state").agg({"age": "mean"}
```

We can also find the minimum and maximum, among performing many other calculations:

```
df_random.groupBy("state").agg(min("age"))
df_random.groupBy("state").agg(sum("age"))
```

Now that we have explored various schemas in Spark, we will explore another important tool in Spark called **User Defined Function (UDF)**.

The UDF

One very powerful tool to consider using with Spark is the UDF. UDFs are custom per-row transformations in native Python that run in parallel on your data. The obvious question is, why not only use UDFs? After all, they are also more flexible. There is a hierarchy of tools you should look to use for speed reasons. Speed is a significant consideration and should not be ignored. Ideally, you should get the most bang for your buck using Python DataFrame APIs and their native functions/methods. DataFrames go through many optimizations, so they are ideally suited for semi-structured and structured data. The methods and functions Spark provides are also heavily optimized and designed for the most common data processing tasks. Suppose you find a case where you just can't do what is required with the native functions and methods and you are forced to write UDFs. UDFs are slower because Spark can't optimize them. They take your native language code and serialize it into the JVM, then pass it across the cluster. I have come across many cases where objects can't be serialized, which can be a pain to deal with. Also, this whole process is much slower for non-JVM languages. I always like to caution against UDFs unless no other choice is possible.

Here, we're creating a simple function that accepts a `string` column and returns a modified version of that string:

```
from pyspark.sql.functions import udf, col
from pyspark.sql.types import IntegerType, StringType
def addString(string):
    return string + "_" + "this_is_added"
```

Now, we will register that function as a UDF using a `lambda` variable:

```
addStringUDF = udf(lambda i: addString(i),StringType())
```

To use our UDF in Python, we only need to invoke it like any other function and pass our desired column:

```
df_random.select(col("State"),\
         addStringUDF(col("name"))\
         .alias("name_and_more") )
```

We can also use this UDF in native SQL statements. We only need to register it using the following method:

```
spark.udf.register("addStringUDF", addString,StringType())
```

This can now be called easily in our SQL statements:

```
df_random.createOrReplaceTempView("my_test")
spark.sql("select state, addStringUDF(Name) as name_and_more from my_test")
```

One nice feature of UDFs is that you can use a Python decorator to define your UDFs. A decorator can be useful for reducing your code. There are pros and cons to using decorators that you must keep in mind. Decorators must be set to `return`, which makes your code clear and easy to read. That being said, I don't normally use decorators often, given that they can be unclear to developers jumping on your project who are not familiar with functional programming.

Here, we're defining our Python UDF using a decorator instead of the function call:

```
@udf(returnType=StringType())
def addString(string):
    return string + "_" + "this_is_added"
```

I have found that it's common to need to work with multiple columns at the same time. It's very easy to do this if you work with structs.

Here, we're creating our UDF with a decorator, as we did before, but we're accessing multiple variables in our function argument using the list syntax:

```
from pyspark.sql.types import IntegerType
from pyspark.sql.functions import udf, lit, struct
@udf(returnType=IntegerType())
def magic_calc(x):
    return x[0] * x[1]
```

Now, we must use our `magic_calc` UDF but pass our column names in a `struct` function. This will combine the values into a passable variable for processing in our UDF:

```
df_random_2 = df_random.select(col("*"), lit(6).alias("height"))
df_random_2.select(col("State"),\
              magic_calc( struct("age", "height"))\
         .alias("name_and_more") ).show()
```

Lastly, there is a unique UDF you can sometimes use to gain some speed improvements. Spark allows you to use what's called a vectorized UDF using pandas. Spark uses Apache Arrow to pass data to `pandas`, and pandas process the data in parallel. This isn't flawless and can often be slower than just using pandas directly. Having all your code in a common API and for the one-off situation where the pandas UDF seems to work better is a very useful tool:

```
from pyspark.sql.functions import PandasUDFType, pandas_udf
from pyspark.sql.types import StringType
```

This is the main difference between a pandas UDF and a normal UDF. You are working with pandas `series` objects. At first, this might seem like a huge difference, but you are stepping outside the world of Spark. There is a significant speed increase for some use cases compared to normal Python UDFs. That being said, we must keep in mind the speed hit we take compared to using normal Spark DataFrame APIs over using UDFs. Just to reiterate, UDFs are edge cases where it's impossible to accomplish something in the normal Spark API and we are okay with the speed hit:

```
@pandas_udf('long')
def how_old(age: pd.Series) -> pd.Series:
    return age + 10



df_random.select(col("State"),\
        how_old(col("age"))\
        .alias("updated_age") ).show()
```

Now that we have explored UDFs, we will check out how to process data so that Spark can utilize it.

Stream processing

Streaming is a very useful mode of processing data and can come with a large amount of complexity. One thing a purist must consider is that Spark doesn't do "streaming data" – Spark does micro-batch data processing. So, it will load whatever the new messages are and run a batch process on them in a continuous loop while checking for new data. A pure streaming data processing engine such as Apache Flink will only process one new load of "data." So, as a simple example, let's say there are 100 new messages in a Kafka queue; Spark would process all of them in one micro-batch. Flink, on the other hand, would process each message separately.

Spark Structured Streaming is a DataFrame API on top of the normal Spark Streaming, much like the DataFrame API sits on the RDD API. Streaming DataFrames are optimized just like normal DataFrames, so I suggest always using structured streaming over normal Spark Streaming. Also, Spark requires schemas to be passed for all reads for performance purposes. Finally, Spark Streaming often requires restarts when various characteristics change, such as location and schema.

Reading from disk

In this first example, we are batch-loading a DataFrame to get the schema for the file and then starting `readStream`. Notice that we are using `readStream`, the streaming method, versus the read method that's used in batch processing:

```
location = "dbfs:/tmp/parquet_fake_data"
fmt = "parquet"
df = spark.read.format(fmt).load(location)
stream_df = spark.readStream.schema(df.schema).format(fmt).
load(location)
```

If you would like to see whether your DataFrame is streaming, you can use the following variable:

```
stream_df.isStreaming
True
```

Streaming transformations

Now that we have a streaming DataFrame, we will do some simple transformations on our data:

```
from pyspark.sql.functions import col, when
streaming_random = stream_df.select(
when(col("state") == "Virginia","Home")
                                    .when(col("state") == "West
Virginia","Vacation")
                                    .when(col("state").isNull()
,"Nothing")
                                    .otherwise(col("state").
alias("relative_location"))
)
```

We have a streaming DataFrame and have formed some work on that data; now, we need to write it somewhere. When working with streaming DataFrames, we must use the streaming write method called `writeStream`. We have two useful ways of troubleshooting streaming DataFames: dumping all data to the console and populating an in-memory table. Also, once you start your writing process, you will get a query object to manage your streaming job:

```
query = streaming_random.writeStream.format("console").
outputMode("append").start()
```

Debugging

Here, we're using an in-memory table that can be accessed like any other. This is not meant to be used in production and should never be used that way:

```
query = streaming_random.writeStream.format("memory").queryName("test_
table") .outputMode("append").start()
test = spark.table("test_table")
```

Once you have your query object, you can check whether it's still streaming using the isActive variable:

```
query.isActive
True
```

You can also see statistics about your query, which can be very useful in understanding how your streaming job is doing:

```
query.status
{'message': 'Waiting for next trigger',
 'isDataAvailable': False,
 'isTriggerActive': False}
```

Lastly, we can stop our job using the stop method:

```
query.stop()
query.isActive
False
```

Writing to disk

We must add a few new components to our code when writing to disk. The first is the checkpoint location. A checkpoint is a location that stores the "state" of the streaming process. This is extremely useful and is used when the stream job is restarted. It ensures, among other things, that you do not reprocess data.

The output mode is another important method we must specify when writing data. There are currently three modes: append, complete, and update. Append mode is used for cases where you will never need to update any current data; it appends to the output sink. On the other hand, complete is used for outputting aggregate data and delivering the entire result data. Finally, update is like complete but delivers just the updated results.

Here is an example of writing a Parquet streaming DataFrame using the append output mode:

```
save_location = "..."
checkpoint_location = f"{save_location}/_checkpoint"
output_mode = "append"
```

```
streaming_random.writeStream.format("parquet").
option("checkpointLocation", checkpoint_location).outputMode(output_
mode).start()
```

Batch stream hybrid

Spark allows a trigger method that defines how the streaming job will be triggered. One issue with streaming jobs is that they require a cluster to be up and resources allocated for the whole lifetime of the streaming job. One way to reduce the wasted resources is to use a trigger once in the streaming job with the `.trigger(once=true)` method. You can then call the job with a scheduled service such as a Databricks jobs scheduler or use some external system to trigger the job when new data is received. We will cover these techniques later in this book:

```
streaming_random.writeStream.format("parquet").trigger(once=True).
option("checkpointLocation", checkpoint_location).outputMode(output_
mode).start()
```

Delta streaming

One major benefit of using Spark Streaming is its support for Delta Lake. In the following code, we're streaming to a Delta table using `trigger` set to `once`:

```
streaming_random.writeStream.format("delta").
option("checkpointLocation", checkpoint_location).trigger(once=True).
outputMode(output_mode).start()
```

Batch processing in a stream

It can be very useful to break out of the streaming API and run a batch write on the streaming input data. Spark API allows for this situation, which is known as `foreachbatch`.

Here, we're creating a function that will do our batch write along with any processing needed for the write:

```
def myfunction(df, batch_id):
    df.write...
```

Now, we will call our function on each element of the streaming data and run our function one ID at a time:

```
streaming_df.writeStream.foreachBatch(myfunction)
```

`foreachbatch` is extremely powerful and can allow you to effectively use streaming in most situations.

Practical lab

Your team has been given a new data source to deliver Parquet files to dbfs. These files could come every minute or once daily; the rate and speed will vary. This data must be updated once every hour if any new data has been delivered.

Setup

Let's set up our environment and create some fake data using Python.

Setting up folders

The following code can be run in a notebook. Here, I am using the shell magic to accomplish this:

```
%sh
rm -rf /dbfs/tmp/chapter_4_lab_test_data
rm -rf /dbfs/tmp/chapter_4_lab_bronze
rm -rf /dbfs/tmp/chapter_4_lab_silver
rm -rf /dbfs/tmp/chapter_4_lab_gold
```

Creating fake data

Use the following code to create fake data for our problems:

```
fake = Faker()
def generate_data(num):
    row = [{"name":fake.name(),
            "address":fake.address(),
            "city":fake.city(),
            "state":fake.state(),
            "purchase_date":fake.date_time(),
            "purchase_id":fake.pyfloat(),
            "sales":fake.pyfloat()
           }]
    return row
panda = pd.DataFrame(generate_data(2))
fake_data = spark.createDataFrame(panda)
fake_data.write.format("parquet").mode("append").save("dbfs:/tmp/chapter_4_lab_test_data")
```

Problem 1

Create a bronze table from the dataset. The data should be streaming but set up to trigger once.

Problem 2

For our silver table, we will need to add the following columns:

- `full_address`: A combination of the address, city, and state
- `Id`: Round up/down `purchase_id` and find the absolute value

Create and use a UDF to create a `first_name` column.

Problem 3

Now, for the gold table, we want to see a table that contains `state`, `mix_sales`, `min_sales`, and `avg_sales`.

Solution

Now, let's explore the solutions to the aforementioned problems.

Solution 1

Here, we're setting up the initial read of our test data. We are dynamically loading the schema from the file. In test cases, this is fine, but in production workloads, this is a very bad practice. I recommend statically writing out your schema:

```
location = "dbfs:/tmp/chapter_4_lab_test_data"
fmt = "parquet"
schema = spark.read.format(fmt).load(location).schema
users = spark.readStream.schema(schema).format(fmt).load(location)
```

Now, the code will populate a bronze table from the data being loaded, and the write process will be appended:

```
bronze_schema = users.schema
bronze_location = "dbfs:/tmp/chapter_4_lab_bronze"
checkpoint_location = f"{bronze_location}/_checkpoint"
output_mode = "append"
bronze_query = users.writeStream.format("delta").trigger(once=True).option("checkpointLocation", bronze_location).option("path", bronze_location).outputMode(output_mode).start()
spark.read.format("delta").load(bronze_location).show()
```

This results in the following output:

```
|                name|             address|       city|         state|
         purchase_date|         purchase_id|       sales|
+--------------------+--------------------+----------+--------------+
--------------------+-----------------+-------------------+
|     Brittney Dalton|533 Lee Trail Sui...|
Jacobfort|Massachusetts|1973-01-27 08:43:30|7088539.53447138|-
8.08676403659487E10|
|Natalie Mclaughlin|745 Moss Pines\nN...|Sandrafort|New
Hampshire|1990-12-07 09:50:41|-7447.2524445945|  5.18255580705486E11|
```

Solution 2

Now, we will create the code to create the silver table from the bronze table. In this manner, we are creating multiple Spark jobs. This process has some benefits and some disadvantages. The main disadvantage is loading the data from disk to memory multiple times.

Here, we're loading our bronze table into memory. This time, we are not required to deal with schemas:

```
from pyspark.sql.types import StringType
from pyspark.sql.functions import udf, lit, struct, concat, col, abs,
floor

bronze_location = "dbfs:/tmp/chapter_4_lab_bronze"
users_bronze = spark.readStream.format("delta").load(bronze_location)
```

We have a UDF that does some small data manipulation on some text:

```
@udf(returnType=StringType())
def strip_name(x):
    return x.split()[0]
```

Now, let's do some data processing by creating a `full_address` column, an `id` column, and a `first_name` column:

```
address_columns = ["address", "city", "state"]
clean = users_bronze.select(col("*"), concat(*address_columns).
alias("full_address"), floor(abs("purchase_id")).alias("id"), strip_
name("name").alias("first_name"))
```

Next, we must write out our silver table, using `append`. Like the bronze table, it will trigger once:

```
silver_location = "dbfs:/tmp/chapter_4_lab_silver"
silver_checkpoint_location = f"{silver_location}/_checkpoint"
fmt = "delta"
output_mode = "append"
```

Batch and Stream Data Processing Using PySpark

```
clean.writeStream.format("delta").option("checkpointLocation",
silver_checkpoint_location).option("path", silver_location).
trigger(once=True).outputMode(output_mode).start()
spark.read.format("delta").load(silver_location).show()
  address|       city|      state|      purchase_date|    purchase_
id|          sales|     full_address|      id|first_name|
+----------------+--------------------+---------+-------------+----
--------------+----------------+--------------------+----------------
----+--------+----------+
|  Brittney Dalton|533 Lee Trail Sui...|
Jacobfort|Massachusetts|1973-01-27 08:43:30|7088539.53447138|-
8.08676403659487E10|533 Lee Trail Sui...|7088539|   Brittney|
|Natalie Mclaughlin|745 Moss Pines\nN...|Sandrafort|New
Hampshire|1990-12-07 09:50:41|-7447.2524445945|
5.18255580705486E11|745 Moss Pines\nN...|    7447|    Natalie|
```

Solution 3

Finally, we will create our gold table.

Here, we're reading in our silver table, with the intent to do some aggregate calculations:

```
from pyspark.sql.types import IntegerType
from pyspark.sql.functions import lit, struct, sum,avg,max, min

bronze_location = "dbfs:/tmp/chapter_4_lab_silver"
schema = spark.read.format(fmt).load(silver_location).schema
users_silver = spark.readStream.format("delta").load(silver_location)
```

We're using the `groupby` API to create some aggregate values for our gold DataFrame:

```
gold = users_silver.groupBy("state").agg(min("sales").alias("min_
sales"), max("sales").alias("max_sales"), avg("sales").alias("avg_
sales"))
gold_location = "dbfs:/tmp/chapter_4_lab_gold"
gold_checkpoint_location = f"{silver_location}/_checkpoint"
fmt = "delta"
output_mode = "complete"
```

Finally, we must write out our DataFrame to our gold table; however, this time, we are not appending but creating a new gold table. In some cases, this can be useful; in others, appending is more appropriate. Gold tables are normally not as large as silver or bronze tables:

```
gold.writeStream.format("delta").option("checkpointLocation",
gold_location).option("path", gold_location).trigger(once=True).
outputMode(output_mode).start()
spark.read.format("delta").load(gold_location).show()
+-------------+--------------------+--------------------+-----------
```

```
--------+
|         state|           min_sales|                max_
sales|            avg_sales|
+-------------+--------------------+--------------------+------------
--------+
|New Hampshire| 5.18255580705486E11| 5.18255580705486E11|
 5.18255580705486E11|
|Massachusetts|-8.08676403659487E10|-8.08676403659487E10|-
8.08676403659487E10|
```

Summary

We have come a long way, friends! In this chapter, we covered batch-processing data, as well as streaming data. We embarked on a comprehensive journey through the world of data processing in Apache Spark with Python. We explored both batch processing and streaming data processing techniques, uncovering the strengths and nuances of each approach.

The chapter began with a deep dive into batch processing, where data is processed in fixed-sized chunks. We learned how to work with DataFrames in Spark, perform transformations and actions, and leverage optimizations for efficient data processing.

Moving on to the fascinating realm of stream processing, we learned about the nuances of Spark Structured Streaming, which enables the continuous processing of real-time data streams. Understanding the distinction between micro-batch processing and true streaming clarified how Spark processes streaming data effectively. This chapter highlighted the importance of defining schemas and using checkpoints for streaming data to ensure data consistency and fault tolerance. We tackled various streaming problems, such as creating bronze, silver, and gold tables, and used UDFs to perform custom transformations on the data.

The concept of streaming was further explored with the usage of pandas UDFs to perform vectorized operations on streaming data. This unique feature allowed us to harness the power of pandas for specific scenarios, aligning Python's strengths with Spark's streaming capabilities.

Finally, we dived into the world of Spark SQL, examining how to create tables and databases, run SQL queries, and leverage SQL-like functionality for data processing.

Throughout this chapter, we emphasized best practices, performance considerations, and optimization techniques for efficient data processing in both batch and streaming modes. By gaining expertise in PySpark, users can build robust data processing pipelines, handle real-time data streams, and develop sophisticated data products.

On concluding this chapter, we have expanded our data processing skills, constructed a solid data platform, and gained valuable insights into the power of Spark and Python in handling large-scale data challenges. Armed with this knowledge, we are well equipped to tackle real-world data processing tasks and deliver impactful data-driven solutions. We are making significant strides in our data processing skills and building our data platform, which will be the topic of the next chapter.

5
Streaming Data with Kafka

There are several streaming platforms on the market, but Apache Kafka is the front-runner. Kafka is an open source project like Spark but focuses on being a distributed message system. Kafka is used for several applications, including microservices and data engineering. Confluent is the largest contributor to Apache Kafka and offers several offerings in the ecosystem, such as Hosted Kafka, Schema Registry, Kafka Connect, and the Kafka REST API, among others. We will go through several areas of Confluent for Kafka, focusing on data processing and movement.

In this chapter, we will cover the following main topics:

- Kafka architecture
- Setting Confluent Kafka
- Kafka streams
- Schema Registry
- Spark and Kafka
- Kafka Connect

Technical requirements

The tooling used in this chapter is tied to the tech stack chosen for the book. All vendors should offer a free trial account.

I will use the following:

- Databricks
- Confluent Kafka

Setting up your environment

Before we begin our chapter, let's take the time to set up our working environment.

Python, AWS, and Databricks

As we have with many others, this chapter assumes you have a working Python 3.6+ release installed in your development environment. We will also assume you have set up an AWS account and have set up Databricks with that account.

Databricks CLI

The first step is to install the `databricks-cli` tool using the `pip` python package manager:

```
pip install databricks-cli
```

Let's validate that everything has been installed correctly. If this command produces the tool version, then everything is working correctly:

```
Databricks -v
```

Now, let's set up authentication. First, go into the Databricks UI and generate a personal access token. The following command will ask for the host created for your Databricks instance and the created token:

```
databricks configure -token
```

We can determine whether the CLI is set up correctly by running the following command, and if no error is returned, you have a working setup:

```
databricks fs ls
```

Lastly, let's set up our `workspace`, `clusters`, and `dbfs` folders:

```
databricks   fs mkdirs    dbfs:/chapter_5
databricks   workspace mkdirs   /chapter_5
databricks   clusters create -json-file    <file_path to tiny.json>
```

Here are the `tiny.json` file contents:

```
{   "num_workers":0, "cluster_name":"tiny",   "spark_version":"10.4.x-scala2.12",
    "spark_conf":{
       "spark.master":"local[*, 4]",    "spark.databricks.cluster.profile":"singleNode"
    },  "aws_attributes":{
       "first_on_demand":1,   "availability":"SPOT_WITH_FALLBACK",   "zone_id":"us-west-2b",
       "instance_profile_arn":null, "spot_bid_price_percent":100,
       "ebs_volume_type":"GENERAL_PURPOSE_SSD",
       "ebs_volume_count":3, "ebs_volume_size":100
    },  "node_type_id":"m4.large",    "driver_node_type_id":"m4.large",
```

```
    "ssh_public_keys":[ ],"custom_
tags":{   "ResourceClass":"SingleNode"}, "spark_env_vars":{   "PYSPARK_
PYTHON":"/databricks/python3/bin/python3"},
    "autotermination_minutes":10, "enable_elastic_
disk":false,   "cluster_source":"UI",   "init_scripts":[ ], "data_
security_mode":"NONE", "runtime_engine":"STANDARD"}
```

Confluent Kafka

Here, we will look at getting a free account and setting up an initial cluster. Currently, Confluent offers $400 of credit to all new accounts, so we should ideally have no costs for our labs, but we will look for cost savings as we move forward.

Signing up

The signup page is `https://www.confluent.io/get-started/`, and it allows for several authentication options, including Gmail and GitHub, asking you for personal information such as your name and your company's name.

You will be presented with the cluster creation page.

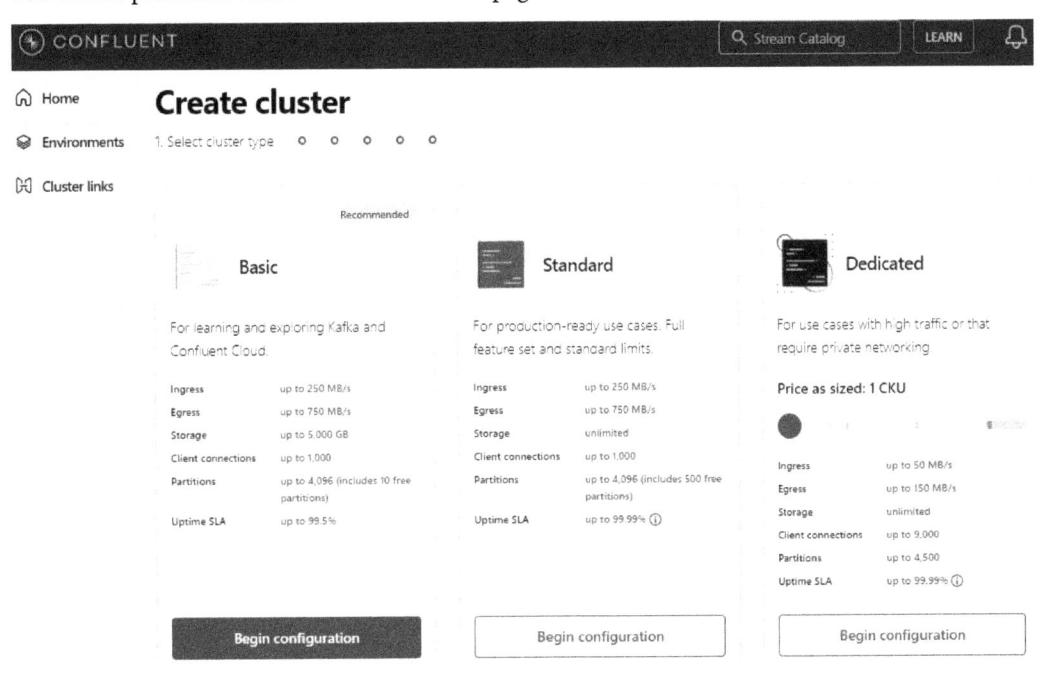

Figure 5.1: The cluster creation page

Here, we will use the **Basic** cluster, which is free at the time of writing.

The next screen allows us to choose a cloud platform and region.

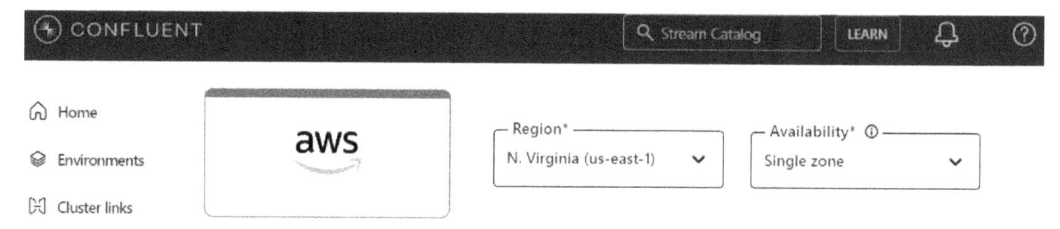

Figure 5.2: Choosing the platform to use

Here, I choose AWS, Northern Virginia, and a single zone. This is a good choice for our labs, but this would need to be more complex for a production system.

We will need to input some payment information.

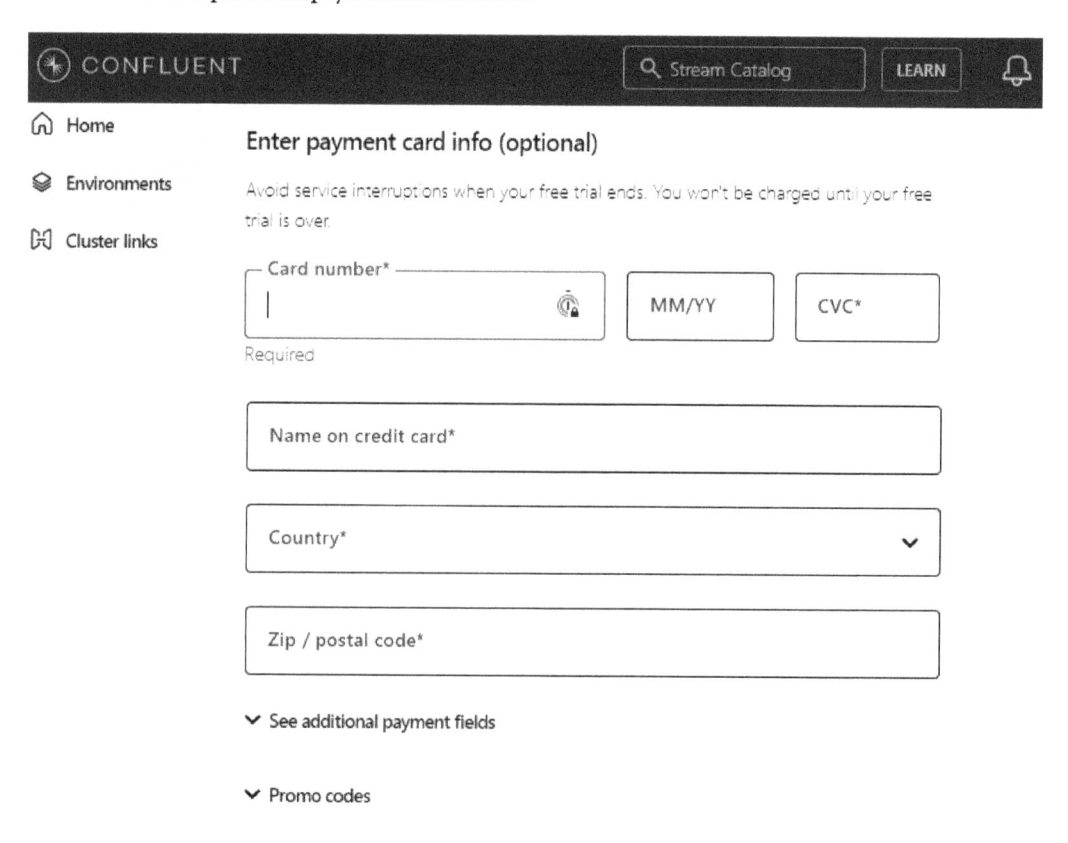

Figure 5.3: The payment info section

Finally, we will be shown a review and confirmation screen.

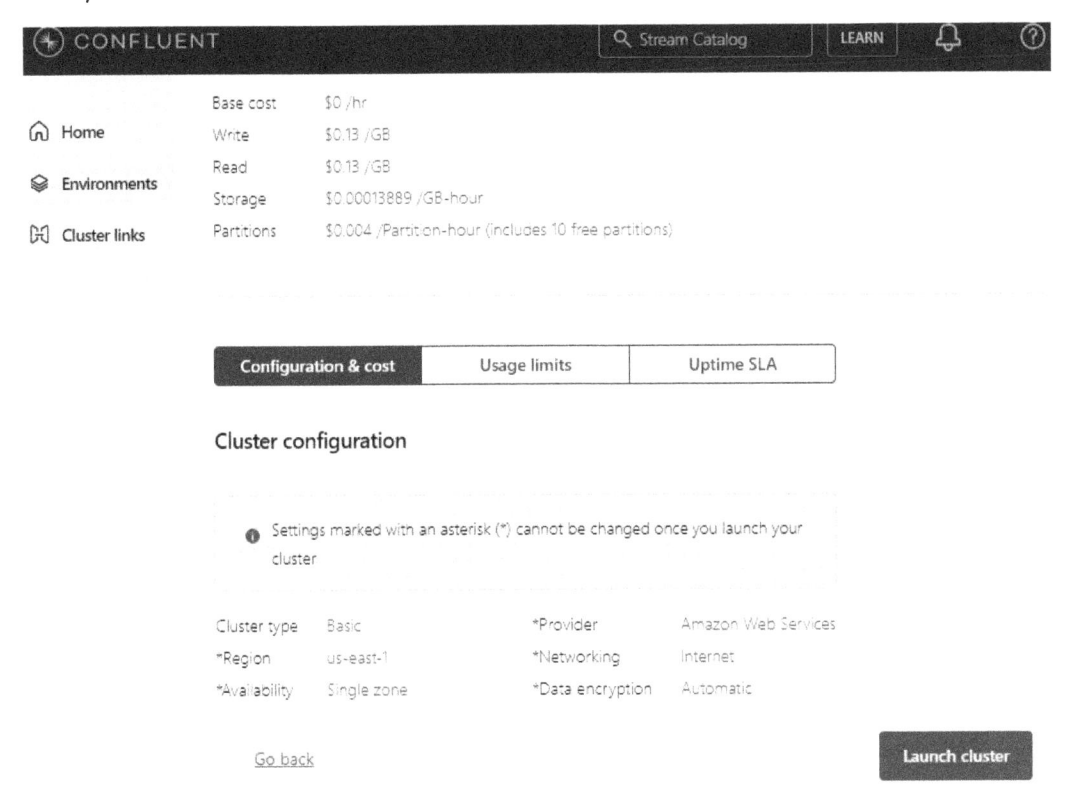

Figure 5.4: The review and confirmation section

Once you launch your cluster, you will be ready to start the chapter.

Kafka architecture

Kafka is an open source distributed streaming platform designed to scale to impressive levels. Kafka can store as much data as you have storage for, but it shouldn't be used as a database. Kafka's core architecture is composed of five main ideas – topics, brokers, partitions, producers, and consumers.

Topics

For a developer, a Kafka topic is the most important concept to understand. Topics are where data is "stored." Topics hold data often called **events**, which means that the data has a key and a value. Keys in this context are not related to a database key that defines uniqueness, but they can be used for organizational purposes. The value is the data itself, which can be in a few different formats such as strings, JSON, Avro, and Protobuf. When your data is written to Kafka, it will have metadata; the most important will be the timestamp.

Working with Kafka can be confusing because the data isn't stored in a database-style semantic. What I mean by this is that your database allows you to perform common tasks such as creating, updating, reading, and deleting entries. This is commonly known as **CRUD**. Kafka doesn't support CRUD; instead, it should be thought of as comprising logs. Logs work because you append new data to your log, and you read from your log at a specific point defined by the reader. Unfortunately, logs cannot be updated or deleted, which can be extremely frustrating for many data professionals. To identify the correct value, you might need to look at the event with the latest timestamp. This isn't to say no data can be deleted; indeed, there are background processes that can remove older events, among other techniques.

Lastly, Kafka events in a topic have an incremental ID called an **offset**. If you want to read the first message, you will look at the earliest offset, but there can be reasons to read from some specific offset. One perfect example is when you are batch-reading from Kafka. In this case, you don't want to read every message whenever you batch-read; instead, you want to continue at the point you stopped prior to. Offsets are relative to a partition of a topic and do not hold significance beyond a partition or even across topics. One side effect of offsets is that events within a partition are ordered.

Partitions

Kafka topics are divided into partitions for a simple reason – parallelism across nodes. One question you might ask is, how does someone know which partition to write into? The rules are that if an event's key is null, it will be written round-robin across all partitions. This will negate any order since offsets are relative to a single partition. Conversely, if there is a key, then the key will be tied to a partition, and the order will be preserved.

Now, when reading from a topic, what will often happen is that multiple consumers will work together in a group for parallelism. In this case, one consumer will read from one partition. When using a single consumer, you will not achieve parallelism, so you will read from more than one partition at a time. Your library handles this process, so it's not something to be concerned about.

Brokers

Brokers are the processing engine of Kafka, but most of the complexity behind the scenes isn't important for a developer to fully understand. What is important to understand is that the Kafka cluster will have multiple brokers to which consumers and producers can connect any specific broker. Brokers will be assigned partitions from topics and handle the replicating partitions across brokers. The clients will automatically get to the correct broker, so you should not worry about knowing which broker has which partition and topic.

Producers

Producers are client machines that want to send messages to a topic. The producer will figure out which partition to write to and what type of compression to use, make retries, callbacks, and transactions (exactly-once semantics), and so on.

There are many versions of clients in various languages that can be used with Kafka. For our lab, we will use the `confluent-kafka` library when writing Python code without Spark.

To install this library, run the following `pip` command:

```
pip install confluent-kafka configparser
```

Here, we will walk through how to use the API:

1. First, we will need to import the `Producer` class:

    ```
    from confluent_kafka import Producer
    ```

2. Next, we will create a configuration dictionary. Do not commit secrets into Git. In production, this could be in a separate file and environment variable, but the ideal is a secret manager where key secrets are stored:

    ```
    config = {'bootstrap.servers': 'XXXXX', 'security.protocol':
    'SASL_SSL', 'sasl.mechanisms': 'PLAIN', 'sasl.username':
    'RG7RDSW7XI4MIXGB', 'sasl.password': 'XXXXX', 'session.timeout.
    ms': '45000', 'basic.auth.credentials.source': 'USER_INFO',
    'basic.auth.user.info': '{{ <KEY>}}:{{ <secret> }}'}
    ```

This information can be easily accessed through the Confluent web guide.

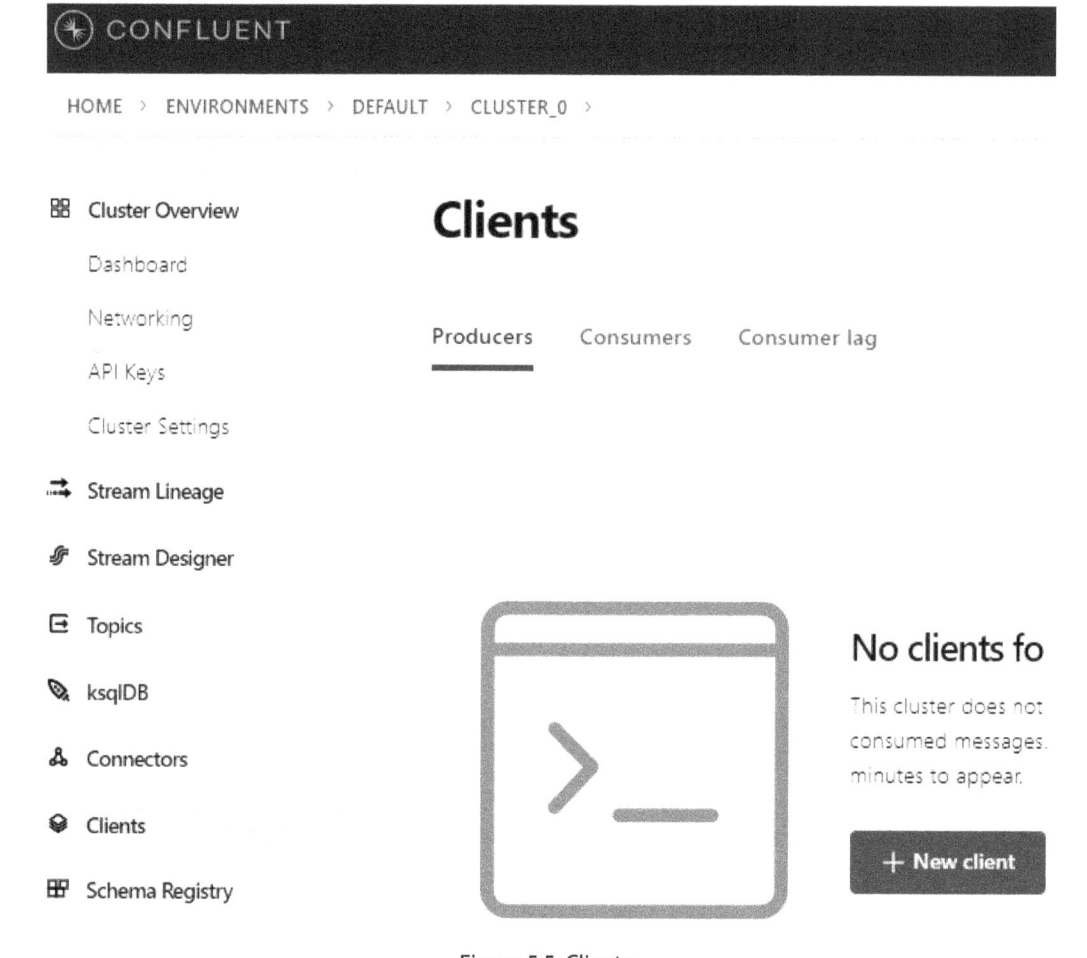

Figure 5.5: Clients

3. You simply need to click **Clients** in the cluster menu and add new clients. It will prompt you to create a new API key. You will also see easy-to-use starter code.

We will now create an instance of the class passing a configuration dictionary:

```
producer = Producer(config)
```

4. Now, we will create a very simplistic callback function; in production, this will need to be more robust:

   ```
   def call_back(error, event):
       if error:
           print(f" Key: {event.key()}, Topic: {event.topic()} failed in write process.")
       else:
           print(f" Sent data to partition {event.partition()}.")
   ```

5. Now, we will send data to Kafka and wait until the message is sent:

   ```
   producer.produce(topic, <key>, <value>, callback=call_back)
   producer.poll(10000)
   producer.flush()
   ```

The preceding code will work with managed Confluent Kafka, but the concepts and API work fine for normal Confluent Kafka.

Consumers

Once data is sent to a topic by the producer, a consumer can read from the topic. Here, we will introduce the basic Python API. The big thing to look at is `group.id`; this is the consumer group we mentioned earlier:

1. First, let's import our `Consumer` class.

   ```
   from confluent_kafka import Consumer
   ```

2. We will reuse the `config` dictionary, but we need a few new elements in the config. Here, we will use the consumer group ID of `chapter_5_test`:

   ```
   config['group.id'] = 'chapter_5_test'
   config['auto.offset.reset'] = 'earliest'
   config['enable.auto.commit'] = False
   ```

3. Now, we will create a `consumer` instance and connect it to a topic:

   ```
   consumer = Consumer(config)
   consumer.subscribe(<topic>)
   ```

4. Now, we will create a simple loop to poll the topic:

   ```
   While True:
       event = consumer.poll(timeout=1.0)
       if event is None:
           continue
   ```

```
          if event.error():
              print( event.error())
          else:
              key = event.key().decode('utf8')
              value = event.value().decode("utf8")
              print(f"Key: {key}, Value: {value}")
```

To make the preceding code more production-ready, it needs to handle the errors more robustly and for some action beyond printing the event to the screen.

A glaring issue might come to mind as we look at Kafka consumers and producers. What happens when we put different data? Data can and often changes; this can happen on purpose or by accident. One solution is to have a guardrail that enforces a specific schema and allows for schema versioning. Confluence created Schema Registry for just this purpose.

Schema Registry

Kafka guarantees the delivery of events sent from producers, but it does not attempt to guarantee quality. Kafka assumes that your applications can coordinate quality data between consumers and producers. On the surface, this seems reasonable and easy to accomplish. The reality is that even in ideal situations, this type of assumed coordination is unrealistic. This type of problem is common among data producers and consumers; the solution is to enforce a data contract.

The general rule of thumb is, garbage in, garbage out. Confluent Schema Registry is an attempt at building contracts for your data schema in Kafka. Confluent Schema Registry is a layer that sits in front of Kafka and stands as the gatekeeper to Kafka. Events can't be produced for a topic unless Confluent Schema Registry first gives its blessing. Consumers can know exactly what they will get by checking the Confluent Schema Registry first.

This process happens behind the scenes, and the Confluent library will do all the hard work for you. It will contact the Confluent Schema Registry via a REST API and guarantee that your schema contracts are valid. As needs change, your schema can evolve with your needs. Care should be taken to keep your schemas backward-compatible.

Confluent Schema Registry supports three formats; your events can be formatted in JSON, Avro, and Protobuf. There are pros and cons to each of these formats; Avro is classically the most popular choice, but Protobuf is becoming very common.

We will now navigate to the cluster in our Confluent cloud account. Again, there is an option for topics.

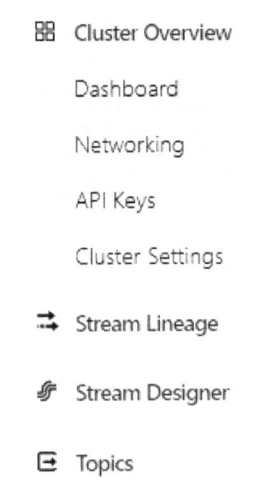

- Cluster Overview
    - Dashboard
    - Networking
    - API Keys
    - Cluster Settings
- Stream Lineage
- Stream Designer
- Topics

Figure 5.6: The Cluster Overview menu

We will now create a new topic; let's call it `chapter_5`.

Once we have a topic created, we'll create a schema. First, there is an option that says **Schema**. Then, it will allow you to pick the value of the events in the topic.

Figure 5.7: An overview of a cluster

You should now see an option to set the schema.

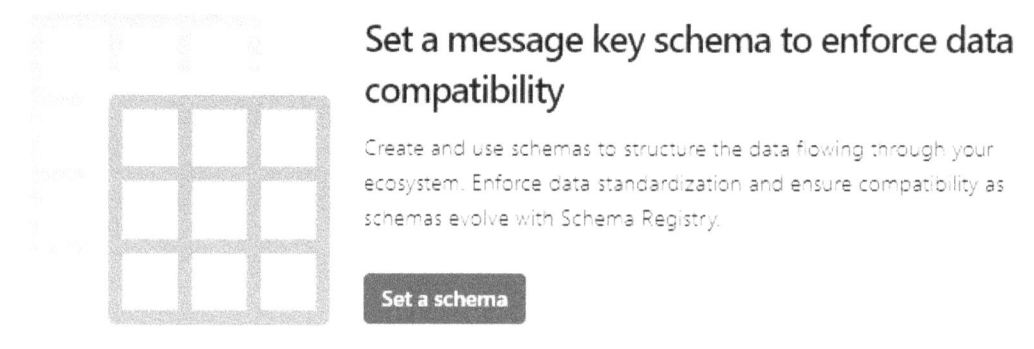

Figure 5.8: Set a schema

You will now see the schema editor; be sure to click **JSON Schema** in the format types menu:

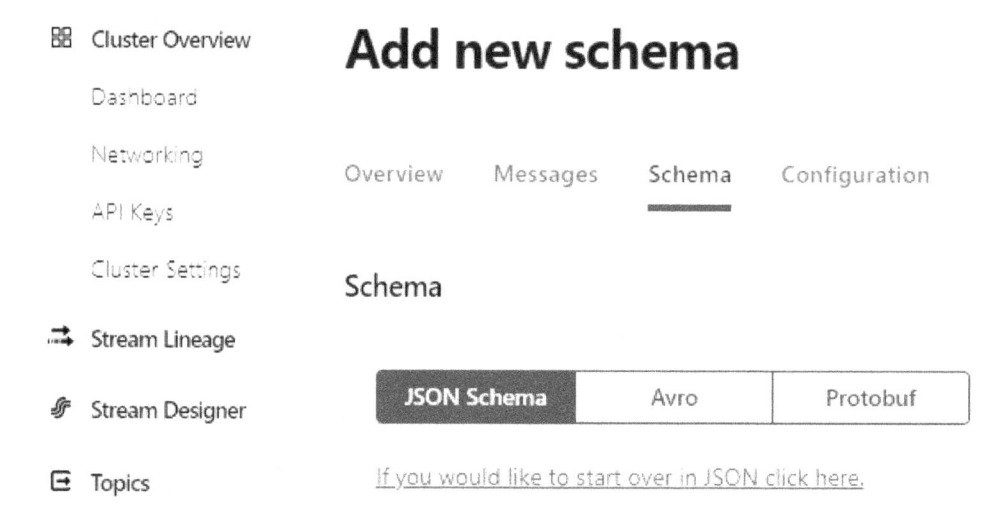

Figure 5.9: The schema type option

The following is a JSON representing the schema we will set for the topic. Paste it into the section for the schema, but make sure you select **JSON Schema** first:

```
{
  "$schema": "http://json-schema.org/draft-07/schema#",
  "$id": "http://example.com/myURI.schema.json",
  "title": "Chapter5",
  "description": "Example Schema for Chapter 5.",
  "type": "object",
  "additionalProperties": false,
```

```
    "properties": {
      "registertime": {
        "type": "integer",
        "description": "time of registration."
      },
      "userid": {
        "type": "string",
        "description": "Users Unique ID."
      },
      "regionid": {
        "type": "string",
        "description": "Users Region."
      },
      "gender": {
        "type": "string",
        "description": "User's Gender."
      }
    }
  }
}
```

Now, we will introduce our Python code for `Producer`. Here, we will define the schema of the topic in a string:

```
schema = """
{
  {
  "$schema": "http://json-schema.org/draft-07/schema#",
  "$id": "http://example.com/myURI.schema.json",
  "title": "Chapter5",
  "description": "Example Schema for Chapter 5.",
  "type": "object",
  "additionalProperties": false,
  "properties": {
    "registertime": {
      "type": "integer",
      "description": "time of registration."
    },
    "userid": {
      "type": "string",
      "description": "Users Unique ID."
    },
    "regionid": {
      "type": "string",
      "description": "Users Region."
```

```
      },
      "gender": {
        "type": "string",
        "description": "User's Gender."
      }
    }
  }
  """
```

Now, let's create a function that will return a dictionary with our data from Kafka:

```
def user_creator(user):
    return {"height":user.height,
            "age":user.age,
            "name":user.name}
```

Here. we will define some simple test data to send to Kafka:

```
data = [50,15,"brian_smith",55,25,"matt_smith"]
```

Let's now create a callback function for when we produce to Kafka:

```
def call_back(error, event):
    if error:
        print(f" Key: {event.key()}, Topic: {event.topic()} failed in write process.")
    else:
        print(f" Sent data to partition {event.partition()}.")
```

We will define the `topic` name as `chapter_5`:

```
topic = "chapter_5"
```

Now, we will create a `schema` object and create a serializer. We will use the serializer to convert the event into the JSON format:

```
schema_registry_client = SchemaRegistryClient(schema)
json_serializer = JSONSerializer(schema, schema_registry_client, user_creator)
```

Next, we will instantiate the `Producer` class and pass the `config` dictionary:

```
producer = Producer(config)
```

Finally, we will walk through our test data and send the messages to Kafka:

```
for event in data:
        producer.produce(topic=topic, key=str(event.height),
                        value=json_serializer(event,
                        SerializationContext(topic, MessageField.
VALUE)),
                        on_delivery=call_back)
producer.flush()
```

Our consumer code is much simpler. First, we will create a function to help convert the data from Kafka:

```
def from_dict(dict):
   return {"age":dict["age"],"height":dict["height"],
"name":dict["name"]}
```

Finally, we will create a deserializer and convert the message:

```
event = consumer.poll(1.0)
json_deserializer = JSONDeserializer(schema, from_dict=from_dict)
message = json_deserializer(event.value(),
            SerializationContext(topic, MessageField.VALUE))
```

Just as Confluent Schema Registry is a huge game-changer for many companies, Confluent has created another technology that has significantly impacted the Kafka ecosystem, called **Kafka Connect**. Connect is an easy-to-use platform for quickly building repurposed building blocks to extract and load data.

Kafka Connect

Confluent noticed that many tasks are almost cookie-cutter and could be shared across projects and clients. One example might be listening to a topic and copying it into a Snowflake table. Confluent created Connect to allow engineers to create very generic tasks and deploy them to a cluster to run those tasks. If you need a source or sink connector that doesn't exist, you can build your own. Connect is a very robust platform that can be a major pipeline component. Connect also offers some basic transformations, which can be very useful. Confluent Cloud offers a hosted connect cluster the same way it offers Schema Registry and Kafka Core.

To access Connect in Confluent Cloud, we will navigate to our cluster and then look for the **Connectors** option in the menu bar.

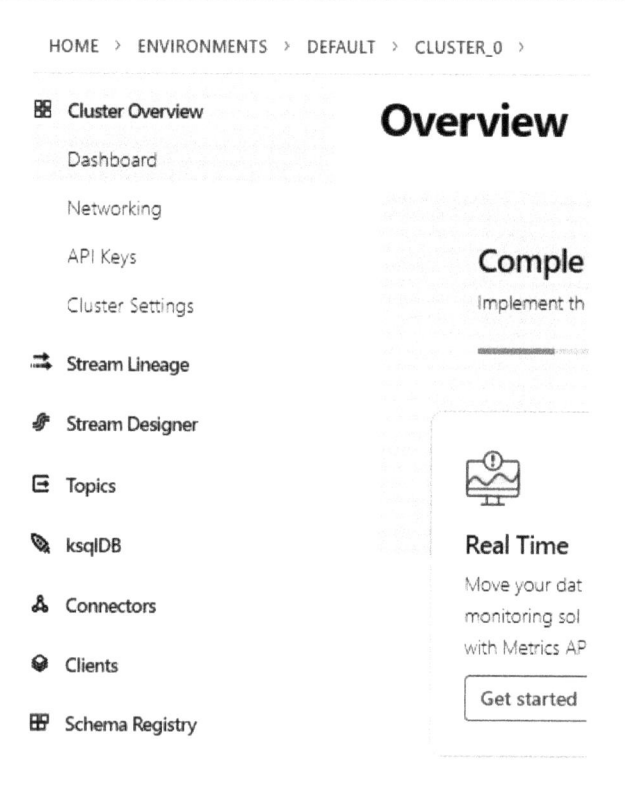

Figure 5.10: The Connectors option in the menu bar

Next, we can set up a simple connector that creates fake data. We will then have the option to add a new connector.

We will then be able to choose our source connector. For example, search for `Datagen Source`, and you should see the **Datagen Source** connector.

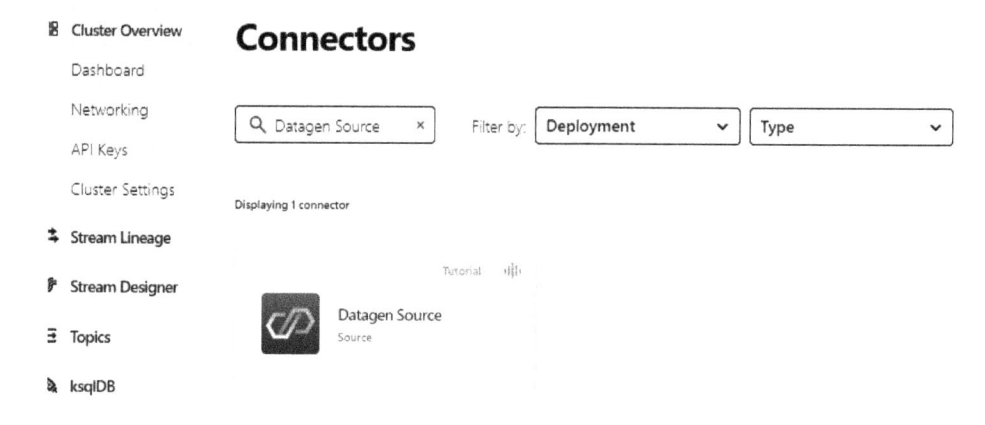

Figure 5.11: Searching for Datagen Source

Next, we will be presented with the topic we will send our fake data. Here, I choose `chapter_5`:

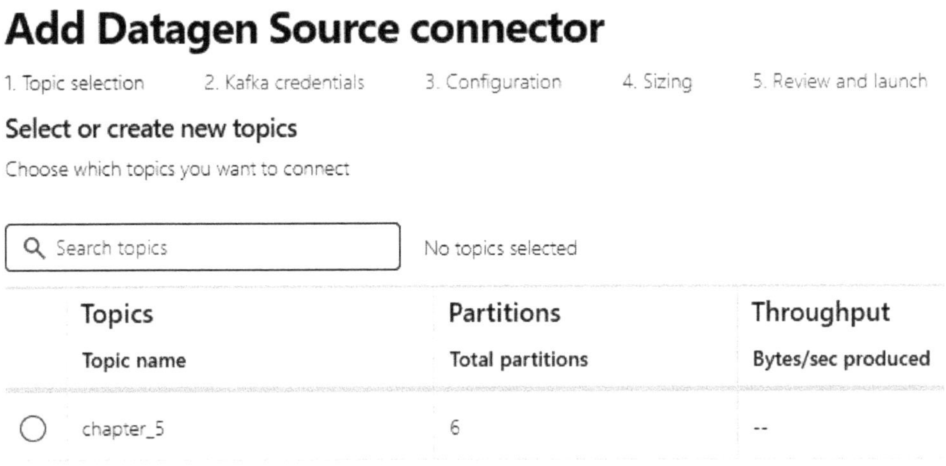
Add Datagen Source connector
1. Topic selection
2. Kafka credentials
3. Configuration
4. Sizing
5. Review and launch
Select or create new topics
Choose which topics you want to connect
Search topics
No topics selected
Topics
Topic name
Partitions
Total partitions
Throughput
Bytes/sec produced
chapter_5
6
--

Figure 5.12: Adding the data

Next, we will choose a non-production-style access model and generate API keys for the connector. I would recommend a granular access model that defines exactly what is needed, but for testing purposes, **Global access** is fine.

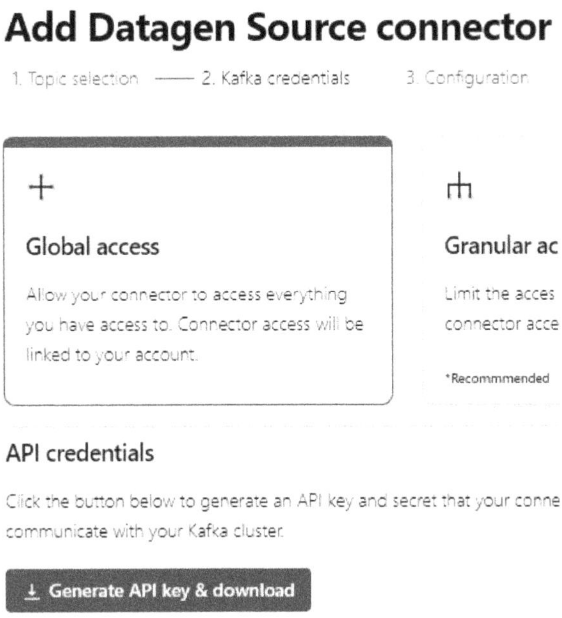
Add Datagen Source connector
1. Topic selection
2. Kafka credentials
3. Configuration
Global access
Allow your connector to access everything you have access to. Connector access will be linked to your account.
Granular ac
Limit the acces
connector acce
*Recommmended
API credentials
Click the button below to generate an API key and secret that your conne
communicate with your Kafka cluster.
Generate API key & download

Figure 5.13: Configuring the model

The next screen presents us with the type of data and the format to send it in. I choose **Users** and the **JSON** format.

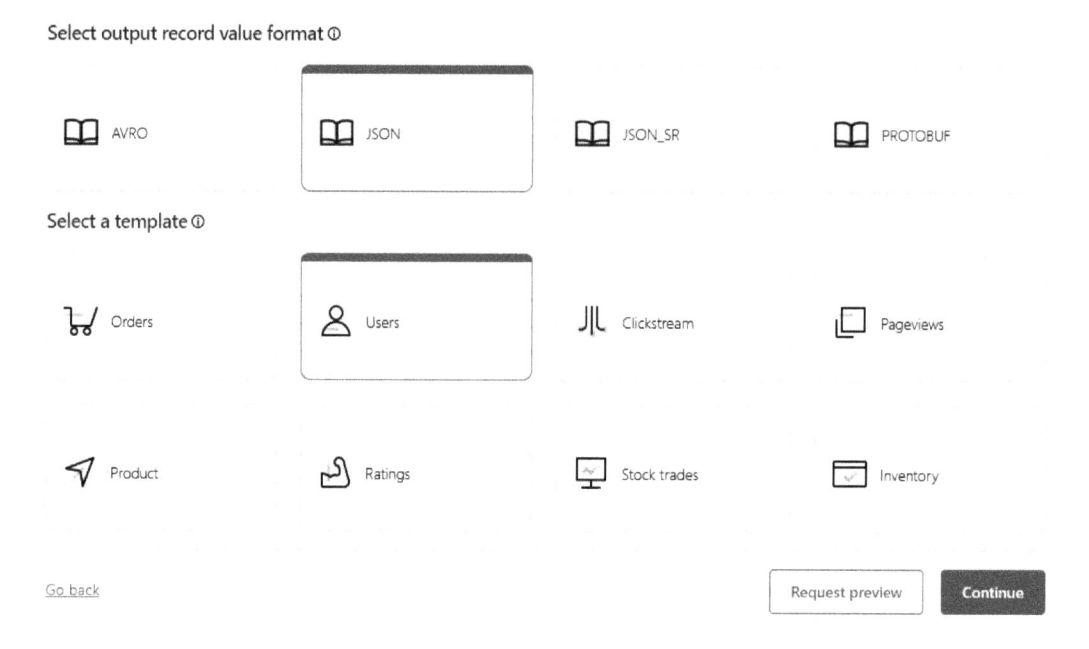

Select output record value format ⓘ

| AVRO | JSON | JSON_SR | PROTOBUF |

Select a template ⓘ

| Orders | Users | Clickstream | Pageviews |

| Product | Ratings | Stock trades | Inventory |

Go back   Request preview   Continue

Figure 5.14: Choosing the format and template

We will finally be asked to name the connector and create it. It will be turned on by default, but it can be paused.

Add Datagen Source connector

1. Topic selection — 2. Kafka credentials — 3. Configuration — 4. Sizing — 5. Review and launch

Connector class*
DatagenSource

Connector name* ⓘ
DatagenSourceConnector_0

Configuration & cost | Topics

Connector configuration

ⓘ Settings marked with an asterisk (*) cannot be changed once you launch your

Go back $0.03472222/hr + $0.03/GB usage   Request preview   **Continue**

Figure 5.15: Naming the connector

You can view your data in the **Topics** section by clicking on the **Messages** tab.

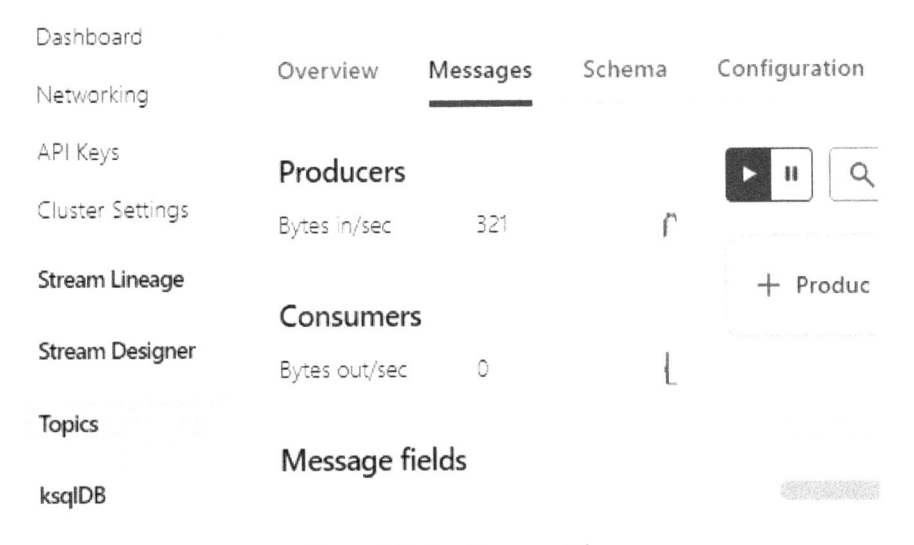

Figure 5.16: The Messages tab

We have gone through the building blocks of Confluent Kafka and how to build pipelines within Kafka. Next, we will look at making Apache Spark interact with Confluent Kafka.

Spark and Kafka

Spark has a long history of supporting Kafka with both streaming and batch processing. Here, we will go over some of the structured streaming Kafka-related APIs.

Here, we have a streaming read of a Kafka cluster. It will return a streaming DataFrame:

```
df = spark \
  .readStream \
  .format("kafka")\
  .option("kafka.bootstrap.servers", "<host>:<port>, <host>:<port>")\
  .option("subscribe", "<topic>")\
  .load()\\
```

Conversely, if you want to do a true batch process, you can also read from Kafka. Keep in mind that we have covered techniques to create a streaming context but using a batch style to avoid rereading messages:

```
df = spark \
  .read \
  .format("kafka") \
  .option("kafka.bootstrap.servers", "<host>:<port>, <host>:<port>")\
  .option("subscribe", "<topic>") \
  .load()
```

Spark can also be a producer for Kafka. For example, I have seen cases where Spark will run a prediction on an event and then send the prediction back to Kafka:

```
stream = df \
  .writeStream \
  .format("kafka") \
  .option("kafka.bootstrap.servers", "<host>:<port>, <host>:<port>") \
  .option("topic", "<topic>") \
  .start()
```

To make this a batch job, simply switch to a `write` method instead of `writeStream`:

```
df.write \
   .format("kafka") \
  .option("kafka.bootstrap.servers", "<host>:<port>, <host>:<port>") \
  .option("topic", "<topic>") \
  .save()
```

Spark now supports Schema Registry, which is something new. You simply need to use the `from_format` methods and input your Schema Registry information:

```
df = spark \
  .readStream \
  .format("kafka") \
  .option("kafka.bootstrap.servers", <URL>) \
  .option("subscribe", "<topic>")
  .load()
   select(
    from_avro($"key", "t-key", Map("schema.registry.url" -> "<schema_reg_url>")).as("key"),
    from_avro($"value", "t-value", Map("schema.registry.url" -> "<schema_reg_url>")).as("value")
  )
```

We have come a long way in learning about Kafka core and the ins and outs of how Kafka and users interact. We have covered Schema Registry and how to enforce contracts with your topics. We have even looked at connecting through Spark and using Connect to build pipelines.

Practical lab

In these practical labs, we will create common tasks that involve integrating Kafka and Spark to build Delta tables:

1. Connect to Confluent Kafka using Spark. Use Schema Registry to create a Spark job. This should ingest data from a topic and write to a delta table.
2. Use the Delta Sink Connector to finalize the table.

It is your task to write a Spark job that ingests events from a Confluent Kafka topic and write it out to a Delta table.

Solution

We will get started as follows:

1. First, we will import our libraries. Also, note that you must install `confluent_kafka` first using `pip`:

    ```
    from confluent_kafka.schema_registry import SchemaRegistryClient
    import ssl
    from pyspark.sql.functions import from_json
    from pyspark.sql.functions import udf, col, expr
    from pyspark.sql.types import StringType
    ```

2. Here, we set up our variables for our initial Kafka connection:

    ```
    kafka_cluster = "see confluent website"
    kafka_api_key = "see confluent website"
    kafka_api_secret = "see confluent website"
    kafka_topic = "chapter_5"
    boostrap_server = "see confluent website"
    schema_reg_url = "see confluent website"
    schema_api_key = "see confluent website"
    schema_api_secret = "see confluent website"
    ```

3. We will create a UDF to convert the value into a string:

    ```
    binary_to_string = udf(lambda x: str(int.from_bytes(x, byteorder='big')), StringType())
    ```

4. Now, we will read our initial DataFrame using our UDF:

    ```
    kafka_df = (
        spark
        .readStream
        .format("kafka")
        .option("kafka.bootstrap.servers", bootstrap_server)
        .option("kafka.security.protocol", "SASL_SSL")
        .option("kafka.sasl.jaas.config", "kafkashaded.org.apache.kafka.common.security.plain.PlainLoginModule required username='{}' password='{}';".format(kafka_api_key, kafka_api_secret))
        .option("kafka.ssl.endpoint.identification.algorithm", "https")
        .option("kafka.sasl.mechanism", "PLAIN")
        .option("subscribe", kafka_topic)
        .option("startingOffsets", "earliest")
        .option("failOnDataLoss", "false")
        .load()
        .select(
            col("topic"),
            col("partition"),
            col("offset"),
            col("timestamp"),
            col("timestampType"),
            col("key").cast(StringType()).alias("key_string"),
            expr("substring(value, 6, length(value)-5)").alias("fixed_value"),
            binary_to_string(expr("substring(value, 2, 4)")).
    ```

```
        alias("value_schema_id")
        )
    )
```

5. Here, we set up our Schema Registry client:

    ```
    schema_registry_conf = { 'url': schema_reg_url, 'basic.auth.
    user.info': f'{schema_api_key}:{schema_api_secret}'}
    schema_registry_client = SchemaRegistryClient(schema_registry_
    conf)
    ```

6. Next, we will create a function to do the for each batch-writing in our stream:

    ```
    table_path = "dbfs:/tmp/kafka_table"
    def kafka_delta_writer(df, ephoch_id):
        cached = df.cache()
        def find_schema(id):
            return str(schema_registry_client.get_schema(id).schema_
    str)
        unque_ids = cached.select(col('value_schema_id').
    cast('integer')).distinct()
        for id in unque_ids.collect():
            current_id = sc.broadcast(id.valueSchemaId)
            current_schema = sc.broadcast(find_schema(current_
    id.value))
            df = cached.filter(col('value_schema_id') == current_
    id.value)
            (df
             .select('topic', 'partition', 'offset', 'timestamp',
    'timestampType', 'key', from_json(col("value").cast("string"),
    current_schema).alias("parsed"))
             .write
             .format("delta")
             .mode("append")
             .option("mergeSchema", "true")
             .save(table_path))
    ```

7. Finally, we will call our foreach function in our write stream:

    ```
    checkpoint_location = "dbfs:/tmp/kafka_table_checkpoint"
    kafka_df.writeStream \
      .option("checkpointLocation", checkpoint_location) \
      .foreachBatch(kafka_delta_writer) \
      .queryName("chapter_5_query") \
      .start()
    ```

It might seem like a good amount of code, but it's rather small and fully supported now in Spark.

110   Streaming Data with Kafka

An alternative solution would be to use a Kafka Connect sink. So, your next task is to create a sink that reads all of a topic and writes it to a Delta table.

First, we will browse the connectors menu in our cluster in Confluent Kafka. Here, I have searched for `databricks`, and we will use the first connector, as shown here.

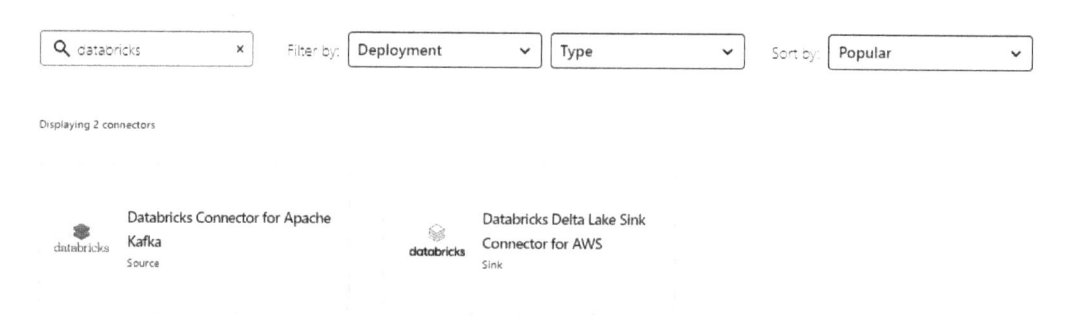

Figure 5.17: Searching for databricks

Next, we will be prompted for a topic to read from; here, I use the `chapter_5` topic we have already created.

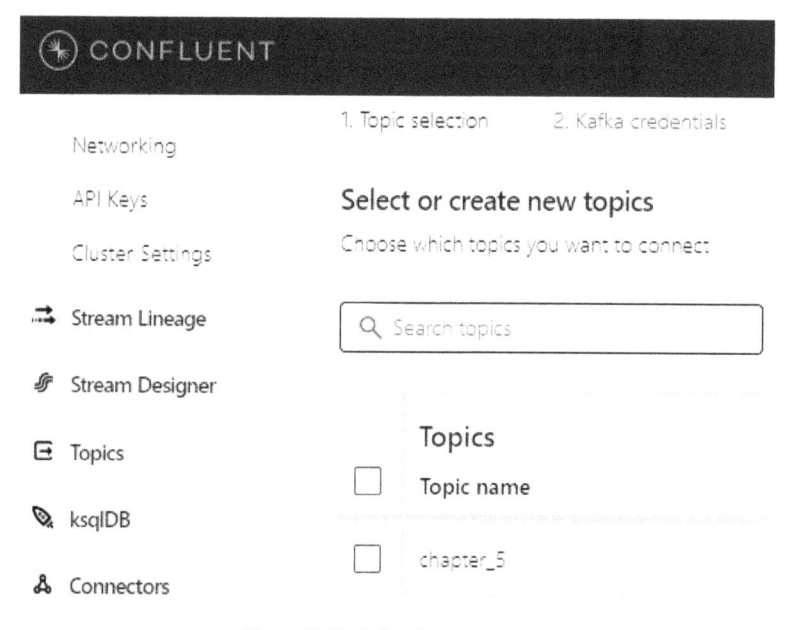

Figure 5.18: Selecting the topic

The next screen will ask us to select the access policy and create an API key. Here, I use the **Global access** policy. This isn't ideal for production, so if you use a policy in production, choose to have a fine-grained security one.

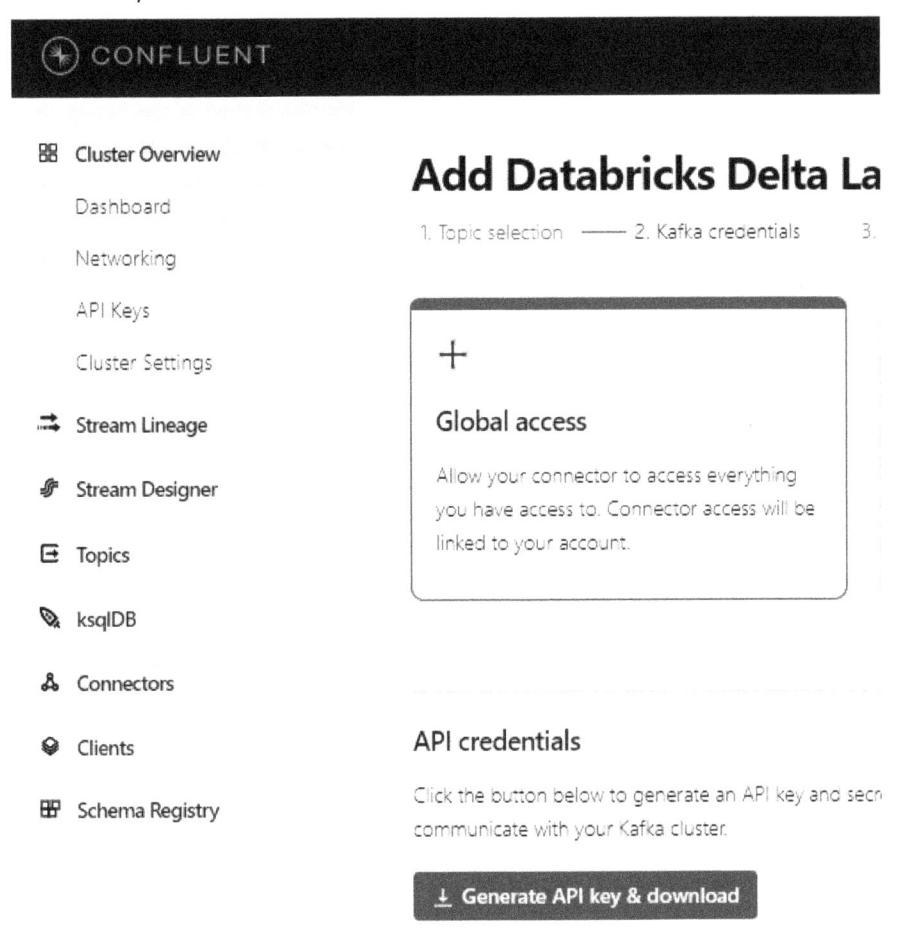

Figure 5.19: Selecting the access policy and API key

Next, we are prompted for a few bits of information. Our URL and folder path can be found in the Databricks menu when selecting the cluster and then browsing for the configuration.

Next, we need to create an access token for Kafka Connect. Here, we will go to the user settings currently located in the top-right corner of the Databricks web UI. There will be a tab for **Access tokens**, as shown in the following screenshot. Create a new token and give it a relevant name.

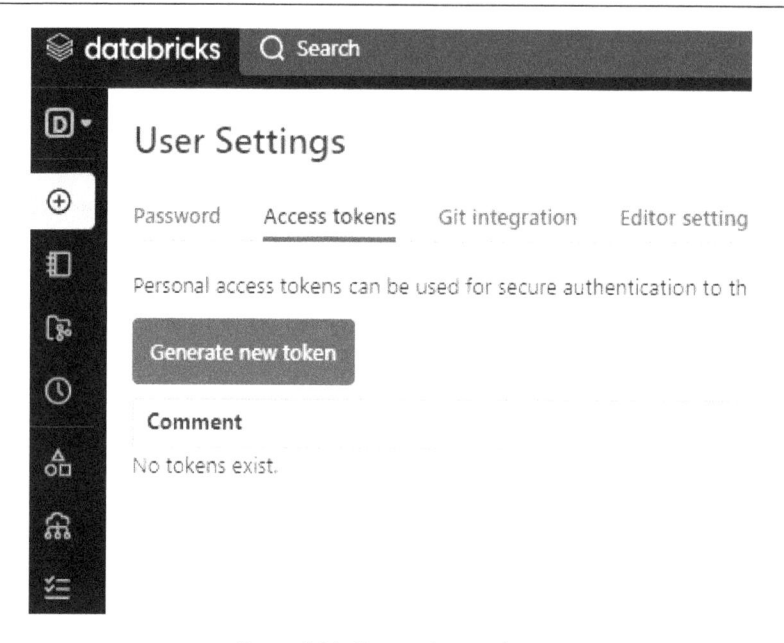

Figure 5.20: Generating a token

The next screen will allow you to name and set a lifetime for the API key. Here, I have set it for one year.

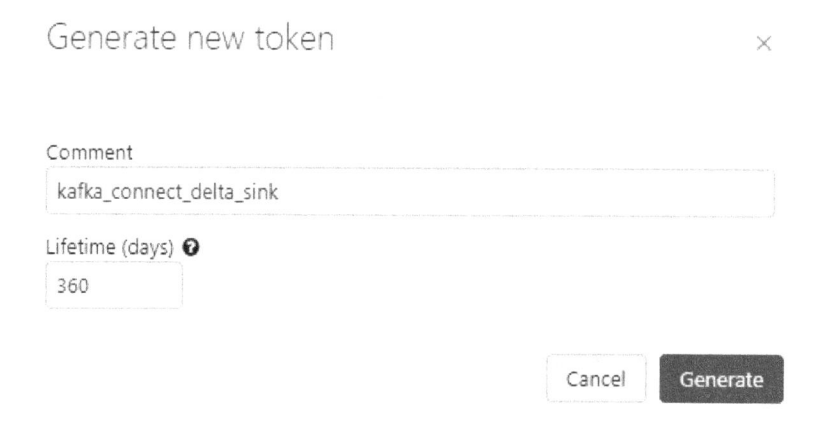

Figure 5.21: The configuration settings for a token

You will be asked for an AWS key and secret.

In the AWS console, under Identity and Access Management (IAM), you will see a section called **Users** and a button to add a user. The web UI should be similar to the following screenshot.

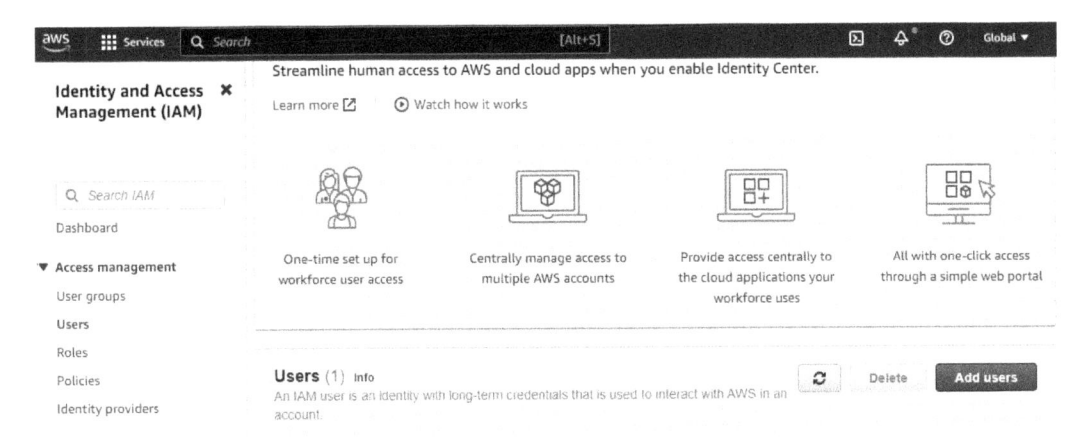

Figure 5.22: The Users section

Once the user is created, you can browse the user and find **Create access keys** under security credentials.

You should now have all the information to complete the initial connect screen. Your next screen will ask you for the format of the events in the topic. In this case, I use the **JSON** format.

Figure 5.23: Selecting the Kafka record value format

Navigate to the **Connectors** section in your cluster and choose the connector you just created. You should see the following advanced configuration. Make sure to set the following settings to match.

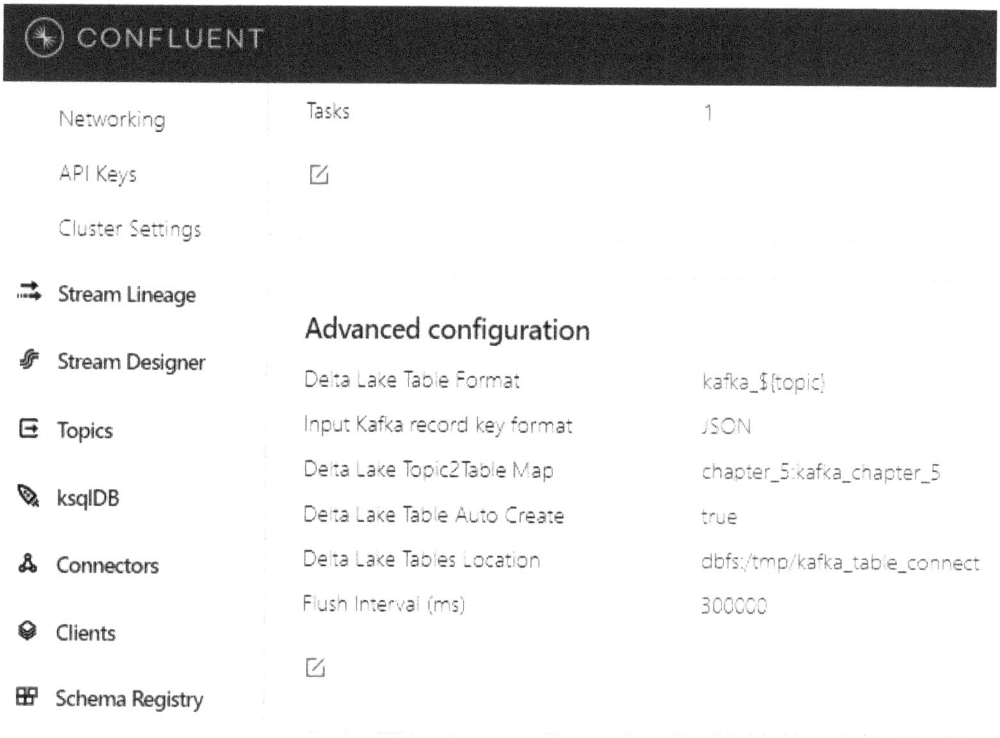

Figure 5.24: Checking the advanced configuration and pipeline

You now have a working pipeline from Kafka to a Delta table.

Summary

So, as our Confluent Kafka Chapter approaches, let's reflect on where we have gone and what we have done. We reviewed the fundamentals of Kafka's architecture and how to set up Confluent Kafka. We looked at writing producers and consumers and working with Schema Registry and Connect. Lastly, we looked at integrating with Spark and Delta Lake. Kafka is an essential component of streaming data. Streaming data has become an in-demand skill and an important technique. We will delve deep into **machine learning operations** (**MLOps**) and several other AI technologies as we advance.

Part 3: Modernizing the Data Platform

In this part, we will look at non-traditional techniques and technologies we have brought into the traditional data platform, like ML/AI and Data Viz. We will then delve into Software best practices like CI and Automation.

This part has the following chapters:

- *Chapter 6, MLOps*
- *Chapter 7, Data and Information Visualization*
- *Chapter 8, Integrating Continous Integration into Your Workflow*
- *Chapter 9, Orchestrating Your Data Workflows*

6
MLOps

ML and AI is one of the most important topics in the past several years. MLOps is the practice of productionizing ML products that have been created from data science research. MLOps is very important not only for reusability but also for clear and accurate data science. In this chapter, we will go through the ins and outs of MLflow, a popular MLOps tool that manages every stage of your data science project and experiments. We will also cover AutoML, which is an automated way to get reasonable ML models and feature stores. These are data management systems that version data for historical purposes.

In this chapter, we're going to cover the following main topics:

- The basics of machine learning
- MLFlow
- HyperOpt
- AutoML
- FeatureStore

Technical requirements

The tooling that will be used in this chapter is tied to the tech stack that's been chosen for this book. All vendors should offer a free trial account.

I will be using Databricks in this chapter.

Setting up your environment

Before we begin this chapter, let's take some time to set up our working environment.

Python, AWS, and Databricks

As in the previous chapter, this chapter assumes you have a working version of Python 3.6+ installed in your development environment. It also assumes you have set up an AWS account and have set up Databricks with that AWS account.

Databricks CLI

The first step is to install the `databricks-cli` tool using the `pip` Python package manager:

```
pip install databricks-cli
```

Let's validate that everything has been installed correctly. If the following command produces the tool version, then everything is working correctly:

```
databricks -v
```

Now, let's set up authentication. First, go into the Databricks UI and generate a personal access token. The following command will ask for the host that's been created for your Databricks instance, as well as the created token:

```
databricks configure -token
```

We can determine whether the CLI has been set up correctly by running the following command. If no error is returned, then you have a working setup:

```
databricks fs ls
```

Lastly, let's set up our `workspace`, `clusters`, and `dbfs` folders:

```
databricks  fs mkdirs   dbfs:/chapter_5
databricks  workspace mkdirs   /chapter_5
databricks  clusters create -json-file    <file_path to tiny.json>
```

The following is the content of the `tiny.json` file. Note the change in runtime and nodes for machine learning usage:

```
{
    "num_workers": 0,
    "cluster_name": "Brian Lipp's Cluster MLOps",
    "spark_version": "13.0.x-gpu-ml-scala2.12",
    "spark_conf": {
        "spark.databricks.cluster.profile": "singleNode",
        "spark.master": "local[*, 4]"
    },
    "aws_attributes": {
```

```
        "first_on_demand": 1,
        "availability": "SPOT_WITH_FALLBACK",
        "zone_id": "auto",
        "instance_profile_arn": "arn:aws:iam::112437402463:instance-
  profile/databricks-workspace-stack-3-access-data-buckets",
        "spot_bid_price_percent": 100,
        "ebs_volume_count": 0
    },
    "node_type_id": "g4dn.xlarge",
    "driver_node_type_id": "g4dn.xlarge",
    "ssh_public_keys": [],
    "custom_tags": {
        "ResourceClass": "SingleNode"
    },
    "spark_env_vars": {},
    "autotermination_minutes": 10,
    "enable_elastic_disk": false,
    "cluster_source": "UI",
    "init_scripts": [],
    "single_user_name": "bclipp21@gmail.com",
    "enable_local_disk_encryption": false,
    "data_security_mode": "LEGACY_SINGLE_USER_STANDARD",
    "runtime_engine": "STANDARD",
    "cluster_id": "0310-000347-et5jgw2a"
}
```

Introduction to machine learning

ML is a discipline that heavily correlates with the discipline of statistics. We will go through the basics of ML at a high level so that we can appreciate the tooling mentioned later in this chapter.

Understanding data

ML is the process of using some type of learning algorithm on a set of historical data to predict things that are unknown, such as image recognition and future event forecasting, to name a few. When you're feeding data into your ML model, you will use features. A feature is just another term for data. Data is the oil that runs ML, so we will talk about that first.

Types of data

Data can come in two forms:

- **Quantitative data**: Quantitative data is data that can be boxed in and measured. Data such as age and height are good examples of quantitative data. Quantitative data can come in two flavors: discrete and continuous. Discrete data is data that is countable and finite or has a limited range of values. An example of discrete data might be the number of students in a class. Continuous data, on the other hand, is data that can represent any value. We are not limited to a set range, or a countable number in continuous data – time is a good example of continuous data. Now that we have quantitative data down, let's move on to qualitative data.

- **Qualitative data**: Qualitative data is data that describes something. Practically, that can be anything from biological sex to income class. Qualitative data comes in two flavors as well: nominal and ordinal. Something that is ordinal has an order to it, such as income class. Nominal data is qualitative data that doesn't have any order to it.

Now that we have explored the basics of data, let's learn how to use that data and feed it to ML.

The basics of feature engineering

We spoke about feature engineering in previous chapters, so I will just review the concept here. A feature is a characteristic of the overall data being used to train your ML model – think age, sex, and BMI. Feature engineering is the process of looking at those characteristics and finding ways to manipulate them to get better performance with your models. These changes would then be applied to your new data as well, so this isn't something that you're doing to cheat. An example might be to group age into child, teen, adult, and elderly. These types of changes might have a positive effect on your model, but that's something you would need to test on a big enough sample to feel confident in your results.

Splitting up your data

When you're training your ML model, you might realize that the more data you feed into your training, the better. The next step might be to take all of your sample data and train on that. This would require you to evaluate your model using the data you have already trained on. At first, this seems okay – after all, it's just data. Right?

So, as a rule, you should never test your model with the data you used to make your model better. This goes for model training, as well as hyperparameter tuning, a topic that will be covered later. You will never get an accurate assessment of your model. The solution is to split your data into two or more groups – one for model training, one for testing, and possibly one for hyperparameter tuning. You can always write code to manually split your data, but many libraries can do this for you. When using `sklearn`, the norm is to use X to represent your features; y will represent the target you are looking to predict.

Here, we are using the `sklearn` library to create a train-test split to create our training and test sets:

```
X_train, X_test, y_train, y_test = train_test_split(X, y, test_
size=0.21, random_state=613)
```

Next, we're using the training data and splitting it to create a validation set:

```
 X_train, X_validation, y_train, y_validation = train_test_split(X_
train, y_train, test_size=0.25, random_state=613)
```

Fitting your data

When looking at how well your model performs, you will be presented with two general concepts: overfitting and underfitting.

Underfitting is the concept of having a model that's too general for your data. Another way to think about it is that it just performs badly on all types of data.

The exact opposite is overfitting, which is when your data performs very well – too well. When you vary the data, suddenly, you will find that its performance is horrible. What's happening is your model is chasing after noise or it's trained to look at details that are not important.

It's ideal to have your models sit somewhere between the two – a model that is both flexible and generalized to varying datasets but focuses on important parts of your data. Again, this is done by performing lots and lots of experiments and testing varying things that go into making your model. This is generally called the bias-variance trade-off. Bias is when your model fits too well to your data and variance is when it doesn't fit enough but will be consistent across varying datasets.

Cross-validation

There is a very interesting technique that's used in ML to increase reliability, even more than just train-test splitting your data: cross-validation. Cross-validation is used when you look at your data and run many train-test split experiments on your data, each using a different sample to test and train with. This process allows you to see what changes have the best results, without you losing any data. This process can be used on your model training data and your validation or hyperparameter data. Depending on how many times you run this experiment, you will call it X-fold validation. For example, if I do this process five times, then it's called 5-fold validation. If I only do this once, it's called leave-one-out cross-validation. Now, you might think that doing more cross-validation is the best choice. You have to weigh time, and also the validity of having a smaller test set in each fold of your validation.

In our case, we will use 10 folds and perform cross-validation using a model we have already trained, and then request the accuracy, precision, recall, and f1 metrics for our model throughout the cross-validation process. We are handing our original X and y to `cross_validation` since it will be testing and training on its own. If you want to have a validation set, then you must split both X and y first.

For our example, X and y will be fake data. Let's create this data using the `make_regression` function:

```
from sklearn.model_selection import cross_validate
from sklearn.datasets import make_regression
X, y = make_regression(n_samples=100, n_features=2, noise=1, random_state=770)
```

X looks as follows:

```
X
array([[-0.21874054,  0.47105943],
       [ 0.35967801,  0.3361914 ],
```

y looks as follows:

```
y
array([  10.25172454,   55.79444101,  -49.88885597, -149.38365502,
        241.06786167,   18.90685562,  -77.81926798, -113.24293344,
```

Let's create an example lasso regression model using `sklearn`:

```
model = linear_model.Lasso()
```

Here, we have set `folds` to `10`:

```
folds = 10
```

Here, we are training our models using the cross-validation technique using the `cross_validation` function:

```
results = cross_validate(model, X, y, cv=folds, return_train_score=True)
```

Now, we can see the output of that function:

```
{'fit_time': array([0., 0., 0., 0., 0., 0., 0., 0., 0., 0.]), 'score_time': array([0.       , 0.       , 0.       , 0.       , 0.0095098,
0.       ,
       0.       , 0.       , 0.       , 0.       ]), 'test_score':
array([0.9997851 , 0.9998334 , 0.99969518, 0.99975864, 0.99948199,
       0.99952154, 0.99950884, 0.99968857, 0.9996008 , 0.99977714])}
```

Now, our `results` variable will be a dictionary that contains all the scoring for both the training and tests:

```
sorted(results.keys())
['fit_time', 'score_time', 'test_score', 'train_score']
```

The following is the test score; you should get something in the same ballpark:

```
results['test_score']
array([0.9997851 , 0.9998334 , 0.99969518, 0.99975864, 0.99948199,
       0.99952154, 0.99950884, 0.99968857, 0.9996008 , 0.99977714])
```

Now that we have explored the ins and outs of ML, let's explore what we can use to train our models.

Understanding hyperparameters and parameters

When we start training our ML models, we will have generally two types of "knobs" to tinker with. The first knob is normally handled by the modeling software – this is typically the parameters of the model. Each modeling technique has parameters that are used within the model to train the model. It's useful to understand what the parameters are when you train your model to see how it compares to other models.

On the other hand, every time you train your model, you can set varying hyperparameters for the software. A simple example of hyperparameters is that, in random forest model training, you can set things such as the number of trees and the number of features. You would need to search through all the varying combinations across your cross-validation to find the best combination for your validation dataset. Many software packages will do most of that heavy lifting for you now, using a grid search or a random search. A grid search is simply a search where you define the variables to search with, and a random search is where the software picks combinations for you. Like anything else, there is no free lunch. The larger your search grid is, the longer and more expensive the training process will take. You must weigh up these variables when you're setting up your experiments.

Training our model

We have mentioned the process of training our model a few times, but it still might seem very vague. For many people, it's a black-box process that happens behind the scenes. What's most important to understand is that the algorithm looks at your training data and then creates a model or a reference structure that you can use to predict against new data. This model will be something in code that you can save, share, and put into production with an application.

Working together

There are endless algorithms to choose from, but my favorite algorithms are ensemble methods, where we use combinations of models to predict results better. I'll mention three popular techniques you might come across – that is, bagging, boosting, and stacking:

- **Bagging** or **bootstrap aggregation** is the process of sampling again and again on your data, with each sample having a model trained on it. We do not remove what we sample, so the process is more robust. Each model votes in an election process to see what the best results are.

A popular example of this process is the random forest algorithm.

- **Boosting**, on the other hand, is the process of building up models sequentially that don't perform as well together to make a better model overall. This process assigns weights to models and their outputs. What happens over several cycles is that a rule structure is created with all the models building off each other.
- **Stacking** is another very popular technique where models are trained; then, meta-models are trained on the output of previous models.

Understanding the basics of ML is a very useful tool, and you will often come into contact with these terms and tools when you're working with data. AutoML takes many of the manual steps and processes we have mentioned here and automates them for us.

AutoML

AutoML is the process of giving an AutoML program your data and having it try to find the best algorithm and hyperparameter for you. This can often give you great general results but typically, it requires more fine-tuning if your AutoML is done well. AutoML can be expensive, so it's important to watch your bill and plan accordingly. Databricks offers a very useful AutoML feature. Databricks AutoML performs data preparation, trains several models, and then finds the best-trained models. Databricks AutoML will use a variety of the most popular ML libraries in the evaluation. So, will AutoML give you the best model possible? No, it's not going to replace the need for further feature engineering and model tuning. Instead, it's going to take a chunk of the work off your plate and try to give you a reasonable model to start with. In some cases, that model will be good enough for what you need.

> **Note**
> You can learn more about AutoML by going to `https://learn.microsoft.com/en-us/azure/databricks/machine-learning/automl/train-ml-model-automl-api` and `https://towardsai.net/p/l/automate-machine-learning-using-databricks-automl%E2%80%8A-%E2%80%8Aa-glass-box-approach-and-mlflow`.

AutoML is a useful technique for jump-starting your data science experiments as it will send you in the right general direction more often than not. AutoML is just one useful component in a data science toolkit, but how do you know what models have been tried or the training performance for a cross-validation process? In these cases, we must use Mlflow.

MLflow

MLflow is an open source MLOps framework that aims to be compatible with whatever other tools you might have. It has libraries in many popular languages and can be accessed via the REST API. MLflow has very few opinions and will not dictate anything related to your tech stack. You don't even need to use the provided libraries; you could choose to use just REST API interactions. This allows teams to customize and pick whatever other tooling they wish. If you want a hosted MLflow, then you can use Databrick's hosted MLflow.

MLOps benefits

There are many useful benefits to MLOps, and they often focus on features and models. MLOps tooling will often record the details of a series of experiments. This type of documentation can include metrics around model training and performance. MLOps tooling often stores your model and, in some cases, has mechanisms for users to interact with that model. Another useful area of MLOps is around features, which often need to be stored or documented so that we can reproduce results as needed in the future.

MLflow has four main features that it offers its users. These are tracking, projects, models, and registry:

- When using tracking, you will come across the concept of a run. A run is simply a case where some small group of code is run, and you need to record metadata about that "run." A run can be organized into an experiment – that is, a group of runs around a specific theme. Tracking is a set of features around saving metrics, code, artifacts, and tagging your ML experiments. You will be able to go back and see how my model performance was and access our model, among other useful features.

- A project is a folder that's used to store relevant information about your experiments. It is normally tied to a Git repository.

- A model is a feature that helps with versioning your models and deploying them into production so that users can take advantage of them.

- Lastly, the registry is a model store that allows you to create a catalog of models being created and used.

The core Python APIs are very simple, as we'll see now.

Here, we are installing the necessary libraries:

```
pip install mlflow
pip install mlflow
pip install scikit-learn
```

Next, we must start our run:

```
with mlflow.start_run():
```

Once we have trained our model, we can log useful metadata about it. This metadata will be displayed alongside your model results in the GUI, so it's very useful to log any needed information for reference and comparison:

```
Mlflow.log_param("ALPHA", alpha)
mlflow.log_metric("MSE", mse)
```

Beyond these basic APIs, you have other useful methods:

```
Search_runs
```

Search runs can be used to find a run within a project. As shown here, you can use several methods to filter as you search:

```
runs = mlflow.MlflowClient().search_runs(
    experiment_ids="13",
    filter_string="_dev",
)
```

I find it very useful to organize runs into experiments. Multiple runs can be placed within an experiment. Here, we're creating an experiment and giving it a few useful tags:

```
experiment = mlflow.create_experiment("my_ml_dev_experiments",
tags={"version": "1.2", "env": "DEV"})
```

If we are using an experiment, then we can pass that ID into our `start_run` method to organize everything very cleanly:

```
with mlflow.start_run(experiment_id=experiment.experiment_id):
```

Note that we are pulling out fields from the `experiment` object. Here are a few other useful ones:

```
experiment.experiment_id
experiment.name
Experiment.tags
```

Here is an example of what you might see in your experiment log:

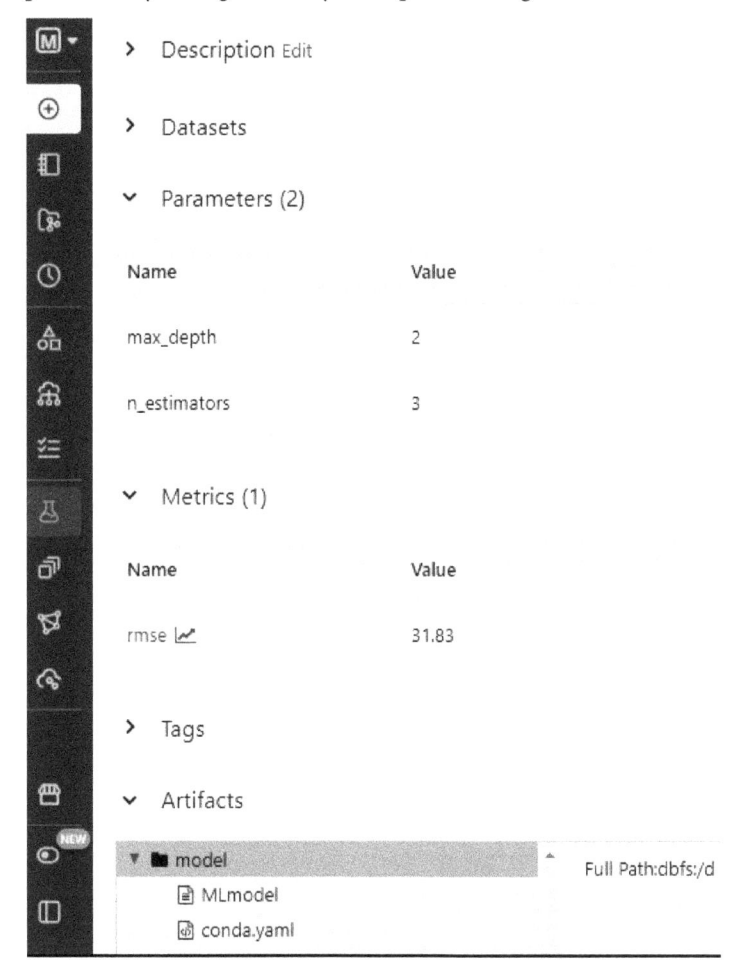

Figure 6.1: Experiment log

MLFlow is a game-changer when it comes to organizing your data science projects. As your projects and experiments grow, MLFlow's power becomes very apparent. Next, we will look at feature stores.

Feature stores

A feature store is a repository of features that have been created and versioned and are ready for model training. Recording features and storing them is critical for reproducibility. I have seen many cases where data scientists have created models with no documentation on how to retrain them other than a mess of complex code. A feature store is a catalog of features, similar to a model store. Feature stores are normally organized into databases and feature tables.

Let's jump right in and go through Databricks feature store's APIs:

1. First, let's import the necessary libraries:

   ```
   from databricks import feature_store
   from databricks.feature_store import FeatureLookup
   import random
   ```

2. Now, let's create our name and record our database and schema. We are using the `users` DataFrame. We will also set our `lookup_key`, which in this case is `user_id`. A lookup key is just the value that identifies the feature store when we're searching for it:

   ```
   table_name = "users_run_" + str(random.randint(0,10000))
   database_name = "sales"
   schema = users.schema
   lookup_key = "user_id"
   ```

3. Now, we can create our database:

   ```
   spark.sql(f"CREATE DATABASE IF NOT EXISTS f{database_name}")
   ```

4. Next, we will create our feature store object and define our feature table. Once we have our table, we will insert our data. This insertion can be done later so that the data is updated as needed:

   ```
   fs = feature_store.FeatureStoreClient()
   fs.create_table(
       name=table_name,
       primary_keys=[lookup_key],
       schema=schema,
       description="user sales features"
   )
   fs.write_table(
       name=table_name,
       df=users,
       mode="overwrite"
   )
   ```

5. If we want to get our feature table, we must create a model feature lookup, as shown here:

   ```
   model_feature_lookups = [feature_store.FeatureLookup(table_name=table_name, lookup_key=lookup_key)]
   ```

6. Lastly, we will create a Spark DataFrame using the `create_training_set` method:

   ```
   training_set = fs.create_training_set(users, model_feature_lookups, label="quality", exclude_columns="wine_id")
   ```

The output should be the same DataFrame that was used initially.

What's so amazing about a feature store? With a feature store, we can easily record and share what version of the data we used to train our model. This is a huge breakthrough. Next, we will look at a distributed tool for hyperparameter tuning called **Distributed Asynchronous Hyperparameter Optimization** (**Hyperopt**).

Hyperopt

Hyperopt is a Python library for managing hyperparameter tuning. Databricks has added useful proprietary features to Hyperopt to enable easy Spark integration. With Hyperopt, you can manage training models that have been created by libraries such as `sklearn` but utilize Spark's clustering capabilities.

Here, we will do a Hyperopt experiment without a cluster first:

1. First, we will import our libraries:

    ```
    from hyperopt import fmin, tpe, hp, SparkTrials, STATUS_OK, Trials
    ```

2. Now, we can create a function that does everything needed to create a score of the performance of the model within the hyperparameter test:

    ```
    def objective(C):
        create our model
        create a metric to measure the model accuracy
        return {'loss': accuracy, 'status': STATUS_OK}
    ```

3. Now, we will create a search space that creates all the permutations of possible hyperparameter combinations:

    ```
    search = hp.lognormal('C', 0, 2)
    ```

4. Let's ask Hyperopt to suggest an algorithm:

    ```
    algorithm=tpe.suggest
    ```

5. Finally, we will tell Hyperopt to start testing each hyperparameter combination:

    ```
    best_value= fmin(
      fn=objective,
      space=search,
      algo=algorithm,
      max_evals=10)
    ```

6. This is wonderful, but what about the Spark cluster? Can't we make it faster? If we just change our code a little, we can tweak it to run across the cluster:

```
from hyperopt import SparkTrials
best_value= fmin(
   fn=objective,
   space=search,
   algo=algorithm,
   max_evals=10,
   trials=spark_trials)
```

With that, we have implemented Hyperopt in our cluster.

Practical lab

So, the first problem is to create a rest API with fake data that we can predict with.

For this, I have used `mockaroo.com`.

Here is the schema I created with Mockaroo:

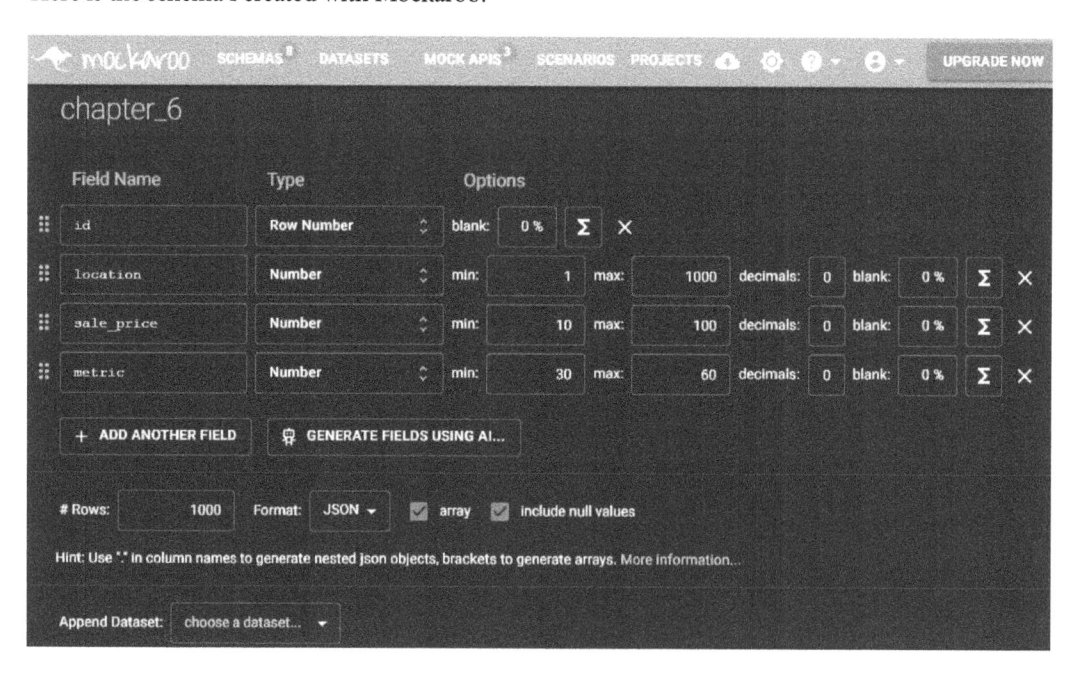

Figure 6.2: Setting fake data

A sample of the data looks like this:

	id	location	sale_price	metric
1	1	445	34	35
2	2	82	54	44
3	3	796	16	42
4	4	245	43	47
5	5	220	98	54
6	6	612	54	39
7	7	481	24	30

10 rows | 0.75 seconds runtime

Figure 6.3: Fake data output

Mockaroo allows you to create a free API – all you need to do is hit **Create API** at the bottom of the schema window.

Next, we will use Python to pull the data and prepare it for modeling.

First, we will import the necessary libraries:

```
import requests
import pandas as pd
import io
import requests
import mlflow
from sklearn import metrics
from sklearn.model_selection import train_test_split
from sklearn.ensemble import RandomForestRegressor
import numpy as np
```

Next, we will use the `requests` package to send a REST GET to our new Mockaroo API:

```
url = "https://my.api.mockaroo.com/chapter_6.json"
```

Note that you must put the key Mockaroo gives you in the header instead of XXXXXXXX:

```
headers = {"x-api-key": "XXXXXXXX"}
response = requests.get(url, headers=headers)
url_data = response.content
json = response.json()
sales = pd.DataFrame(json)
```

Lastly, we will create the train-test split for our data:

```
y = sales["sale_price"]
X =  sales.drop('sale_price', axis=1)
X_train, X_test, y_train, y_test = train_test_split(X, y, test_size=0.34, random_state=613)
```

At this point, we are ready to do our modeling.

Create an MLflow project

Creating a new MLflow project is very simple:

1. You only need to define your experiment and the path to save your model. Replace the fake email user with your username:

    ```
    experiment = mlflow.create_experiment("/Users/XXXX@gmail.com/chapter_6/experiments/", tags={"version": "1.0", "env": "DEV"})
    model_path = f"/Users/XXXX@gmail.com/chapter_6/experiments/model"
    ```

2. Train a model to predict the sales prices by logging your activity in MLflow.

    Here, we will set our single hyperparameter to 2:

    ```
    max_depth = 2
    ```

3. Next, we will set up our run and train our model:

    ```
    with mlflow.start_run(experiment_id=experiment):
        rf = RandomForestRegressor(max_depth=max_depth,
                                   n_estimators=n_estimators,
                                   random_state=0)
        rf.fit(X_train, y_train)
        y_pred = rf.predict(X_test)
        rmse = np.sqrt(metrics.mean_squared_error(y_test, y_pred))
        mlflow.log_param("max_depth", max_depth)
        mlflow.log_param("n_estimators", n_estimators)
        mlflow.log_metric("rmse", rmse)
        mlflow.sklearn.log_model(rf, "model")
        mlflow.sklearn.save_model(rf, model_path)
    ```

4. Let's see what the GUI looks like after we have trained our model.

As you can see, there are two runs. I added a failed run to give the UI a little more information:

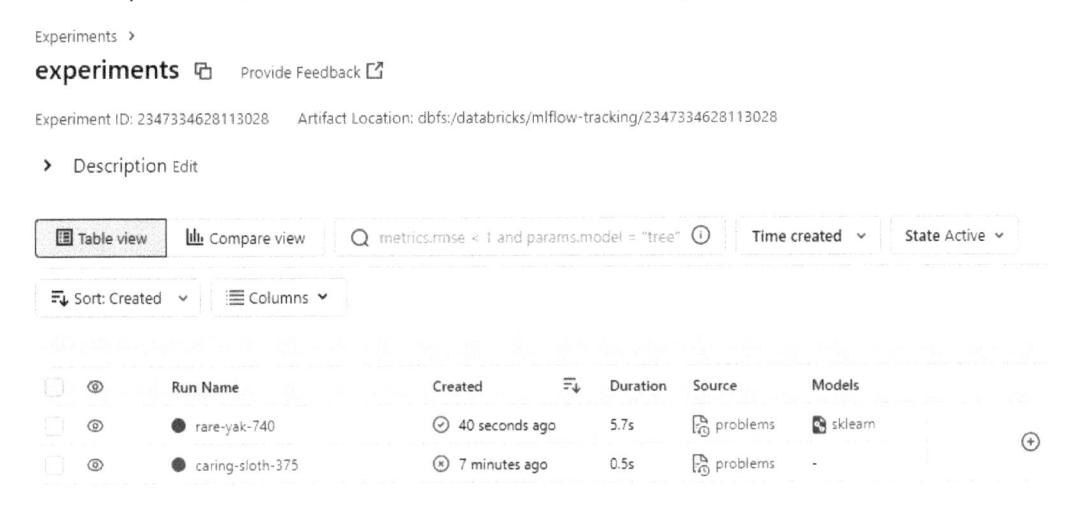

Figure 6.4: Experiments

As you can see, there are two runs, with a model available to access. We can see the notebook we used to create the run. If we were to click on the random name MLflow gave the run, we could reproduce the run. However, here, we will click on the model called `sklearn`:

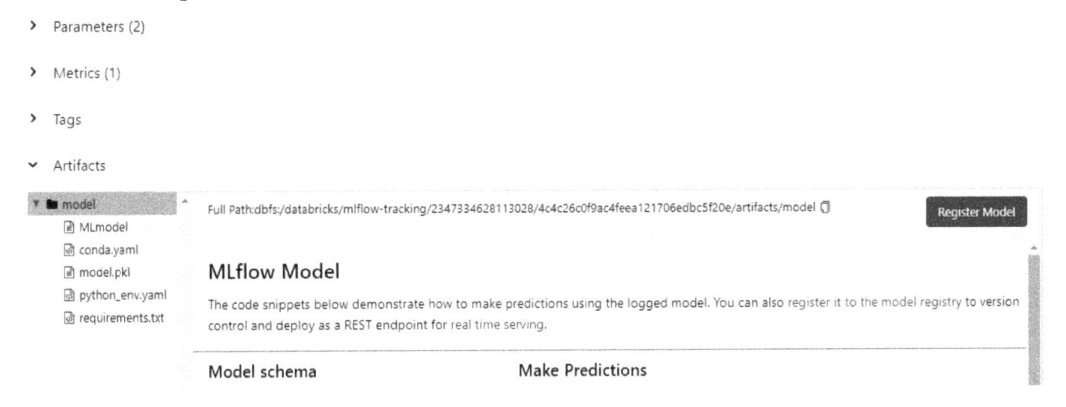

Figure 6.5: Models

At this point, we'll be given the choice to see the metrics, what parameters were used, how to use the model with example Python code, and a button to register the model in the registry. Let's register our model.

134   MLOps

We will be taken to a window where we can name our model. When we click **Register**, it will be available for others to use:

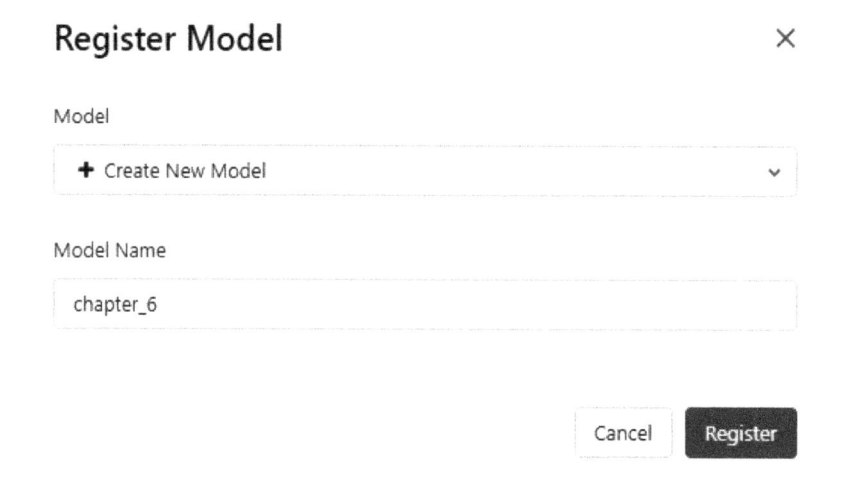

Figure 6.6: Registering a model

As we can see, our model has been registered and is available for use in the **Registered Models** section:

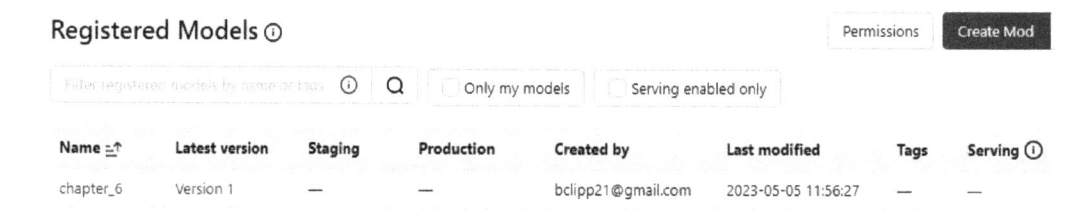

Figure 6.7: List of registered models

If we click on the model and then go to the **Serving** tab, we will be presented with the option to set our model behind a REST API.

Finally, we can set our model up for production use:

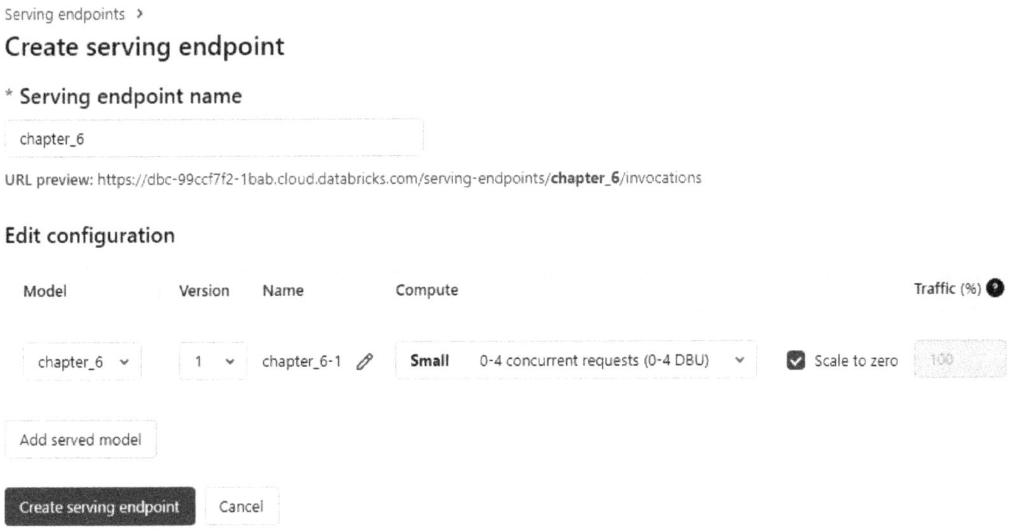

Figure 6.8: Model endpoints

Summary

Phew – that was a ton of information! It's been a long chapter, so let's discuss what we have covered. First, we looked at the basics of ML and how it can be used. Then, we looked at the importance and usage of data in ML. We explored AutoML and managing ML projects with MLFlow. Lastly, we looked at how we can better manage our training data with a feature store. In the next chapter, we will look at managing our data workflows.

7
Data and Information Visualization

The core use for much of an enterprise's data is data visualization. Data visualization can be used for anything, from data analysis and BI dashboards to charts in web apps. A data platform must be flexible enough to effectively handle all data visualization needs. We have chosen tooling that supports various languages, including SQL, R, Java, Scala, Python, and even point-and-click data visualizations. We will focus on Python, SQL, and point-and-click, but feel free to explore other tools. R, for example, has a wide range of excellent data visualizations.

In this chapter, we will cover the following main topics:

- Python-based charts using plotly.express
- Point-and-click-based charts in Databricks notebooks
- Tips and tricks for Databricks notebooks
- Creating Databricks SQL analytics dashboards
- Connecting other BI tooling to Databricks

Technical requirements

The tooling used in this chapter is tied to the tech stack chosen for the book. All vendors should offer a free trial account.

I will be using the following:

- Databricks
- AWS
- Tableau Desktop

- Python
- SQL
- dbt

Setting up your environment

Before we begin our chapter, let's take the time to set up our working environment.

Python, AWS, and Databricks

As we have with previous chapters, this chapter assumes you have a working version of Python of 3.6 or above release installed in your development environment. We will also assume you have set up an AWS account and Databricks with that account.

Databricks CLI

The Databricks CLI is used to create our Databricks infrastructure; before we can create anything, we must first make sure it's set up correctly.

Installation and setup

The first step is to install the `databricks-cli` tool using the `pip python` package manager:

```
pip install databricks-cli
```

Let's validate that everything has been installed correctly. If the following command produces the tool version, then everything works correctly:

```
Databricks -v
```

Now, let's set up authentication. First, go into the Databricks UI and generate a personal access token. The following command will ask for the host created for your Databricks instance and the created token:

```
databricks configure -token
```

We can determine whether the CLI is set up correctly by running the following command, and if no error is returned, you have a working setup:

```
databricks fs ls
```

Lastly, let's set up our workspace, cluster, and `dbfs` folder:

```
databricks   fs mkdirs   dbfs:/chapter_7
databricks   workspace mkdirs   /chapter_7
databricks   clusters create -json-file    <file_path to tiny.json>
```

The `tiny.json` file contents should be as follows:

```
{    "num_workers":0, "cluster_name":"tiny",   "spark_version":"10.4.x-scala2.12",
    "spark_conf":{
        "spark.master":"local[*, 4]",    "spark.databricks.cluster.profile":"singleNode"
    },   "aws_attributes":{
        "first_on_demand":1,   "availability":"SPOT_WITH_FALLBACK",   "zone_id":"us-west-2b",
        "instance_profile_arn":null, "spot_bid_price_percent":100,
        "ebs_volume_type":"GENERAL_PURPOSE_SSD",
        "ebs_volume_count":3, "ebs_volume_size":100
    },   "node_type_id":"m4.large",    "driver_node_type_id":"m4.large",
    "ssh_public_keys":[ ],"custom_tags":{   "ResourceClass":"SingleNode"},   "spark_env_vars":{   "PYSPARK_PYTHON":"/databricks/python3/bin/python3"},
    "autotermination_minutes":10, "enable_elastic_disk":false,   "cluster_source":"UI",   "init_scripts":[ ], "data_security_mode":"NONE",  "runtime_engine":"STANDARD"}
```

We should now have our Databricks environment all set up and ready for our chapter. We will now look at data visualization.

Principles of data visualization

Data is present everywhere. It's in every aspect of our lives, and one of the most profound methods of understanding that data is through our visual senses. We can better summarize, explain, and predict our data using charts and dashboards. However, before we go through some possible ways to create data visualizations, we will delve into some background knowledge on data visualization.

Understanding your user

When creating data visualizations, it's essential to understand how they will be used. Understanding who's using your data visualization is one of the most fundamental requirements. What is their purpose for your data visualization? Is this for strategic decision-making, or is it used for operational usage? Are you making an analytical data visualization? Understanding that a dashboard is used for critical decisions or a site reliability engineer's operational dashboard will allow you to focus on accomplishing a user-friendly data visualization that supports your user's primary goals. It will also let you further ask which vital data, goals, and KPIs will enable your users. It's important to remember that the data you present will allow you to bring insight and enlighten your users. You will take on the data storyteller role, giving you a unique position to affect critical decisions.

Validating your data

It's always important to check the data you use to create your visualizations. Validating the scale of your data and other fundamental information is an essential component of good data visualizations. It's also OK to run automated tests before using your data. Tests create a network of confidence in your data and allow users to trust the decisions they make using your data visualizations.

As we start to understand our data and our users, we will have a better picture of our data persona. Let's now discuss different types of data visualizations.

Data visualization using notebooks

Here, we will discuss the main types of visualization charts and give examples for each, using `plotly.express` and the Databricks notebook GUI.

Line charts

Line charts are used with varying data points that move over an endless plain. A perfect example of data on a continuous plain is time-series data. One thing to consider with line charts is that it's best to show small changes over a more extended period.

Bar charts

Bar charts help compare significant changes and show differences between groups of data. A key detail to remember is that bar charts are not used for contiguous data and typically represent categorical data.

Histograms

Histograms can be thought of as bar charts for continuous data. Histograms are often used with frequency over, for example, sales data.

Scatter plots

Scatter plots are essential charts showing relationships between two datasets and the correlation between data.

Pie charts

Pie charts often have a bad rap, but I feel they are great to show percentages of a larger picture. The name comes from taking a slice of pie and visually seeing the leftover proportion.

Bubble charts

Bubble charts are very good at showing relationships between three or more numerical values. By displaying the data on an *X* and *Y* plane and varying the size of each data point, you can see the relationships of multiple datasets.

Here, we introduced several charting types, and now, we will go through some examples of using them with plotly.express.

Plotly is a popular data visualization library that creates interactive and visually pleasing charts with little effort. We'll now explore various charts that can be created with it.

A single line chart

Here, we will create a single-line chart using provided stock data and the Plotly package. We will use data provided by Plotly for all Plotly examples to keep things simple. Once we have pre-processed our data to make it look how we need it, the process to create the chart is simple. We will use the `line` method of the `px` class. Finally, we will use the `show` method when the chart is ready. One item to note is that in the chart produced, we will see a widget to interact with, and the chart itself is responsive to mouse movements:

```
import plotly.express as px
import pandas as pd
stock_prices: pd.DataFrame =  px.data.stocks().melt("date", var_name="listing", value_name="price").sort_values(["date","listing"])
figure = px.line(stock_prices, x="date", y="price", color = "listing",animation_frame="listing",title='2018 & 2019 Tech Stocks')
figure.show()
```

This results in the following output:

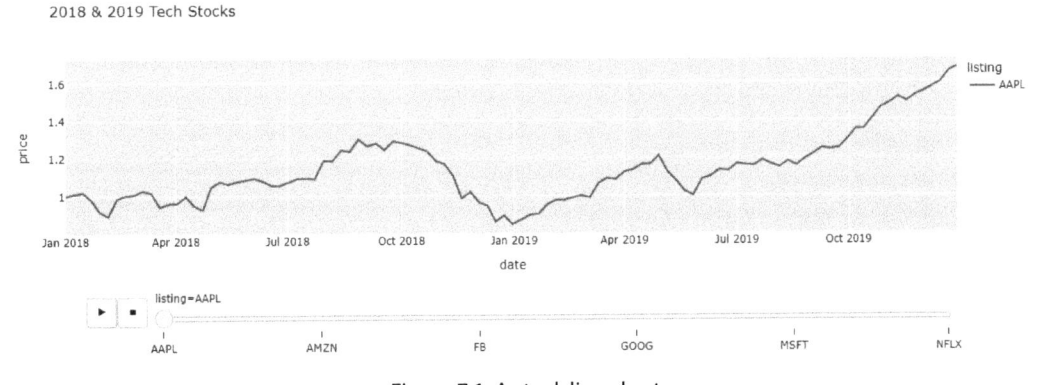

Figure 7.1: A stock line chart

A multiple line chart

Like our single line chart, we will use the `line` method and `show` the method to the class. Using the `color` argument in the line, the method can dynamically create multiple lines and choose a pattern to deviate from each effectively:

```
import plotly.express as px
import pandas as pd
stock_prices =  px.data.stocks().melt('date', var_name='listing',
value_name='price').sort_values(['date','listing'])
fig = px.line(stock_prices, x="date", y="price", color =
"listing",title='2018 & 2019 Tech Stocks')
fig.show()
```

This results in the following output:

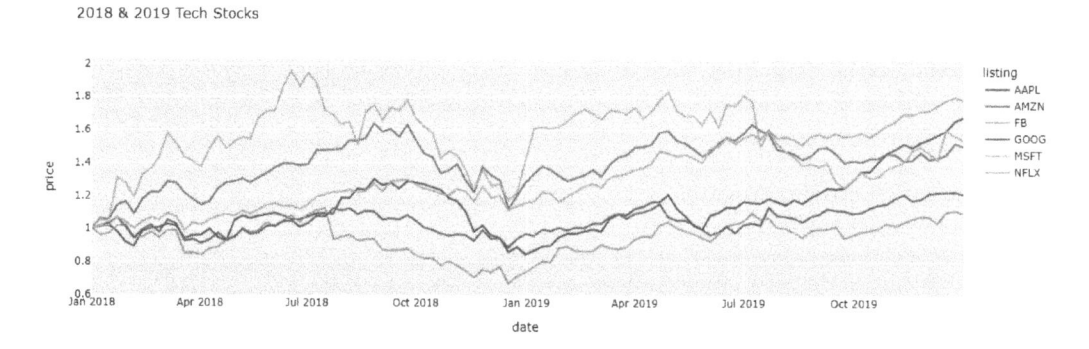

Figure 7.2: A multiple line chart

A bar chart

Now, we will move on to bar charts; the main difference will be that we use the `bar` method. Here, we will use a `tips` dataset and create an interactive bar chart:

```
import plotly.express as px
import pandas as pd
tips: pd.DataFrame = px.data.tips()
figure = px.bar(tips, x='size', y='tip')
figure.show()
```

This results in the following output:

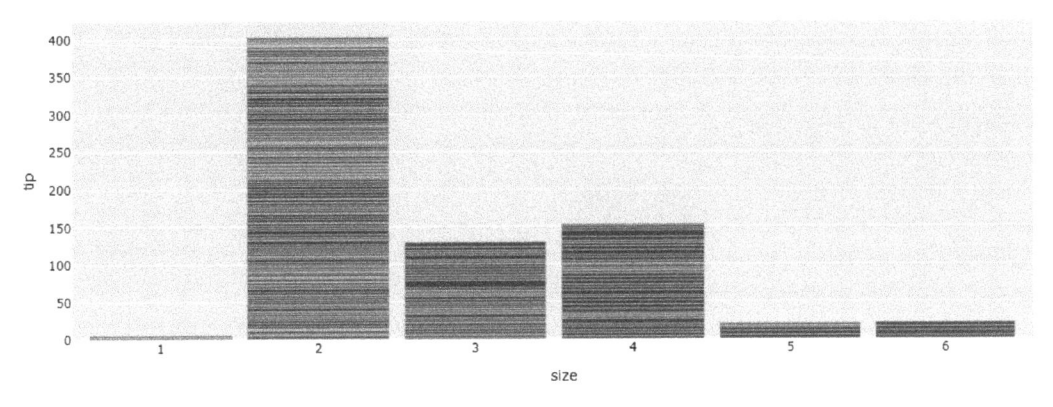

Figure 7.3: A bar chart

A scatter plot

With the following chart, we will create a scatter plot using the `scatter` method. We will set the hover data, color, and size to make the chart interactive and show data on multiple layers:

```
import plotly.express as px
import pandas as pd
iris: pd.DataFrame = px.data.iris()
figure = px.scatter(iris, x="sepal_width", y="sepal_length", hover_
data=["petal_width"], color="species",size="petal_length")
figure.show()
```

This results in the following output:

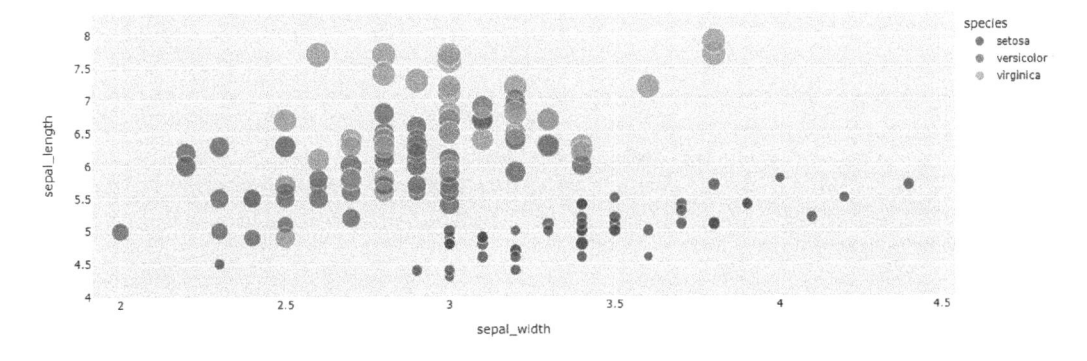

Figure 7.4: A scatter plot

A histogram

We will now create a classic histogram using the `tips` data. So, here, we will use the `histogram` method and assign the color as `green`:

```
import plotly.express as px
import pandas as pd
tips: pd.DataFrame = px.data.tips()
figure = px.histogram(tips, x="tip", nbins=25, color_discrete_
sequence=['green'])
figure.show()
```

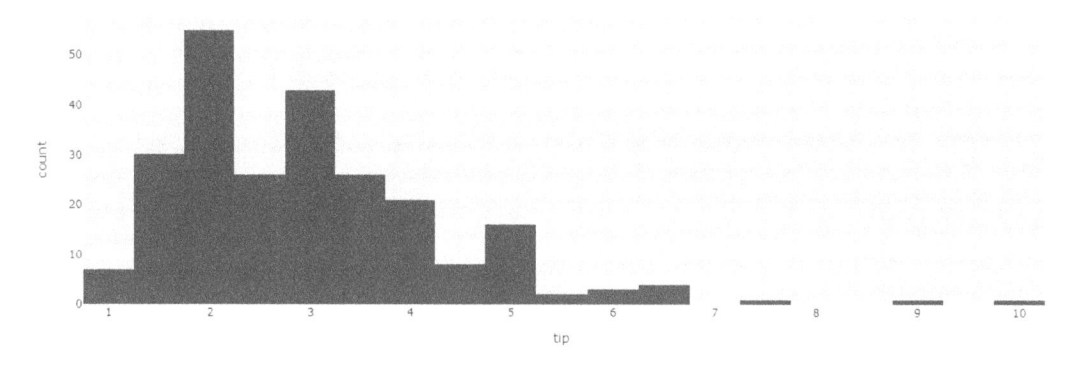

Figure 7.5: A histogram

A bubble chart

Lastly, we will create a version of the classic Gapminder chart. We will use a scatter plot and select the year 1952. This is a perfect example of creating a complex chart that visually meets our needs with only a small line of code:

```
import plotly.express as px
import pandas as pd
population = px.data.gapminder()
figure = px.scatter(population.query("year==1952"), y="lifeExp",
x="gdpPercap",size="pop", color="continent",hover_name="country", log_
x=True, size_max=80)
figure.show()
```

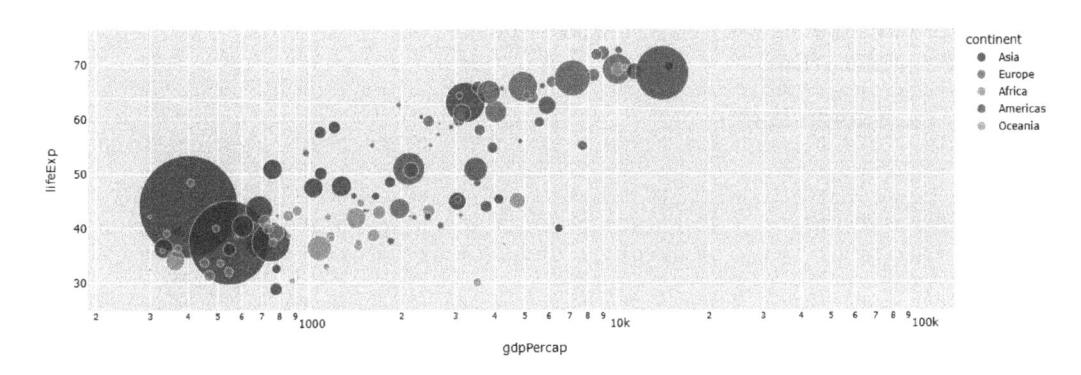

Figure 7.6: A Gapminder chart

GUI data visualizations

Now that we have seen how to create data visualizations in Databricks notebooks using `plotly`, we will go over creating similar charts using the GUI visualization menu. To access the notebook visualization menu in a notebook cell, display your `pyspark` DataFrame as follows:

```
data_frame = spark.read.csv("...")
display(data_frame)
```

You will be presented with the following menu:

Figure 7.7: Notebook Create wizard

146　Data and Information Visualization

Once you click **Visualization**, you will be presented with the DataViz editor. Here is an example of how to create a multiline chart.

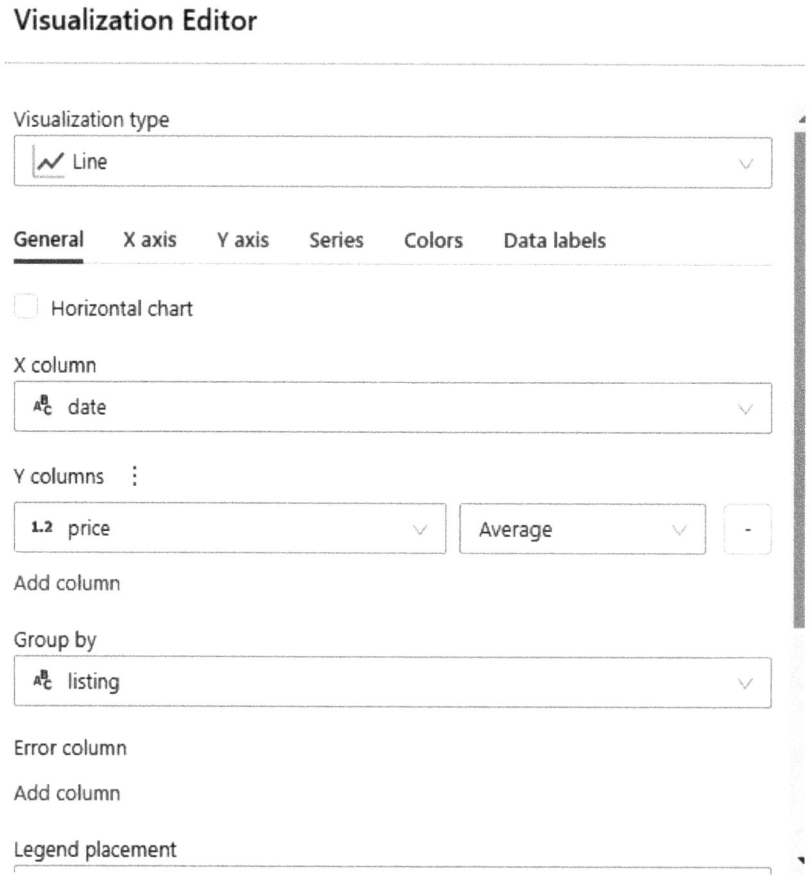

Figure 7.8: Visualization Editor

Here is the code to run in the cell:

```
import plotly.express as px
import pandas as pd
stock_prices =  px.data.stocks().melt('date', var_name='listing',
value_name='price').sort_values(['date','listing'])
display(stock_prices)
```

This creates the following chart:

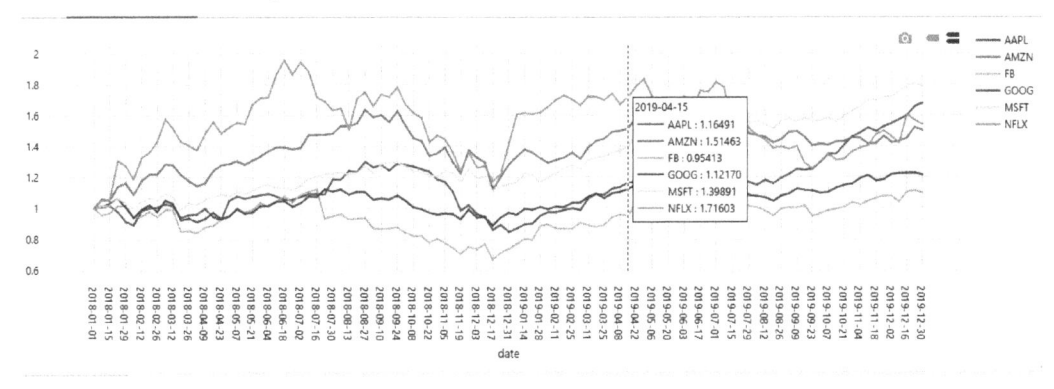

Figure 7.9: The notebook multiline chart

The GUI has a long list of charts, so you will likely be able to create whatever meets your needs. The question is, when would you use the GUI over a library such as Plotly? It's a question of how much customization and tweaking you need. Building charts without the GUI will always give more control to the engineer.

We have now gone through creating visualizations using both Plotly and Databricks's in-notebook tool. We will now take a look at some tricks to work with notebooks.

Tips and tricks with Databricks notebooks

Since we will go through notebooks, it makes sense to mention a few tricks you can do with Databricks notebooks.

Magic

Databricks notebooks can use **magic**, which involves mixing in some type of non-Python component using the % syntax.

Markdown

Markdown is an advantageous way to format text, much like HTML, but it's much simpler to write and learn. To invoke a Markdown cell, simply type %md at the start of your cell.

Other languages

When working with notebooks, it can be handy to run a command in a language other than what the notebook is set up to run. The language magic works by typing %[language] at the start of the notebook cell. For example, you can invoke %sql, %r, %scala, and %python using the language magically. Keep in mind that it is impossible to pass variables between languages, and the context of the language magic is limited to the cell itself.

Terminal

To gain terminal access to the driver node, use the %sh magic at the start of the cell. This can be extremely useful to validate file locations or run dbutils commands, for example. If you would like the cell to fail if the command fails, use %sh -e at the start of the cell.

Filesystem

This magic will give you direct access to dbutils fs when you use %fs at the start of the cell. This can be very helpful when you need to validate that a file has been saved or deleted.

Running other notebooks

When you want to run another notebook in a makeshift chain, you can use %run for that task. This can be very useful if you separate functionality into different notebooks. When you run the second notebook, it runs as if it were in the parent notebook, so all variables, classes, and functions defined will be in the same namespace. Remember that this is not a best-practice approach to building workflows. Alternative patterns such as Databricks workflows and Databricks jobs should be used in most cases.

Widgets

Widgets allow you to get input at the execution of the notebook and use that data in your code. There are four types of widgets supported – dropdown, text, combo, and multi-select.

Here is an example of a drop-down box using the input values:

```
dbutils.widgets.dropdown("last_name", "smith",["lee", "smith", "johnson"])
last_name = dbutils.widgets.get("last_name")
print(last_name)
Output: smith
```

We have gone through useful tricks to get more out of your notebook experience; now, we will tackle working with SQL analytics.

Databricks SQL analytics

Databricks SQL analytics is an evolved section of Databricks adapted for SQL-only analysis and BI access. What makes SQL analytics unique is the tight integration between all the other tooling. So, when your Databricks pipelines publish tables, SQL analytics will be able to access all those artifacts.

Accessing SQL analytics

At the time of writing, Databricks SQL analytics is offered with only premium-tier accounts. Once you have switched to the premium tier, you will see SQL in the area drop-down menu.

Once you have enabled the premium tier or higher, to access SQL analytics, use the dropdown at the top left of the screen. You will be given three choices – **Data Science & Engineering**, **Machine Learning**, and **SQL**. For now, we will use SQL analytics, but switch to **Data Science & Engineering** if you need access to your notebooks anytime.

Figure 7.10: The SQL menu option

SQL Warehouses

Databricks has minimized the cluster configuration, among many other configuration options, to simplify the interface a SQL analyst might interact with. For example, in the SQL analytics section, you only have the choice of setting up a SQL warehouse.

SQL warehouses are easy to create but offer some customization, such as AWS instance profile access. A key detail to remember is that SQL warehouses are nothing more than Databricks Spark clusters with a functional wrapper. The most critical choice for SQL warehouses is the sizing, and they use t-shirt sizes to make things easy to understand.

Here, we will create a new 2X-Small SQL warehouse using the web GUI:

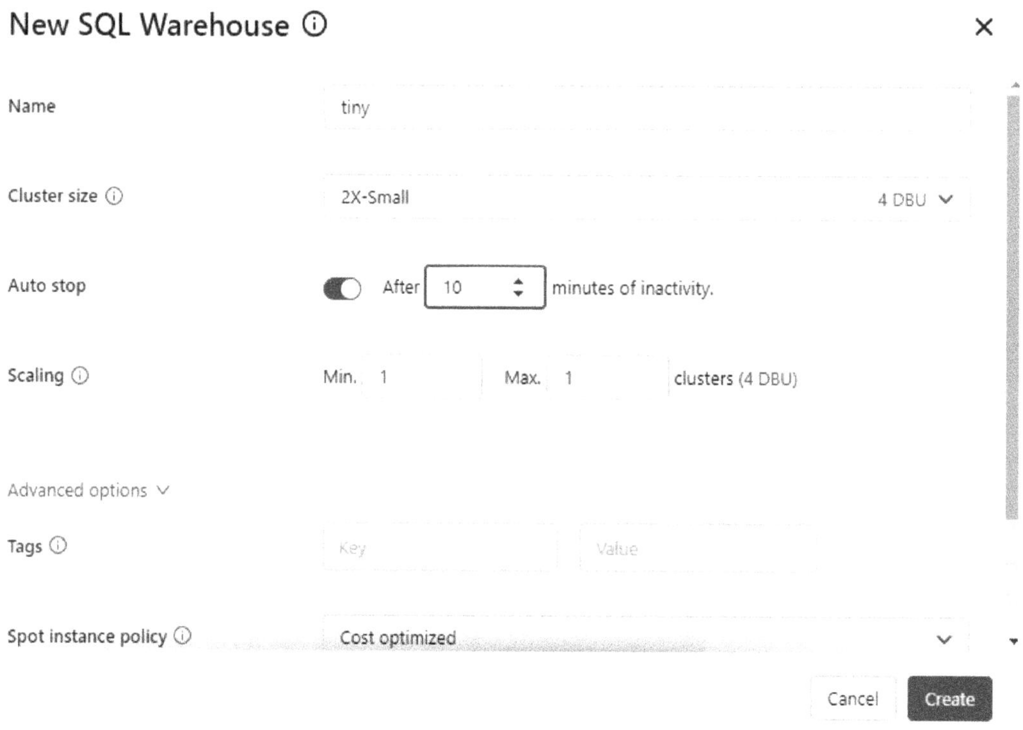

Figure 7.11: A new SQL warehouse

SQL editors

A SQL editor is a functional IDE-like interface for writing SQL. It will suggest SQL functions for you and tables or fields based on what has been created.

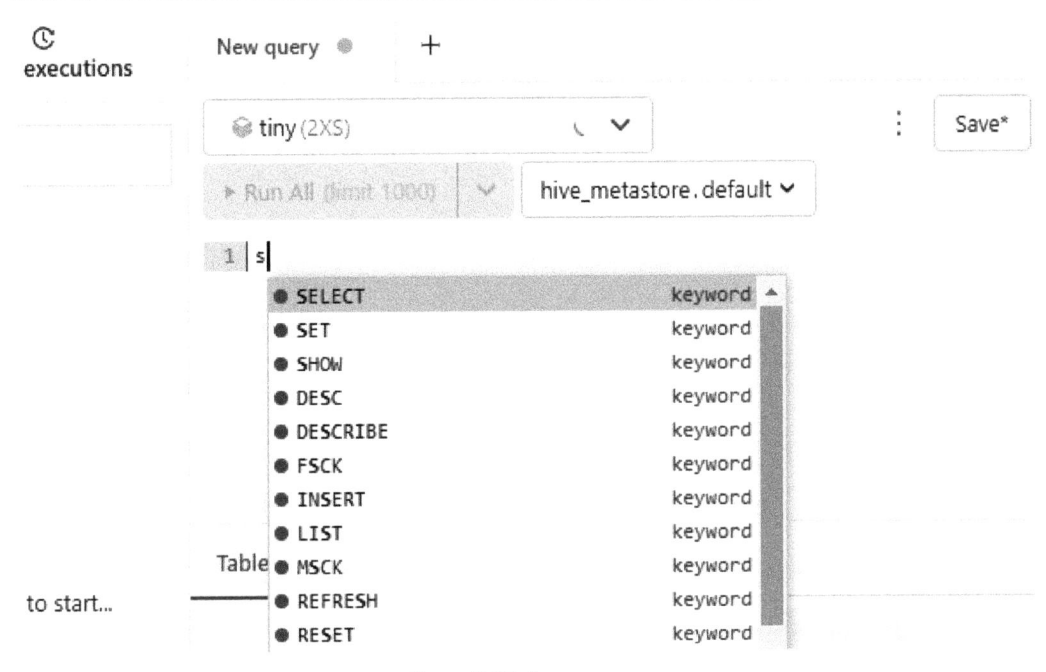

Figure 7.12: A new query

When ready, you can hit **Save**, and the query will appear in the **Queries** section.

Queries

Queries are used in SQL analytics as the fundamental building block of dashboards and charts. What's helpful is that metadata is collected for your queries, and you can share it across teams.

Queries

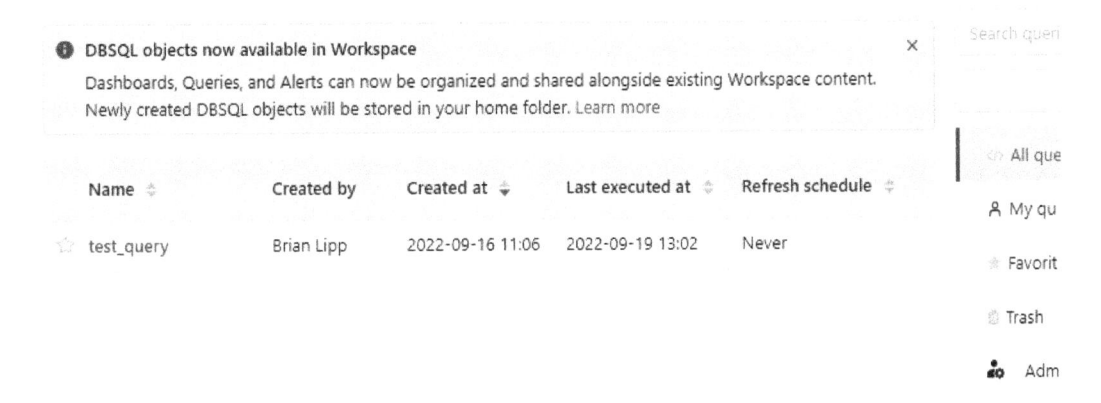

Figure 7.13: The Queries menu

Dashboards

Dashboards are collections of charts built off queries. In the *Practical lab* section, we will go through creating charts and dashboards. Now, it's essential to understand that once you develop your queries, you should create charts from them and then build dashboards with them. Dashboards can be updated on a schedule or manually.

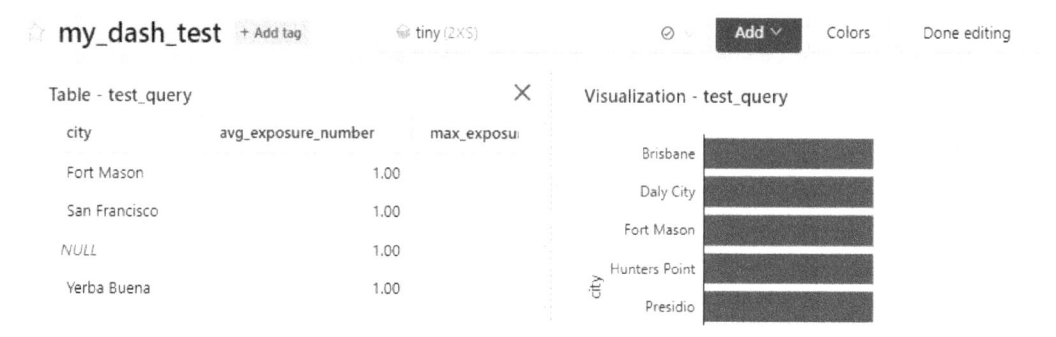

Figure 7.14: A new dashboard

Alerts

Alerts are a beneficial addition to SQL analytics tooling. You can create scheduled runs that trigger an alert based on a query's output. This feature will not replace an enterprise monitoring system, but it can be critical for a SQL analyst.

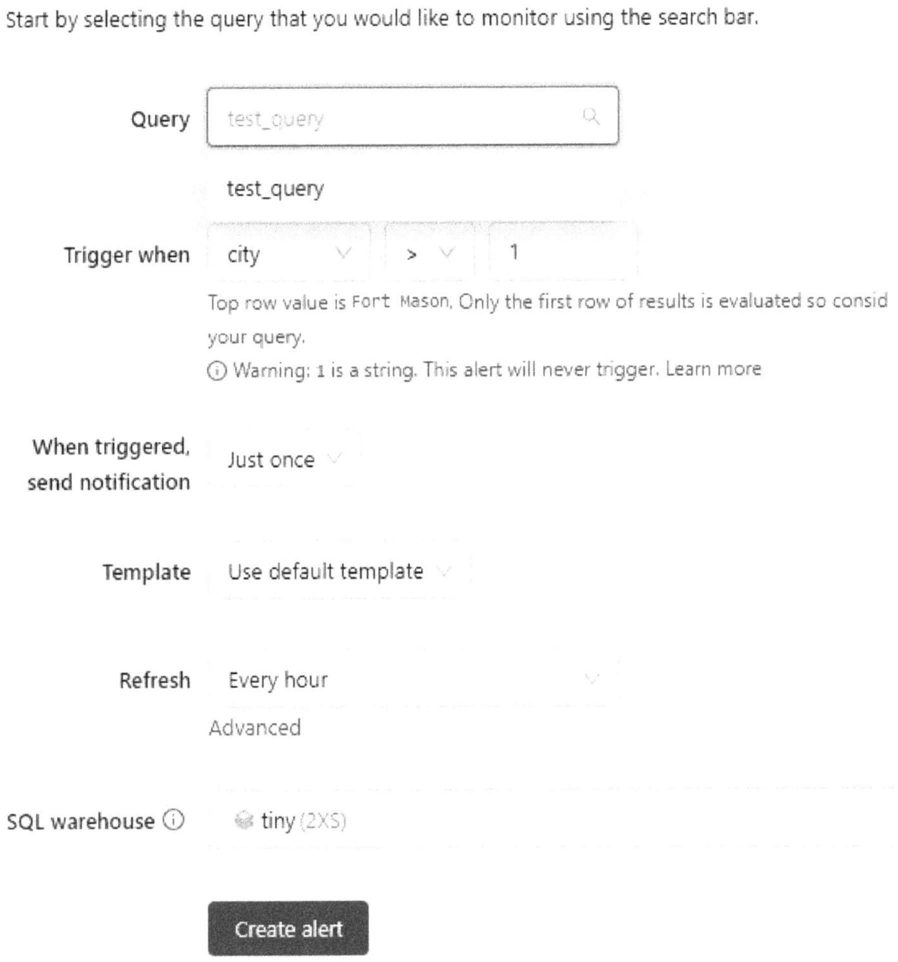

Start by selecting the query that you would like to monitor using the search bar.

Figure 7.15: A new alert

Query history

Lastly, Databricks creates rich metadata on your query, including your history and SQL performance. This can be useful when understanding your user's workloads and optimizing tables.

Here, we can see in the query history the time spent and the process the query went through.

Figure 7.16: Query history

Having gone through SQL analytics, we are now familiar with using the built-in dashboarding tooling, but we can connect other BI tools.

Connecting BI tools

Although the dashboards for SQL analytics are excellent, you will often find that other BI tooling is needed for some workflows. Here, I will show you how to connect Tableau Desktop to Databricks SQL analytics. Tableau is one of the most common BI dashboarding tools found on the market. However, the setup process is typically very similar if your situation requires a different tool:

1. The first step is to click the **Partner Connect** button on the toolbar. The **Partner Connect** section lists automated and simplified connectors for common BI tooling.

Figure 7.17: Partner Connect

2. You will be presented with the **Tableau Connect** screen, as shown here. On this screen, you will be able to choose your SQL warehouse.

Figure 7.18: Tableau

3. Now, you will be given the connection file for Tableau Desktop to use.

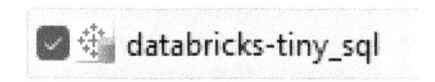

Figure 7.19: The connection file

4. Once you run that connection file, you will be presented with a sign-in screen. Follow all directions provided by Databricks on the Tableau **Partner Connect** screen. Keep in mind that any SQL warehouses you use must either have started; otherwise, wait until they have completed the startup process to use them.

Figure 7.20: The SQL warehouse password

Once you have successfully connected to Databricks, you can access all your data from Databricks in Tableau Desktop.

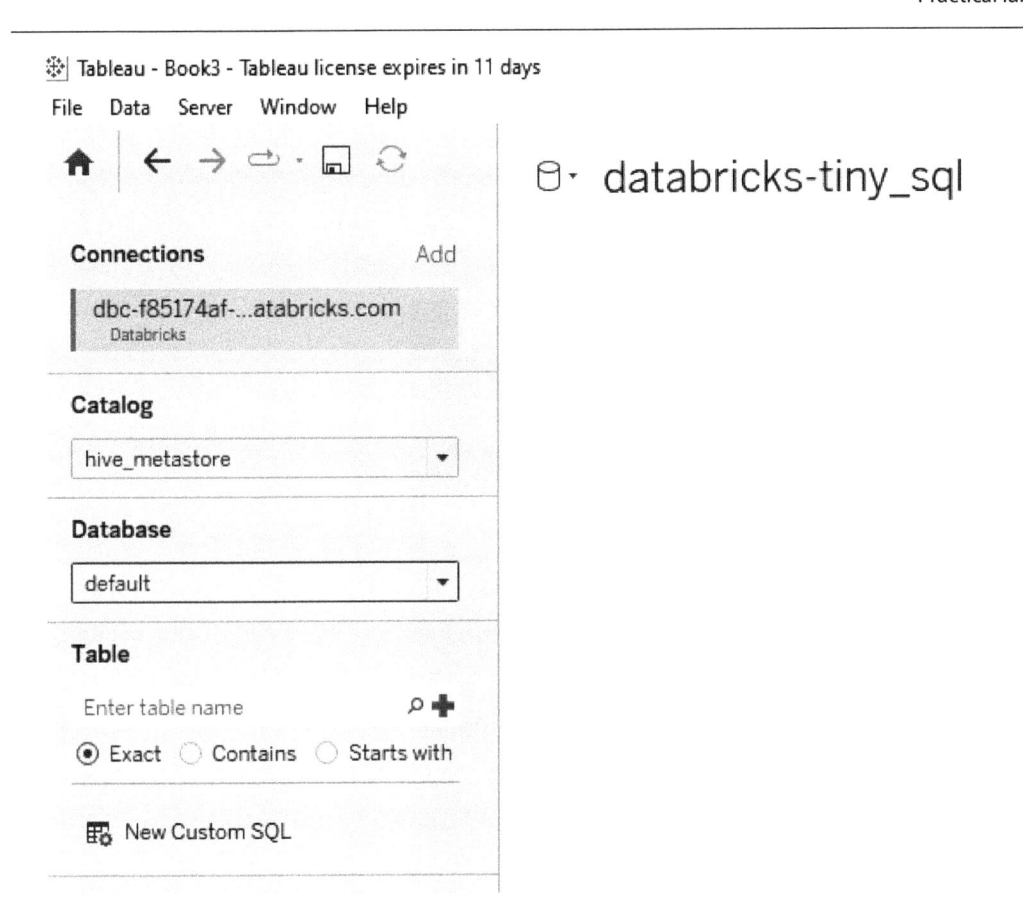

Figure 7.21: The working setup

We have covered a ton of information and opened the door to a wealth of tools. It's essential to understand the users' needs and your company's capabilities and then match the tooling that best fits your users. We covered notebook-based data visualizations and dashboards using SQL analytics. We also went through how to set up access from BI tools such as Qlik, Tableau, and Power BI. Now, we will work on a practical lab, expanding what we have worked on.

Practical lab

In this practical lab, we will explore adding the tool DBT and creating several dashboards.

Loading problem data

We will use the following three datasets for our labs – `error_codes.json`, `factory.json`, and `factory_errors.json`. For this lab, we will use the web GUI to load the data; in a production environment, we would have a pipeline to handle this process:

1. First, click **Create** on the toolbar to load data using the web GUI.

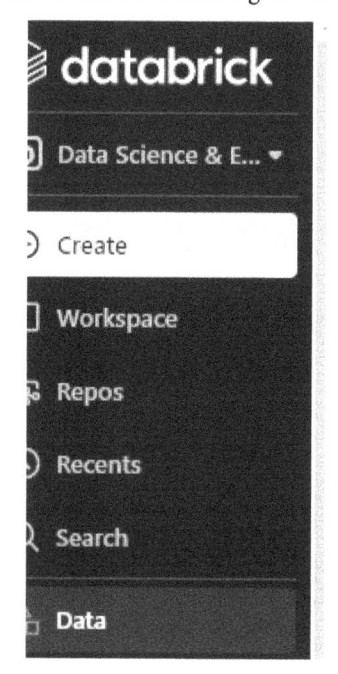

Figure 7.22: Create

2. Now, we will click the **Create table** button, and then we must select the cluster to use; any available cluster is acceptable.

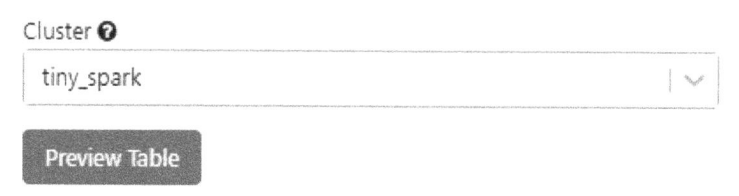

Figure 7.23: Selecting a cluster

3. We will use the GUI to load the table and not use a notebook this time. You will be presented with the following menu. Be sure to name your tables consistently, use the **default** database/schema, and select the **JSON** file type, **Infer schema**, and **Multi-line**.

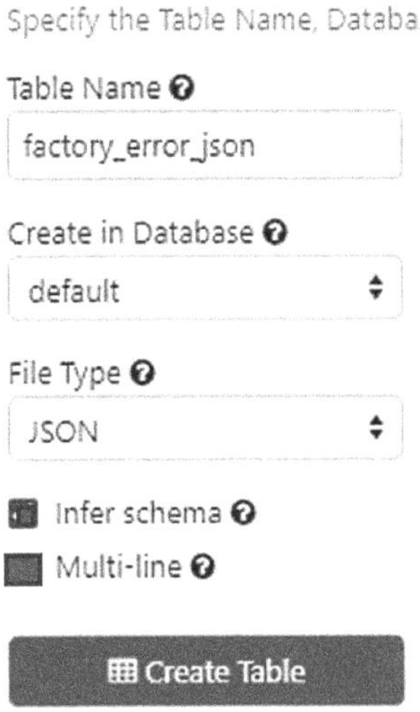

Figure 7.24: Create Table

Follow this process for all three datasets.

Problem 1

New technology trends sweep through your company, with several updates to the preferred tooling. For example, several analytics engineers request access to dbt Cloud, a popular tool used to create data models.

Your task is to set up access from Databricks to DBT Cloud.

Solution

In this solution, we will go through the steps to connect the partner with DBT Cloud and log in to it to validate that the data is accessible.

If you don't have a DBT Cloud account, create an account using the email associated with your Databricks login:

1. Once you have a DBT account, follow the steps from earlier to access Partner Connect by pulling up the DBT menu.

Figure 7.25: Connecting the partner

2. Once we have selected the **DBT partner to connect** menu, we will be presented with several options. Here, we will choose our tiny SQL warehouse, and we will use the default schema.

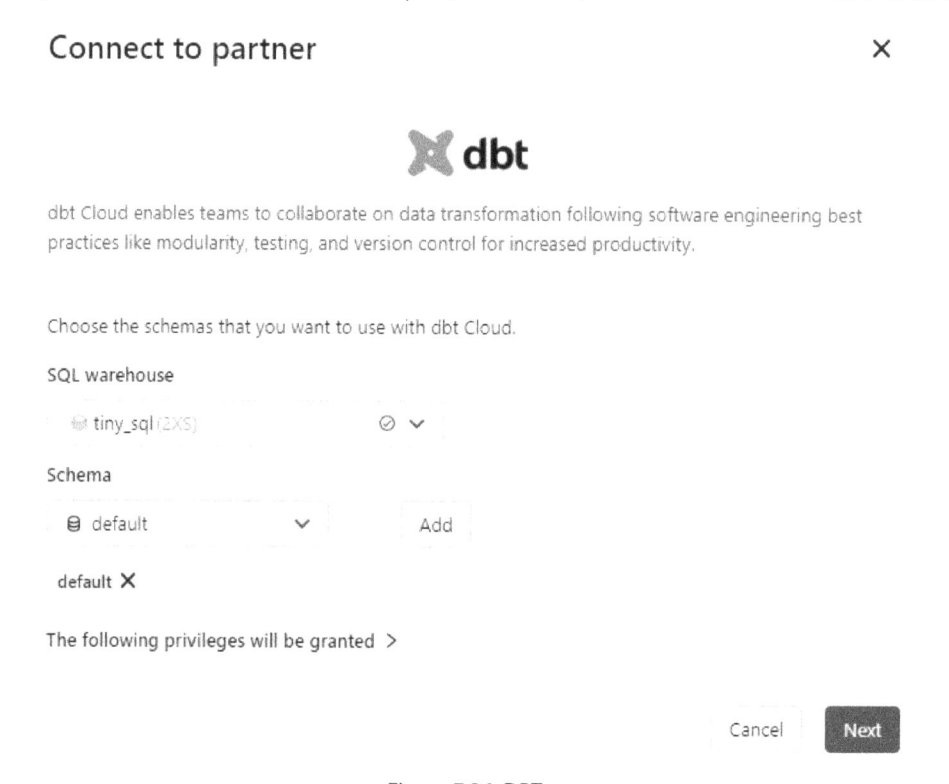

Figure 7.26: DBT

3. Once you click **Next**, a loading screen should be displayed. Now, if you do not have DBT enabled for your email, associated with the Databricks user you are using, then an email from DBT will be sent from DBT Cloud. DBT Cloud currently still offers a free tier for single developers.

Figure 7.27: DBT signup

4. Once everything has been configured and your account created, you should be able to log in and see the Databricks Partner Connect project.

Figure 7.28: DBT Connect

We have set up DBT Cloud and have opened the door to using DBT to manage our data platform.

Problem 2

Your team has requested to monitor factory errors. They are primarily concerned with factory one and the types of mistakes they see there. They would like some dashboards to help them handle the factory errors.

162   Data and Information Visualization

Solution

Here, we will create the following SQL queries in SQL analytics:

- **Query 1**:

    As requested, the first query will isolate all errors and show only factory one.

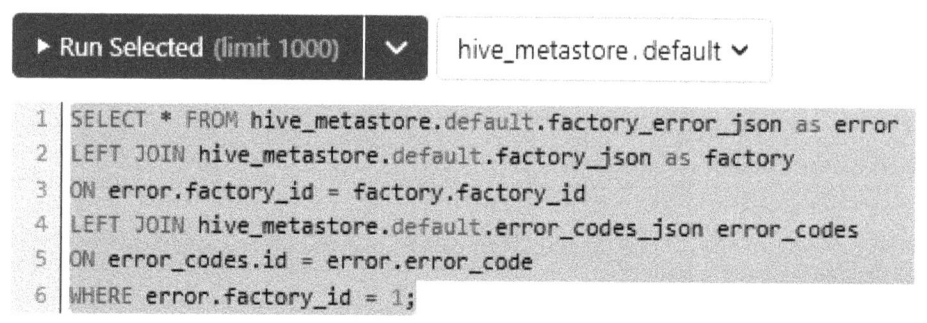

```
problem_7

▶ Run Selected (limit 1000)   ⌄    hive_metastore.default ⌄

1  SELECT * FROM hive_metastore.default.factory_error_json as error
2  LEFT JOIN hive_metastore.default.factory_json as factory
3  ON error.factory_id = factory.factory_id
4  LEFT JOIN hive_metastore.default.error_codes_json error_codes
5  ON error_codes.id = error.error_code
6  WHERE error.factory_id = 1;
```

Figure 7.29: SQL 1

- **Query 2**:

    This query will give us a big picture of all of our errors.

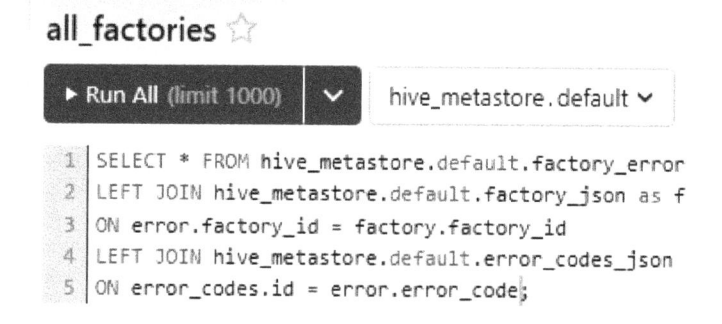

```
all_factories

▶ Run All (limit 1000)   ⌄    hive_metastore.default ⌄

1  SELECT * FROM hive_metastore.default.factory_error
2  LEFT JOIN hive_metastore.default.factory_json as f
3  ON error.factory_id = factory.factory_id
4  LEFT JOIN hive_metastore.default.error_codes_json
5  ON error_codes.id = error.error_code;
```

Figure 7.30: SQL 2

Now, we will create a bar chart using the first query in a new dashboard.

Dashboards

Figure 7.31: SQL 2

Practical lab 163

We will create a new dashboard called `Chapter_7`. Next, we will see an **Add** button on the right.

Figure 7.32: The Add button

Databricks then prompts us for the query to use. For the first chart, we will use `query_1`. Here is the bar chart configuration:

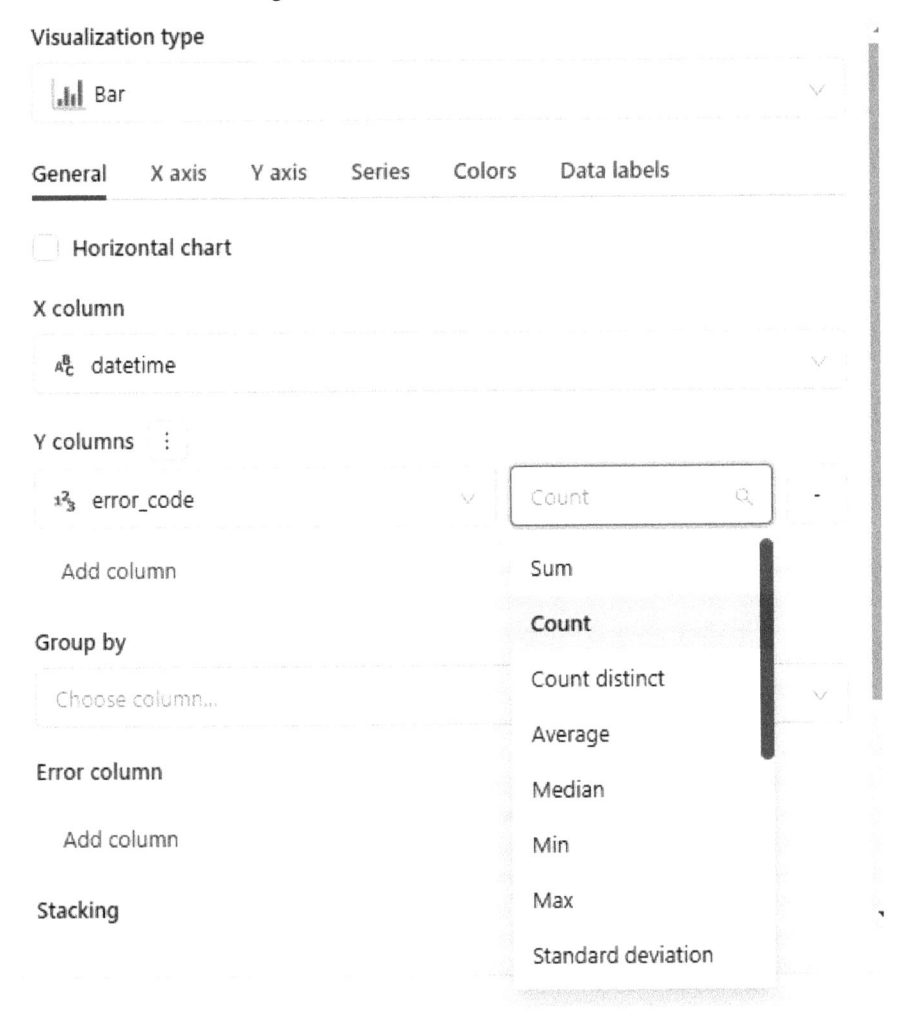

Figure 7.33: The bar chart setup

Here, we see the updated dashboard with our bar chart.

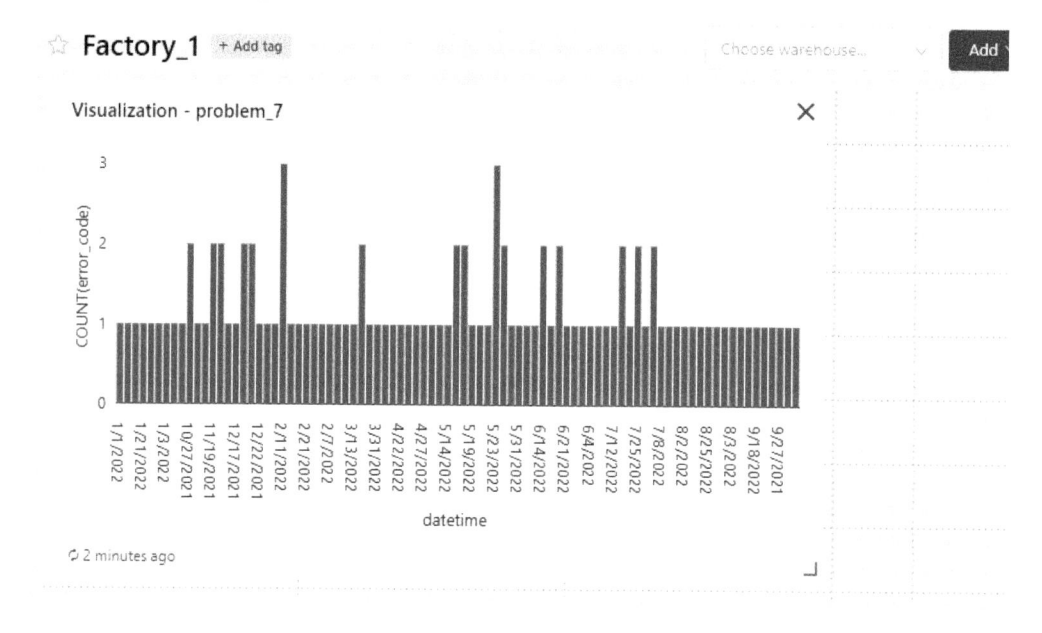

Figure 7.34: The bar chart

Now we will add a pie chart, as shown here.

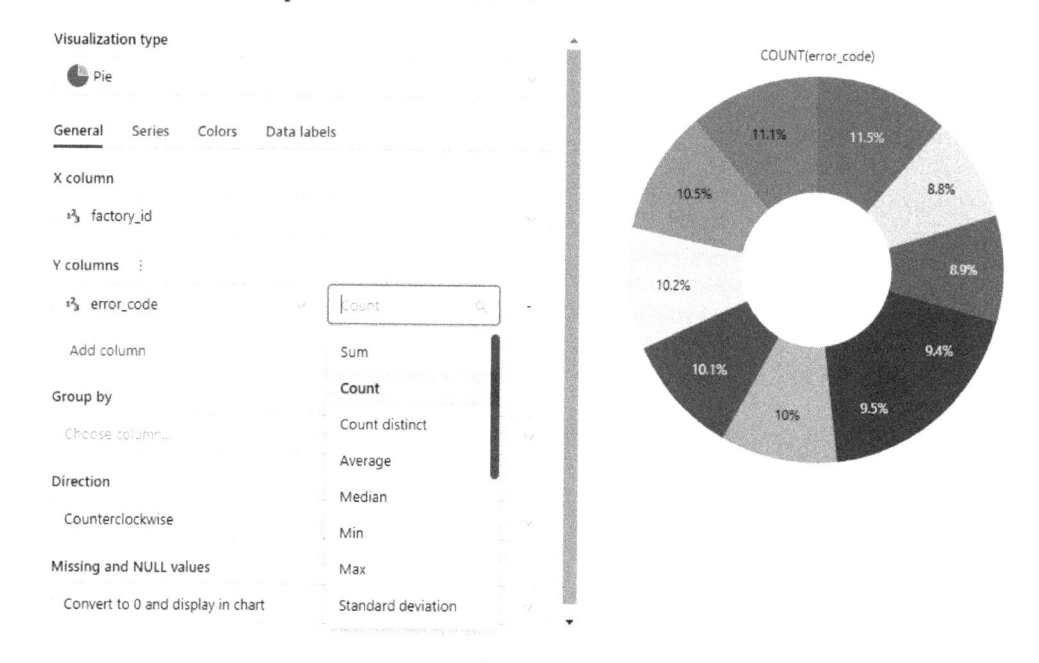

Figure 7.35: A dashboard

We now have a simple dashboard to monitor factory one's errors and a general picture of all errors across factories.

We will now create an alert for errors coming from `query_1`.

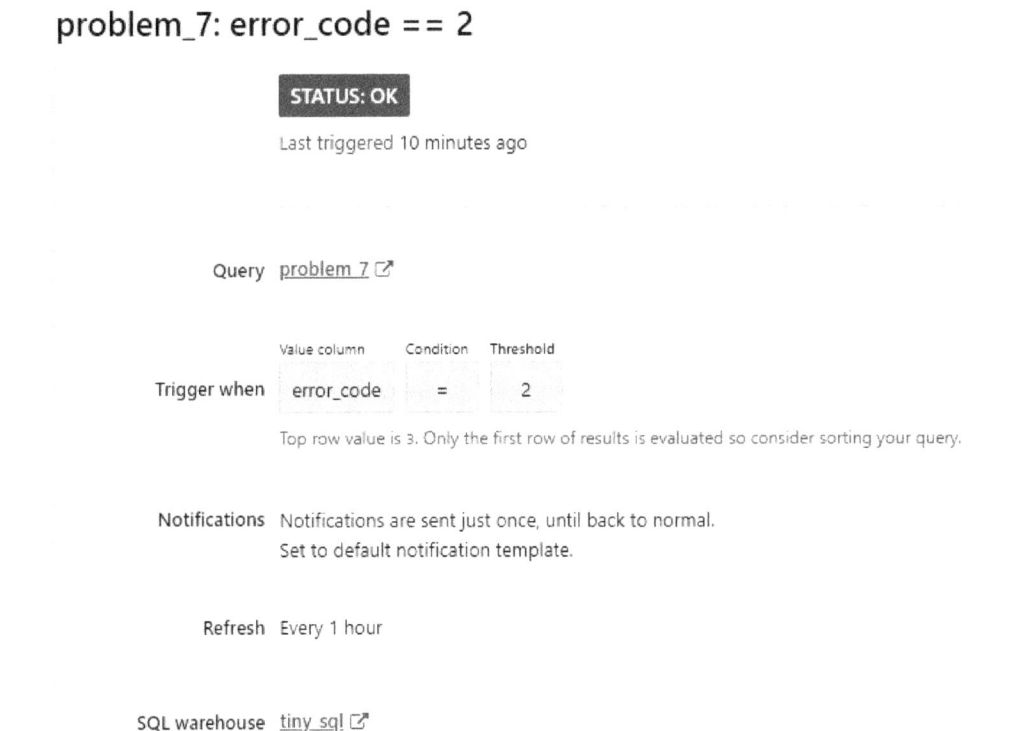

problem_7: error_code == 2

STATUS: OK

Last triggered 10 minutes ago

Query problem 7

Trigger when — Value column: error_code, Condition: =, Threshold: 2

Top row value is 3. Only the first row of results is evaluated so consider sorting your query.

Notifications Notifications are sent just once, until back to normal. Set to default notification template.

Refresh Every 1 hour

SQL warehouse tiny_sql

Figure 7.36: An alert

Summary

We covered a lot of material. To summarize, we talked about the importance of data visualizations and how to create them using a variety of tooling. We went over tips and tricks for notebooks in Databricks. We delved into SQL analytics and connecting BI Tools such as Tableau and DBT. With the knowledge you now possess, you should be able to design and implement complex data visualization systems.

In the upcoming chapter, we will see how to organize our data projects and build them into continuous integration projects using Jenkins and GitHub. As we write our code, we will look at techniques for automating checks of our code. We will then discuss how to deploy our code into production.

8

Integrating Continous Integration into Your Workflow

As we grow our projects, many data projects go from being a scattering of notebooks to a **continuous integration** (**CI**)-driven application. In this chapter, we will go through some of the tooling and concepts for stringing together your Python scripts and notebooks into a working data application. We will be using Jenkins for CI, GitHub for source control, workflows for orchestration, and Terraform for **Infrastructure as Code** (**IaC**). Those tools can be swapped out for your preferred tool without much effort.

In this chapter, we're going to cover the following main topics:

- Python wheels and creating a Python package
- CI with Jenkins
- Working with source control using GitHub
- Creating Databricks jobs and controlling several jobs using workflows
- Creating IaC using Terraform

Technical requirements

The tooling used in this chapter is tied to the technology stack chosen for the book. All vendors should offer a free trial account.

I will be using the following:

- Databricks
- AWS
- Terraform Cloud

- GitHub
- Jenkins
- Docker

Setting up your environment

Before we begin our chapter, let's take the time to set up our working environment.

Databricks

As we have with many others, this chapter assumes you have a working version of Python 3.6 and the preceding tooling installed in your development environment. We will also assume that you have set up an AWS account, and have set up Databricks with that AWS account.

Databricks CLI

The first step is to install the `databricks-cli` tool using the `pip` Python package manager:

```
pip install databricks-cli
```

Let's validate that everything has been installed correctly. If this command produces the tool version, then everything is working correctly:

```
Databricks -v
```

Now let's set up authentication. First, go into the Databricks UI and generate a personal access token. The following command will ask for the host created for your Databricks instance and the created token:

```
databricks configure --token
```

We can quickly determine whether the CLI is set up correctly by running the following command; if no error is returned, you have a working setup:

```
databricks fs ls
```

Lastly, let's set up our `workspace`, `clusters`, and `dbfs` folder:

```
databricks   fs mkdirs    dbfs:/chapter_7
databricks   workspace mkdirs   /chapter_7
databricks   clusters create -json-file    <file_path to tiny.json>
```

Here are the `tiny.json` file contents:

```
{   "num_workers":0, "cluster_name":"tiny",   "spark_version":"10.4.x-scala2.12",
    "spark_conf":{
        "spark.master":"local[*, 4]",    "spark.databricks.cluster.profile":"singleNode"
    },  "aws_attributes":{
        "first_on_demand":1,   "availability":"SPOT_WITH_FALLBACK",   "zone_id":"us-west-2b",
        "instance_profile_arn":null, "spot_bid_price_percent":100,
        "ebs_volume_type":"GENERAL_PURPOSE_SSD",
        "ebs_volume_count":3, "ebs_volume_size":100
    },  "node_type_id":"m4.large",    "driver_node_type_id":"m4.large",
    "ssh_public_keys":[ ],"custom_tags":{  "ResourceClass":"SingleNode"}, "spark_env_vars":{   "PYSPARK_PYTHON":"/databricks/python3/bin/python3"},
    "autotermination_minutes":10, "enable_elastic_disk":false,   "cluster_source":"UI",   "init_scripts":[ ], "data_security_mode":"NONE",  "runtime_engine":"STANDARD"}
```

The DBX CLI

DBX will use the credentials file from the Databricks CLI you created. You only need to install the `pip` library:

```
pip3 install dbx
```

Docker

We will use Docker to run Jenkins locally; this isn't the setup you would do in production but, for our testing purposes, this should be perfect.

First, you must download and install Docker Desktop from the following URL:

https://docs.docker.com/engine/install/

Docker Desktop supports Windows, Linux, and macOS, so whatever your preference is, it has you covered. Follow the installation directions as provided by Docker, and run the following to test that your Docker setup is working:

```
docker run docker/whalesay cowsay Chapter_8
```

You should see an ASCII image of a whale on the screen; if you do, then everything is set up correctly.

Git

Git will be used in this chapter and there are many ways to install it; I recommend using `https://git-scm.com/download/`.

When you run the Git version, you should see a message explaining what it is.

I also prefer to set the color of the output when using the Git CLI:

```
git config --global color.ui auto
```

Once installed, you should set up authentication with your GitHub account (if you do not have one, you will need to create one for this chapter):

```
git config --global user.name <>
git config --global user.email <>
```

If you prefer to set the username for a specific repository, browse the repository and run the following:

```
git config color.ui auto
git config user.email <>
```

GitHub

I will be using GitHub and its CLI for *Chapter 8*. First, let's create a **personal access token** (**PAT**). I believe SSH is more secure, but for simplicity, a PAT is easier to work with in this book.

Now let's set up the GitHub CLI from `https://cli.github.com/` and follow the directions to install it.

You should see a help menu when you now run the `gh` command.

Let's now set up authentication for the GitHub CLI:

```
gh auth login
```

You will get the following set of questions:

```
PS C:\Users\bclip> gh auth login
? What account do you want to log into? GitHub.com
? What is your preferred protocol for Git operations? HTTPS
? Authenticate Git with your GitHub credentials? Yes
? How would you like to authenticate GitHub CLI?  [Use arrows to move, type to filter]
> Login with a web browser
  Paste an authentication token
```

Figure 8.1: Question set

The CLI will give you an access code; when your browser opens up, type that code into the browser. You will then be presented with the following screen:

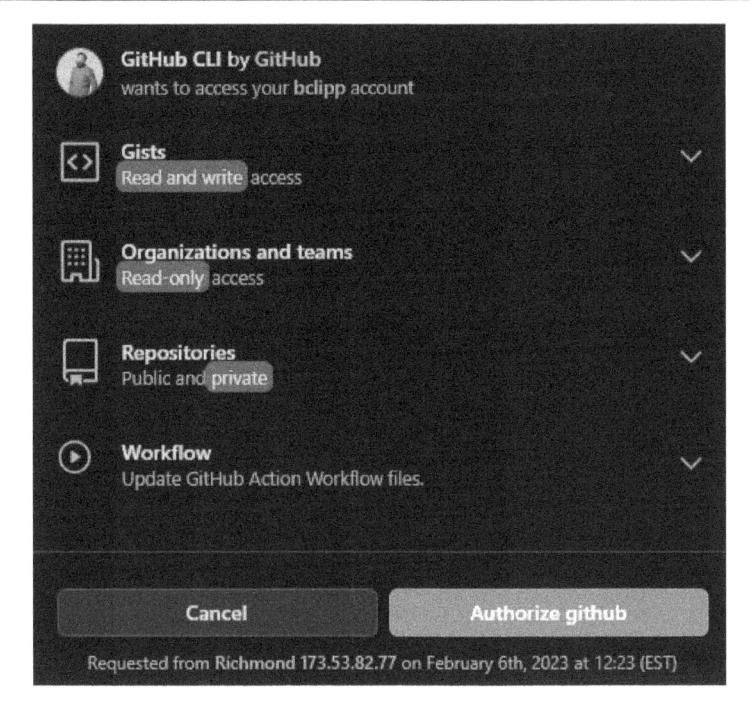

Figure 8.2: GitHub authorization

You are now set up for the GitHub CLI.

Let's create our repository using the GitHub CLI:

Figure 8.3: GitHub repo creation

Pre-commit

We will be using `pre-commit` to run basic quality checks on our code before committing them to GitHub. This uses hooks or triggers in our Git workflow to run processes we define in our configuration file. Traditionally, `pre-commit` will be used with Python-only code, but there are options for much more – such as Terraform, for example.

Let's install `pre-commit` and our code quality tools using `pip`:

```
pip install pre-commit pylint, flake8, black, mypy
```

Terraform

We will use Terraform Cloud and the Terraform CLI. Let's first set up the Terraform CLI using the following URL: https://developer.hashicorp.com/terraform/tutorials/aws-get-started/install-cli.

Then, we will need to create a Terraform Cloud account at https://app.terraform.io/session.

Next, let's connect the CLI to our Cloud account and run `terraform login`. You will see the following screen:

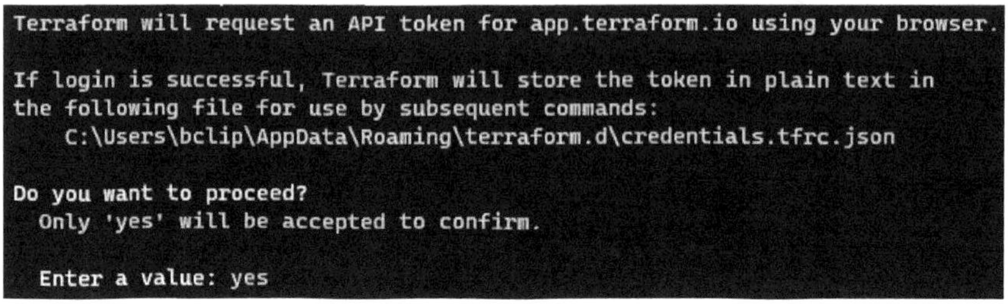

Figure 8.4: Terraform

You will be presented with a web browser screen asking you to create an API token.

Figure 8.5: Creating an API token

Now, you should see a success screen.

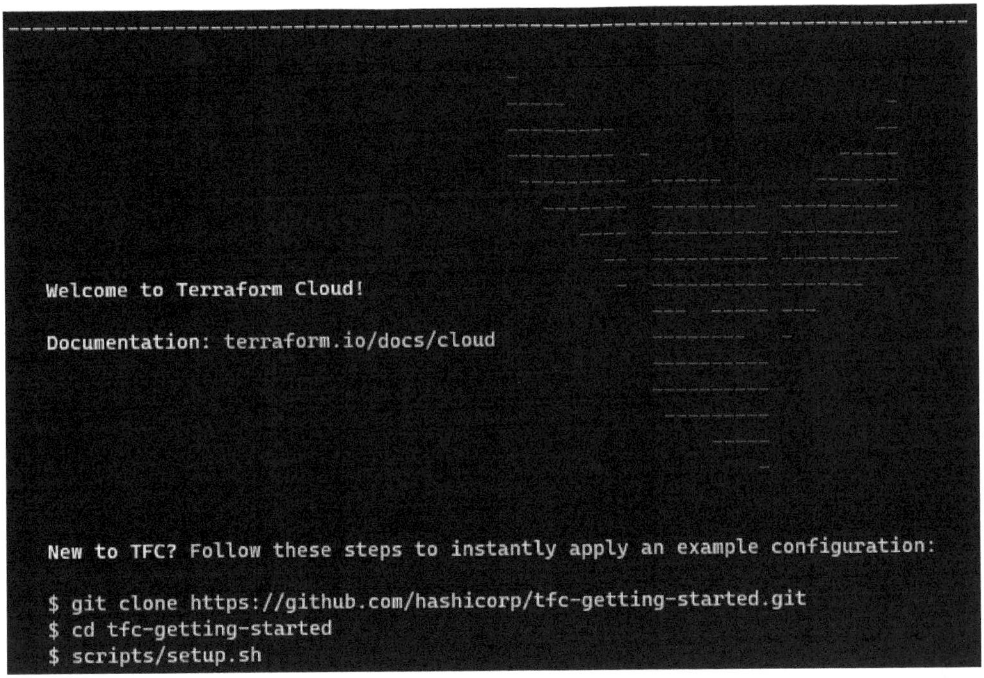

```
Welcome to Terraform Cloud!

Documentation: terraform.io/docs/cloud

New to TFC? Follow these steps to instantly apply an example configuration:

$ git clone https://github.com/hashicorp/tfc-getting-started.git
$ cd tfc-getting-started
$ scripts/setup.sh
```

Figure 8.6: Terraform Cloud success screen

Docker

Here are some basic commands in Docker:

- `docker run <>`: This will run a container after specifying the image
- `Docker stop <>`: This will stop a container that is running
- `docker ps`: This lists all running containers
- `docker image prune --all -force`: This is a very useful command that will clean up several components of Docker

Install Jenkins, container setup, and compose

You can use the following command:

```
docker run -it -p 8080:8080 jenkins/jenkins:lts
```

174 Integrating Continous Integration into Your Workflow

In your console, you should see a similar output to the following figure, displaying the loading processes. Look out for the password for the admin user, which will be displayed on the screen:

Figure 8.7: Jenkins console

Now, connect to this URL in your browser to see the management console:

`http://localhost:8080/`

You will now see a login screen in which you paste the password you copied from the startup messages.

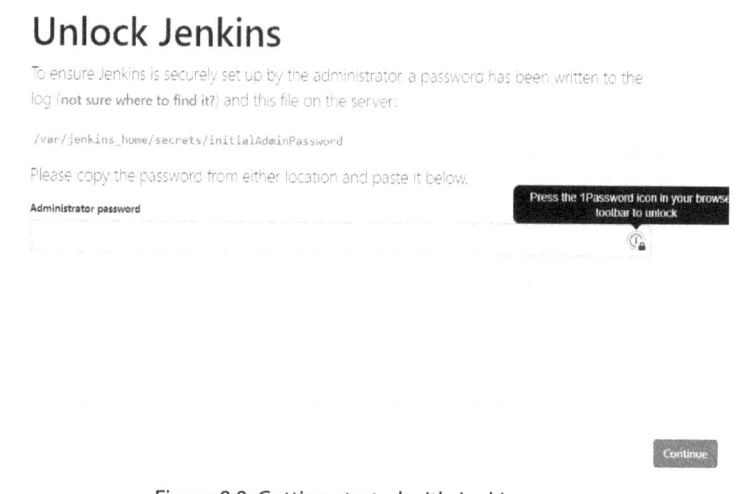

Figure 8.8: Getting started with Jenkins

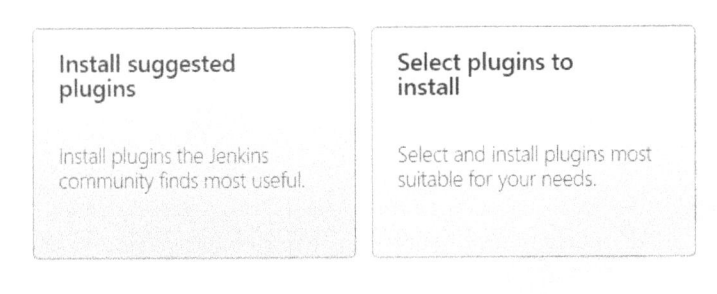

Next, you will be presented with a plugin installation screen; choose **Install suggested plugins**.

Figure 8.9: Customizing plugins

Finally, you will be asked to create a user; make sure to remember the password.

Figure 8.10: Creating the user

Now that we have set up our tools, let's start going through using these tools to automate our data platform.

CI tooling

When making the development transition to a more organized project, the tooling we will go through is organized around what is known as the **software development life cycle**. This is generally understood as the preferred path when writing software. This life cycle isn't always a good fit – for example, in research-style projects such as data science projects.

We have set up a large number of tools, but let's now take a look first at Git and GitHub.

Git and GitHub

Source control is a fundamental component in writing software and managing technology. When you write your code, you check it into source control. When you are ready to bring that code into the main branch, you create a pull request. A **pull request** is a process where other members of the team will review your code, discuss portions of that code, and work together with you. The output of a pull request is confidence in the new feature you are bringing into your project.

Let's look at the basic commands in Git.

This is the command for creating a local copy of your repository or project:

```
git clone <git project url>
```

This is the command for creating a feature branch:

```
git checkout -b <branch name>
```

This is the command for stage-changed files to be committed to GitHub:

```
git add <file name>
```

Once you have all your files staged, you can create a commit to GitHub:

```
git commit -m "my message explaining what I am committing"
```

Use the following command to push your changes to GitHub:

```
git push
```

This command gets updates locally from GitHub:

```
git pull
```

This is the command for creating a pull request in GitHub:

```
gh pr create --web
```

And this is the command for approving a pull request in GitHub:

```
gh pr review --approve
```

As we complete Git and GitHub, the natural progression is to set up `pre-commit`, a tool that allows you to set standards for your GitHub repos. The `pre-commit` tool will proactively ensure that there are no errors in your code based on the policies and criteria that were set in it. It will not allow code to be committed unless the code adheres to the standards that have been set.

Pre-commit

When you commit code to Git, it would be nice to first run through some checks on your code to validate that it meets your team's standards. Git allows you to hook in tools that are triggered when your try to commit code to Git – such as `pre-commit`, which will allow you to write a YAML-based file that runs other tools to check your code.

The following code is an example of the common tooling triggered with `pre-commit`:

```
repos:
-   repo: https://github.com/psf/black
    rev: stable
    hooks:
    - id: black
      language_version: python3.6
-   repo: https://github.com/PyCQA/isort
    rev: 5.10.1
    hooks:
    -   id: isort
-   repo: https://gitlab.com/PyCQA/flake8
    rev: 4.0.1
    hooks:
    - id: flake8
-   repo: https://github.com/adamchainz/blacken-docs
    rev: v5.4.2
    hooks:
    -   id: blacken-docs
        additional_dependencies:
        - black==22.12.0
-   repo: https://github.com/PyCQA/isort
    rev: 5.10.1
    hooks:
```

```
          -   id: isort
    -   repo: https://github.com/PyCQA/pylint
        rev: v2.15.9
        hooks:
          -   id: pylint
```

Now, let's run the following command to set up `pre-commit`:

```
pre-commit install
```

If we want to do a commit but avoid `pre-commit`, we can run the following:

```
git commit --no-verify
```

Lastly, if you want to run `pre-commit` on all files, such as in Jenkins, run the following:

```
pre-commit run --all-files
```

We have looked at `pre-commit` and how to enforce standards with your Git repos. Now, we will look at building Python wheels and packages.

Python wheels and packages

A Python wheel file is a ZIP file that holds a Python package, which is another way to say it is ready to install and use. Often, when you use something from `pip`, it is a wheel. When you build a Python application and store it on a PyPI server, it's a wheel.

Anatomy of a package

The typical entry point for your Python application is `__main__.py`.

The `__init__.py` file is found in every folder you use. It can have special purposes such as holding the version – for example, `__version__ = "1.0.0"`.

An alternative to `setup.py` is `pyproject.toml`; both are central places to put project-wide configurations. You can specify requirements, among other things. Here is an example:

```
PACKAGE_REQUIREMENTS = ["pyyaml"]
LOCAL_REQUIREMENTS = [
    "pyspark==3.2.1",
    "delta-spark==1.1.0",
    "scikit-learn",
    "pandas",
    "mlflow",
    "faker",
```

```
]
TEST_REQUIREMENTS = [
    "pytest",
    "coverage[toml]",
    "pytest-cov",
    "dbx>=0.8"
]
```

This command is used to install requirements from `setup.py`:

```
pip install -e ".[local,test]"
```

We will be working with wheels with the `dbx` tool, which is a project management tool for Databricks.

As we come to the end of learning about Python wheels and packages, we will now take a look at a new tool that has come out to manage your Databricks projects, called DBX.

DBX

DBX is a central tool meant for CI workloads when working with Databricks. You can use it to create a project template and deploy and launch your workflows. Since DBX uses Databricks APIs, it is able to use Databricks workflows. A workflow is a grouping of `dbt` notebooks or jobs meant to flow together.

These are some of the most important files:

- `.dbx/project.json`: Organized by environments; used to manage configuration across your project.
- `project_folder`: Used to store your Python code that isn't included in notebooks or tests.
- `conf/deployment.yml`: A YAML-based configuration file that allows you to define the details of Databricks workflows. You can define tasks for `dbt` notebooks and jobs at the moment.
- `notebooks`: Used to hold Databricks notebooks.
- `tests`: Should be used for integration and unit tests, with each in its own subfolder structure.

Important commands

To create your shell project (not required but useful), run the following command but add your project name:

```
dbx init \
    -p "cloud=AWS" \
    -p "project_name=<name of project>" \
    -p "profile=<databricks config profile name>" \
    --no-input
```

When you are ready, you can deploy your workflow, identified in the `deployment.yml` file. Keep in mind that you can have multiple workflows in one project. A simple reason could be your ETL pipeline and your integration tests:

```
dbx deploy <workflow-name>
```

Now, once the workflow is deployed, you can launch your workflow using the following:

```
dbx launch <workflow-name>
```

A very useful option is to pass runtime information to your workflow, which you can do using the following command:

```
dbx launch <workflow_name> --assets-only <workflow_name>
--parameters='[
    {"task_key": "<name>", "base_parameters": {"B": 4, "A": 10}}
]'
```

One huge part of DBX and data pipelines is running tests. What are the types of tests and how do we know what to test? We will discuss this next.

Testing code

It's important to test your code, and there are many theoretical beliefs that people have about writing and testing code. Some people feel you need to write tests with or before your code. Some people feel you should have a test for every "group" of code you write. This is typically a decision for the development team to make, but understanding why is often very useful. When we write tests before or with our code, we force ourselves to write testable code, in smaller chunks. Code coverage is an emotional discussion, but I have always found that it's an easy way to improve the quality of code.

Unit tests

A unit test is a test that doesn't exceed the bounds of the system running your code and looks to validate an assumption for a group of code. Unit tests are generally for functions, methods, and classes that do not interact with the "outside" world. When you have a function that interacts with the outside world but you want to test some part of that function that doesn't, you are forced to refactor your code so that those outside-world interactions are separate. Generally, the scope of unit testing is limited to functional testing.

Integration tests

An integration test is a test that looks to validate an assumption on an interaction between two or more entities. This could be a data pipeline that talks to the source and destination data storage devices, for example. A more simplistic example might be a data pipeline that uses sample data and produces a dataset with unique characteristics. Even in the last case, since we are producing data on disk, it would be considered an integration test. Integration tests are great for validating REST APIs and cluster interactions, among other things.

My go-to tool for testing in Python is Pytest, which is very flexible and easy to use. What makes Pytest my favorite is that it is designed to help you write your tests.

Understanding what to test in a data pipeline is very important. We will now venture into an extremely useful tool called Terraform. Terraform can be used to deploy infrastructure and your Databricks components, such as workflows.

Terraform – IaC

Terraform is a vendor-neutral tool and library for deploying and managing infrastructure. Terraform is written in the Hashicorp language, which is a high-level declarative language. The one key component that makes Terraform work is the state file. The state file is basically a transaction log for your resources. The transaction log is the way Terraform knows what to build, modify, and delete. If you lose your state file, you will have to manually manage the infrastructure that was created.

It is also possible to create small reusable modules of Terraform code and break up your state files into smaller units. In cases where you break your state file up, you can define other state files to use in your configuration file.

IaC

Many of us have been there: walking through GUI interfaces and building out our servers, clusters, and workspaces. How do we validate that we built out the correct infrastructure? Repeating the same step repeatedly can be difficult and error-prone. Translating your infrastructure into simple code opens the door to peer reviews, automated deployments, and a standard way to manage your infrastructure across many domains. Terraform is one of the most popular IaC tools and should be your first choice when doing IaC.

Terraform runs through a CLI, which can connect to the cloud to store the state file.

The CLI

The Terraform CLI has a few very useful commands, which are as follows:

- `terraform init`: Used to set up your environment based on the Terraform configuration files created.
- `terraform plan`: Based on the configuration files, explains in simple terms what's going to change on the target resource.
- `terraform validate`: Goes through the configuration file and makes sure there are no syntax issues.
- `terraform apply`: Runs the plan, confirms that the explained actions are what you expect, and then attempts to talk to the resource and make those changes. There can often be problems in the resource that block the `apply` process midway. One example is a conflicting resource with the same name. This can be tricky to work through at times, which is why it's best to use Terraform for all your resource management.
- `terraform destroy`: Defines what actions it will make – in this case, destroying resources outlined in the configuration file, and then once accepted, deleting them. If the resources have been changed by another entity and not Terraform, this might result in partial deletions.
- `terraform fmt`: Formats your code for you with proper indentation, which, at first, might seem not important, but if you put it in your CI/CD pipeline, you will find your code is easier to read.
- `terraform login`: Used to set up your local Terraform to connect to the cloud services.

HCL

When you write your Terraform code, you are faced with two main types of code blocks: providers and resources. A provider is defined to give Terraform direction on where to connect for some of your resource changes.

Here is an example Databricks `providers` block:

```
required_providers {
    databricks = {
      source = "databricks/databricks"
      version = "1.0.0"
    }
  }
}
```

You can separate this into a separate file, which can be useful when organizing. Often, you will see that file called `terraform.tf`.

A resource code block for Databricks might look like this:

```
data "databricks_spark_version" "latest_lts" {
  long_term_support = true
}
resource "databricks_cluster" "tiny" {
  cluster_name = "tiny"
  spark_version = data.databricks_spark_version.latest_lts.id
  node_type_id = "m4.large"
  driver_node_type_id = "m4.large"
  autotermination_minutes = 10
  autoscale {
    min_workers = 1
    max_workers = 2
  }
  aws_attributes {
    first_on_demand = 1
    availability = "SPOT_WITH_FALLBACK"
    zone_id = "us-west-2b"
    spot_bid_price_percent = 100
    ebs_volume_type = "GENERAL_PURPOSE_SSD"
    ebs_volume_count = 3
    ebs_volume_size = 100
  }
}
```

First, we define a block of data that sets the data defining whether we want the long-term support version of the runtime. We can reuse this data block throughout our HCL code. Next, we define a Databricks cluster. This might seem like more work than it's worth, but as soon as you start adding libraries to install `init` scripts and instance profiles, having your cluster in code form and deployed in an automated fashion can be very useful.

We have gone through the basics of Terraform and how to deploy cloud components using Terraform Cloud. We will now look at automating our software workflows with Jenkins. Jenkins is one of the most popular CI automation tools you will ever find, and having some experience with it is useful.

Jenkins

Jenkins is one of the many CI tools to automate deploying your code. Jenkins allows for a declarative language written in a file in the Git repository.

Jenkinsfile

Here is a basic example of a declarative pipeline that would live in a Jenkinsfile:

```
pipeline {
    agent any
    stages {
        stage('first stage') {
            steps {
                echo 'Step 1'
            }
        }
    }
}
```

In the preceding code, we first define which agent the work will be done on – for our use case, we will use any agent. In other cases, you might have work organized by teams, production, or other possible choices.

Next, we define one stage; this could in reality be test, deploy, or any other step in our CI pipeline:

```
pipeline {
    agent any
    stages {
        stage('first stage') {
            steps {
                echo 'Step 1'
                withCredentials([usernamePassword(credentials: 'mycreds', usernameVariable: 'USER', passwordVariable: 'PWD')])
                { sh 'my_tool  -u $USERNAME -p $PASSWORD'}
            }
        }
    }
}
```

In the preceding pipeline, we pull credentials from the server that have already been defined and then run a "tool" using those credentials:

```
pipeline {
    agent any
    parameters {
        choice(name: 'Environment', choices: ['Dev', 'Prod'], description: 'Choose Environment')
    }
    stages {
        stage('See Parameters') {
```

```
        steps {
            echo "Environment ${params.Environment}"
        }
      }
    }
}
```

Another option you have is to create parameter choices that are answered at the start of the pipeline run. This can be used to affect the path of the pipeline – for example, we might deploy our code in a dev environment if dev is chosen:

```
steps {
                script {
                    def env = "${params.Environment}"
                    def branch = "${params.Branch}"
                    if(env == "dev") {
                        echo "Dev"
                    } else {
                        echo "Prod"
                    }
                }
            }
```

You can also have if/then-like expressions that adjust the flow of your pipeline, such as the following code. If branch is master, then it will deploy to Prod:

```
pipeline {
     agent any
     stages {
        stage('Build') {
            Expression {
                BRANCH_NAME == 'master'
            }
            steps {
                echo "Deploying to Prod Env"
            }
        }
```

If you need multiple stages to run at the same time, you can use the parallel keyword:

```
parallel {
                stage('stage A') {
```

Lastly, you always have the option to write helper functions in Groovy and call them in your pipeline:

```
pipeline {
    agent any
    triggers {
        cron('H/12 * * * *')
    }
pipeline {
agent any
stages {
    stage('build') {
        agent any
        steps {
            script {
                helperFunction('chapter_8')
            }
        }
    }
}
}
def helperFunction(String a) {
        echo a
}
```

Practical lab

We'll now use this lab to implement everything we have learned.

Problem 1

Create a repo and use Terraform to create a new cluster.

We now use the gh CLI to create the repository in GitHub:

```
gh repo create
? What would you like to do? Create a new repository on GitHub from scratch
? Repository name chapter_8_infra
? Description used for infrascture
? Visibility Public
? Would you like to add a README file? Yes
? Would you like to add a .gitignore? Yes
? Choose a .gitignore template Python
? Would you like to add a license? Yes
? Choose a license GNU Affero General Public License v3.0
```

```
? This will create "chapter_8_infra" as a public repository on GitHub.
Continue? Yes
✓ Created repository bclipp/chapter_8_infra on GitHub
? Clone the new repository locally? Yes
```

Next, we create an organization, workspace, and project with Terraform Cloud:

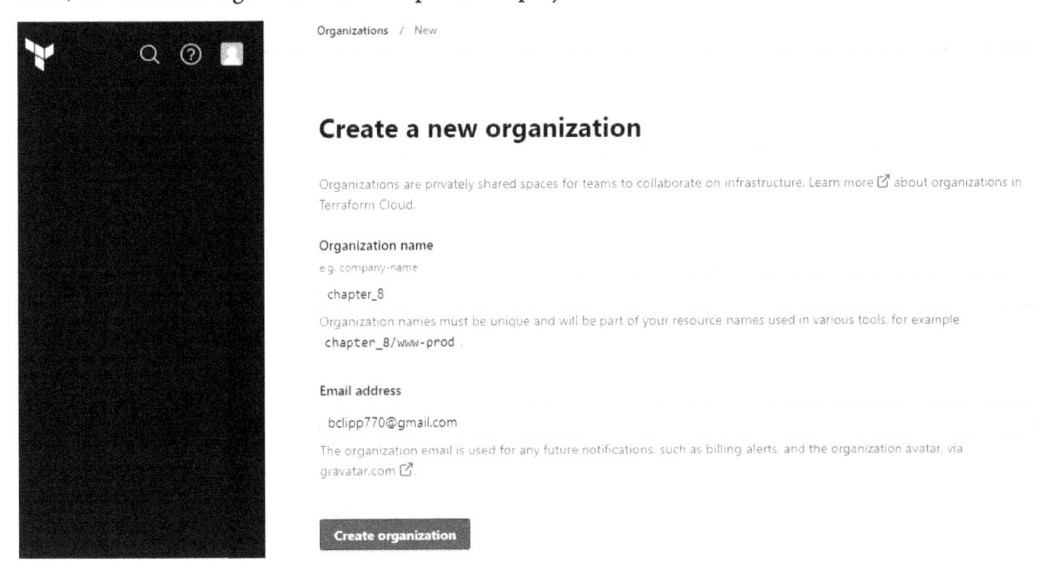

Figure 8.11: Creating an organization

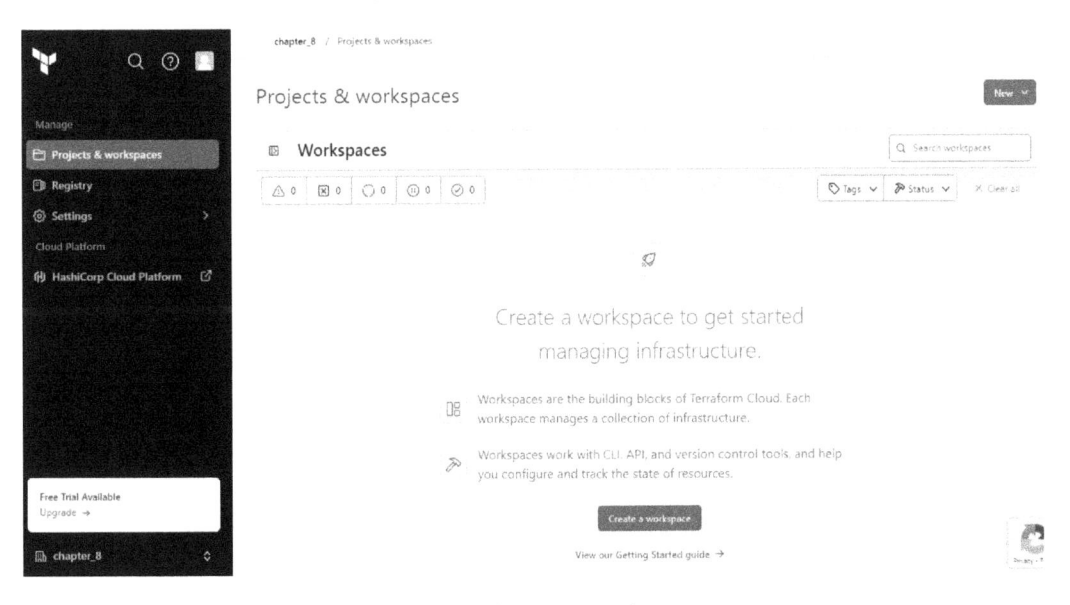

Figure 8.12: Creating a workspace

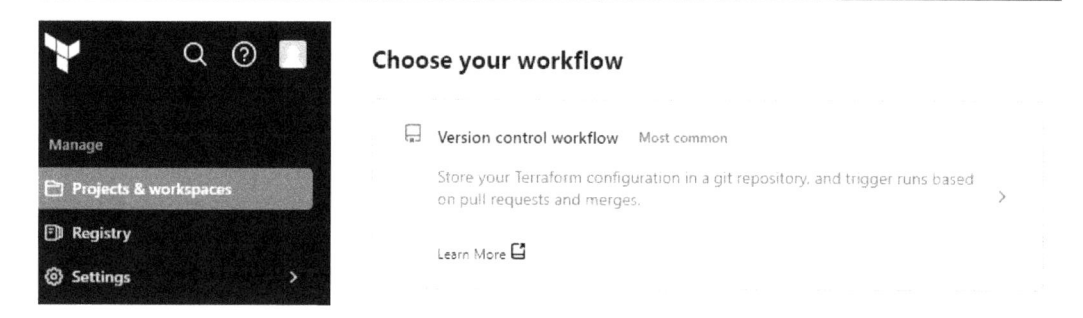

188   Integrating Continous Integration into Your Workflow

Figure 8.13:

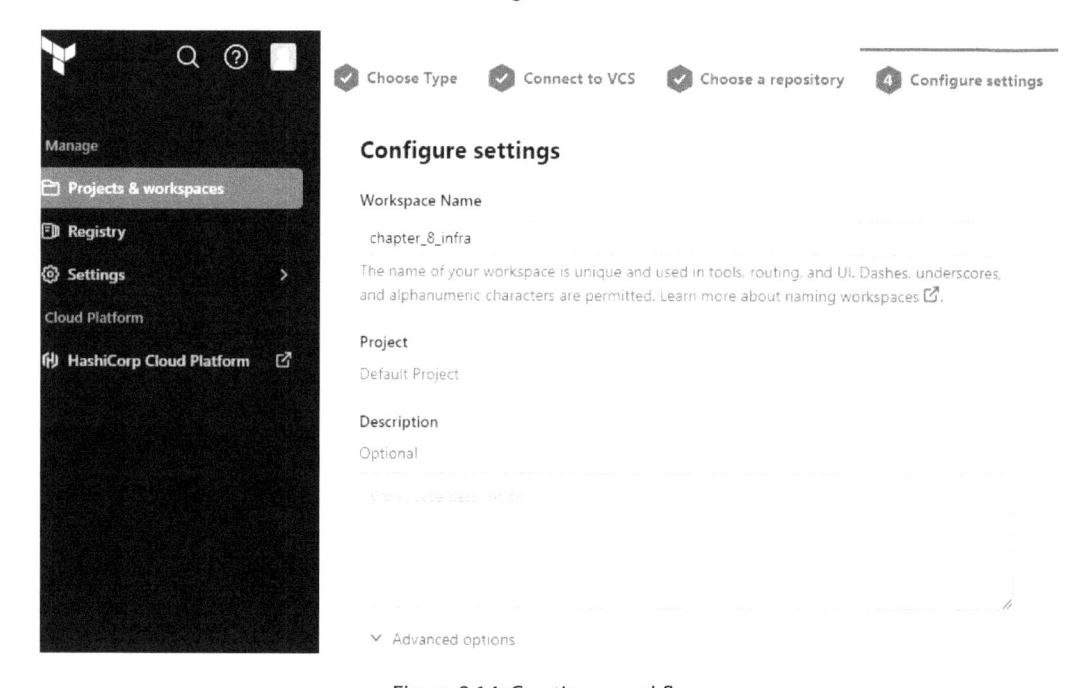

Figure 8.14: Creating a workflow

In our repo, we add the following code (`terraform.tf`); notice how we separate the provider from the rest of the code:

```
variable "HOST" {
  type = string
}
variable "TOKEN" {
  type = string
}
provider "databricks" {
  host = var.HOST
```

```
    token = var.TOKEN
}
terraform {
  cloud {
    organization = "chapter_8"
    workspaces {
      name = "cli"
    }
  }
  required_providers {
    databricks = {
      source = "databricks/databricks"
      version = "1.0.0"
    }
  }
}
```

Here, we now add our `main.tf` with variables for `host` and `token`. Later, we will create those variables in the Terraform cloud:

```
data "databricks_spark_version" "latest_lts" {
  long_term_support = true
}
resource "databricks_cluster" "tiny" {
  cluster_name = "tiny"
  spark_version = data.databricks_spark_version.latest_lts.id
  node_type_id = "m4.large"
  driver_node_type_id = "m4.large"
  autotermination_minutes = 10
  autoscale {
    min_workers = 1
    max_workers = 2
  }
  aws_attributes {
    first_on_demand = 1
    availability = "SPOT_WITH_FALLBACK"
    zone_id = "us-west-2b"
    spot_bid_price_percent = 100
    ebs_volume_type = "GENERAL_PURPOSE_SSD"
    ebs_volume_count = 3
    ebs_volume_size = 100
  }
}
```

Lastly, we will create two variables exactly matching the ones we are using in our code, but with `TF_VAR_` prepended to the name.

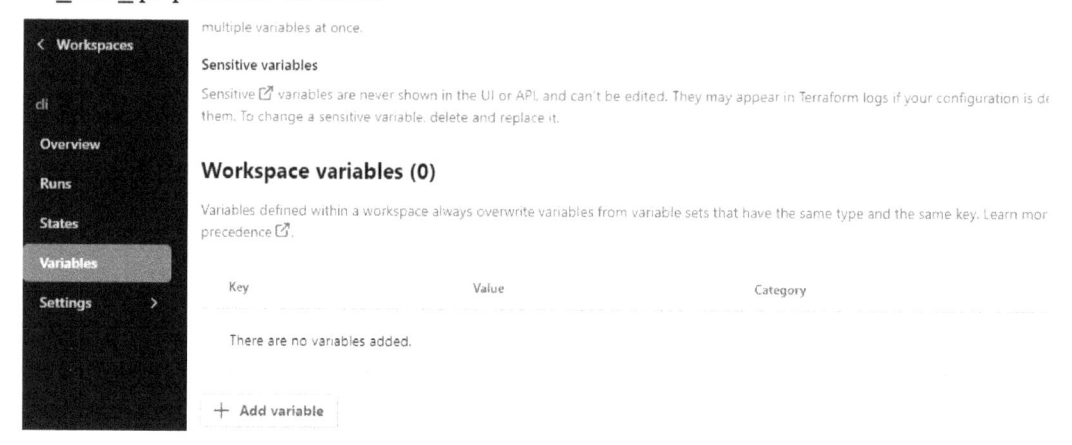

Figure 8.15: Creating variables for the workspace

We have now created our repo and we have our Terraform ready to be deployed.

We can run `terraform init` and deploy to create our new clusters.

Problem 2

Create a small pipeline that creates data and writes to the **Databricks Filesystem** (**DBFS**) in a GitHub repository using `dbx`.

First, we will create the repository for our code:

```
gh repo create
? What would you like to do? Create a new repository on GitHub from scratch
? Repository name chapter_8_pipeline
? Repository name chapter_8_pipeline
? Description pipeline code
? Description pipeline code
? Visibility Public
? Would you like to add a README file? Yes
? Would you like to add a .gitignore? Yes
? Choose a .gitignore template Python
? Would you like to add a license? Yes
? Choose a license GNU Affero General Public License v3.0
? This will create "chapter_8_pipeline" as a public repository on GitHub. Continue? Yes
```

```
✓ Created repository bclipp/chapter_8_pipeline on GitHub
? Clone the new repository locally? Yes
```

Next, we will set up our template for our dbx project:

```
dbx init \
    -p "cloud=AWS" \
    -p "project_name=chapter8" \
    -p "profile=chapter_8" \
    --no-input
```

Before we do anything, it's a good idea to create our pre-commit setup:

```
.pre-commit-config.yaml
repos:
-   repo: https://github.com/psf/black
    rev: stable
    hooks:
    - id: black
      language_version: python3.6
-   repo: https://github.com/PyCQA/isort
    rev: 5.10.1
    hooks:
    -   id: isort
-   repo: https://gitlab.com/PyCQA/flake8
    rev: 4.0.1
    hooks:
    - id: flake8
-   repo: https://github.com/adamchainz/blacken-docs
    rev: v5.4.2
    hooks:
    -   id: blacken-docs
        additional_dependencies:
        - black==22.12.0
-   repo: https://github.com/PyCQA/isort
    rev: 5.10.1
    hooks:
    -   id: isort
-   repo: https://github.com/PyCQA/pylint
    rev: v2.15.9
    hooks:
    -   id: pylint
```

Finally, we add our code.

This is our entry point for the etl job. It's using some shared libraries:

```
chapter_8/tasks/bronze_1.py
from chapter_8.job.config.pipeline_configs import
JobConfigureSales1Bronze
from chapter_8.job.utils.db import autoloader_read, autoloader_write
def ingest_file_write_job_type(config):
    data_frame = autoloader_read(config)
    query = autoloader_write(data_frame,config)
def entrypoint():
    ingest_file_write_job_type(JobConfigureSales1Bronze)
if __name__ == '__main__':
    entrypoint()
```

This is our fake data generator task. It will create data for us to "consume." Notice that we are using the entry point method. This will allow for dbx to properly interact with our code:

```
chapter_8/tasks/fake_data.py
from chapter_8.job.config.pipeline_configs import
JobConfigureSales1Bronze
from chapter_8.job.utils.db import write_pandas_dataframe_file
from chapter_8.job.utils.fake_data import get_fake_data_frame
def create_panda_data_job_type(config):
    data_frame = get_fake_data_frame()
    write_pandas_dataframe_file(data_frame, config.file_location)
def entrypoint():
    create_panda_data_job_type(JobConfigureSales1Bronze)
if __name__ == '__main__':
    entrypoint()
```

Here, we have a central place to store our task configurations. I chose a data class for this role; in practice, you might have many configurations stored in one or more files:

```
chapter_8/job/config/pipeline_configs.py
@dataclass
class JobConfigureSales1Bronze:
    egress_table_name = "sales_1_bronze"
    file_location = "/tmp/sales_chapter_8/"
    database_name = "chapter_8"
    schema = sales_1_bronze_schema
    checkpoint_location = "/tmp/sales_chapter_8_checkpoint"
```

Here, we have shared functions that interact with the database and other similar types of APIs. It is best to group your code into similar modules and specific functions:

```
chapter_8/job/utils/db.py
from dataclasses import dataclass
import time
import os
def autoloader_read(config):
    return spark.readStream.format("cloudFiles") \
        .option("cloudFiles.format", "csv") \
        .option("delimiter", ",") \
        .schema(config.schema) \
        .load(config.file_location)
def autoloader_write(data_frame, config):
    return data_frame.writeStream.format("delta") \
        .outputMode("append") \
        .option("checkpointLocation", config.checkpoint_location) \
        .trigger(availableNow=True) \
        .toTable(config.egress_table_name)
def write_pandas_dataframe_file(data_frame, location):
    time_string = time.strftime("%Y%m%d-%H%M%S")
    path = location + f"fake_data{time_string}.csv"
    data_frame.to_csv(path)
    print(path)
def create_database(database_name):
    spark.sql(f"CREATE DATABASE IF NOT EXISTS {database_name};")
def create_table(table_name, database_name):
    empty_rdd = spark.sparkContext.emptyRDD()
    empty_data_frame = spark.createDataFrame(data=empty_rdd,
                                             schema=sales_1_bronze_schema)
    empty_data_frame.write.saveAsTable(table_name + "." + database_name)
def setup_tables():
    create_database(JobConfigureSales1Bronze.database_name)
    create_table(JobConfigureSales1Bronze.egress_table_name,
JobConfigureSales1Bronze.database_name)
```

Here are the fake data functions used by our task. Notice it is generating fake data using `faker` and pandas:

```
chapter_8/job/utils/fake_data.py
from faker import Faker
import pandas as pd
import os
```

```python
def get_fake_data_frame():
    fake = Faker()
    def generate_data(num):
        row = [{"name": fake.name(),
                "address": fake.address(),
                "city": fake.city(),
                "state": fake.state(),
                "date_time": fake.date_time(),
                "friend": fake.catch_phrase()} for x in range(num)]
        return row
    panda = pd.DataFrame(generate_data(10000))
    # return spark.createDataFrame(panda)
    return panda
```

Next, we are building the schema for our table in a structured way. If we have other tables that share a field, then we can group that field and adjust the changes in a uniform manner:

```
chapter_8/job/utils/schema.py
from pyspark.sql.types import StructField, StringType, FloatType, StructType
sales_location = StructField("location", StringType())
sales_name = StructField("name", StringType())
sales_price = StructField("price", FloatType())
sales_1_bronze_schema = StructType([
    sales_location,
    sales_name,
    sales_price
])
```

Here we adjust the `setup.py` file and add our two new entry points:

```
setup.py
    entry_points = {
        "console_scripts": [
            "bronze_1= chapter_8.tasks.bronze_1:entrypoint",
            "fake = chapter_8.tasks.fake_data:entrypoint",
        ]},
```

Lastly, we create an entry in the `deployment.yaml` file to represent our new workflow:

```
conf/deployment.yml
    - name: "chapter_8_workflow"
      job_clusters:
        - job_cluster_key: "default"
          <<: *basic-static-cluster
```

```yaml
tasks:
  - task_key: "bronze_user_1"
    job_cluster_key: "default"
    python_wheel_task:
      package_name: "chapter_8"
      entry_point: "entrypoint"
      parameters: []
  - task_key: "etl"
    depends_on:
      - task_key: "fake_data"
    job_cluster_key: "default"
    python_wheel_task:
      package_name: "chapter_8"
      entry_point: "ml"
      parameters: []
```

To deploy our workflow, we run `dbx deploy` and then launch.

Summary

We covered a vast number of topics in one chapter, yet we have only touched the surface of CI. CI can be complex, but it doesn't have to be. Hopefully, you have some working knowledge of some tools and techniques for automating your workloads across your data platform. In the next chapter, we will explore various ways to orchestrate our data workflows.

9
Orchestrating Your Data Workflows

We have covered a wealth of techniques and knowledge in building our data platforms. However, there are some missing components in fully orchestrating everything. We've mentioned Databricks Workflows, but we didn't dive deep into how it works; we also haven't mentioned logging or secrets management. Workflows is an orchestration tool that's used to manage data pipelines in Databricks. Orchestration tools normally allow for common data tasks and provide the history of each pipeline run, which is specific to the pipeline. Having a central place to manage all your pipelines is a critical step to having reliable, scalable data pipelines. So, this chapter will discuss these topics in detail and create more stability in our data platform.

In this chapter, we're going to cover the following main topics:

- Logging and monitoring with Datadog
- Secrets management
- Databricks Workflows
- Databricks REST APIs
- Secrets management

Technical requirements

The tooling that will be used in this chapter is tied to the tech stack that's been chosen for this book. All vendors should offer a free trial account.

I will be using Databricks in this chapter.

Setting up your environment

Before we begin this chapter, let's take some time to set up our working environment.

Databricks

As in the previous chapters, this chapter assumes you have a working version of Python 3.6 or above installed in your development environment. It also assumes you have set up an AWS account and that you have set up Databricks with that AWS account.

Databricks CLI

The first step is to install the `databricks-cli` tool using the `pip` Python package manager:

```
pip install databricks-cli
```

Let's validate that everything has been installed correctly. If the following command produces the tool's version, then everything is working correctly:

```
Databricks -v
```

Now, let's set up authentication. First, go into the Databricks UI and generate a personal access token. The following command will ask for the host that was created for your Databricks instance and the token that was created:

```
databricks configure --token
```

We can quickly determine whether the CLI has been set up correctly by running the following command. If no error is returned, then you have a working setup:

```
databricks fs ls
```

Lastly, let's set up our `workspace`, `clusters`, and `dbfs` folders:

```
databricks   fs mkdirs    dbfs:/chapter_9
databricks   workspace mkdirs   /chapter_9
databricks   clusters create -json-file    <file_path to tiny.json>
```

The following is the content of the `tiny.json` file:

```
{    "num_workers":0, "cluster_name":"tiny",   "spark_version":"10.4.x-scala2.12",
    "spark_conf":{
        "spark.master":"local[*, 4]",    "spark.databricks.cluster.profile":"singleNode"
     },   "aws_attributes":{
```

```
        "first_on_demand":1,   "availability":"SPOT_WITH_
FALLBACK",    "zone_id":"us-west-2b",
        "instance_profile_arn":null, "spot_bid_price_percent":100,
        "ebs_volume_type":"GENERAL_PURPOSE_SSD",
        "ebs_volume_count":3, "ebs_volume_size":100
    }, "node_type_id":"m4.large",   "driver_node_type_id":"m4.large",
    "ssh_public_keys":[ ],"custom_
tags":{ "ResourceClass":"SingleNode"}, "spark_env_vars":{  "PYSPARK_
PYTHON":"/databricks/python3/bin/python3"},
    "autotermination_minutes":10, "enable_elastic_
disk":false,  "cluster_source":"UI",  "init_scripts":[ ], "data_
security_mode":"NONE",  "runtime_engine":"STANDARD"}
```

The DBX CLI

dbx will use the credentials file from the Databricks CLI you created. You only need to install the pip library:

```
pip3 install dbx
```

Orchestrating data workloads

Now that we have all the pre-setup work done, let's jump right into organizing and running our workloads in Databricks. We will cover a variety of topics, the first of which is managing incremental new additions via files.

Making life easier with Autoloader

Spark Streaming isn't something new and many deployments are using it in their data platforms. Spark Streaming has rough edges that Autoloader resolves. Autoloader is an efficient way to have Databricks detect new files and process them. Autoloader works with the Spark structured streaming context, so there isn't much difference in usage once it's set up.

Reading

To create a streaming DataFrame using Autoloader, you can simply use the cloud file format, along with the needed options. In the following case, we are setting the schema, delimiter, and format for a CSV load:

```
spark.readStream.format("cloudFiles") \
    .option("cloudFiles.format", "csv") \
    .option("delimiter", ",") \
    .schema(schema) \
    .load(file_location)
```

Writing

Once we have processed our data, we can write it to a Delta table using the following code. This code should be familiar to you at this point. We will delve into some of its nuances in a minute:

```
data_frame.writeStream.format("delta") \
    .outputMode("append") \
    .option("checkpointLocation", checkpoint_location) \
    .trigger(availableNow=True) \
    .toTable(egress_table_name)
```

Two modes

Autoloader has two ways to detect new files – directory listing and file notification. We'll cover them here.

Directory listing

Directory listing mode allows Autoloader to use the current directory listing APIs available in your cloud provider to find new files. This approach is good for data that has less velocity since a very large amount of files in a folder will be harder to parse. There is a charge for listing files on cloud storage. You can use lexical ordering to reduce some of the costs.

To set up a file notification autoloader, include this as an option in your `readStream`:

```
cloudFiles.useIncrementalListing =True
```

File notification

File notification is a scalable and more complex mode that creates a notification and queue service for you. File notification mode is designed to scale with high-velocity data streams. There is a charge for these setups, so be sure to price out what your setup will cost and monitor billing.

To set up a file notification autoloader, include this as an option in your `readStream`:

```
cloudFiles.useIncrementalListing =False
```

Useful options

Beyond the basics of Autoloader, there are a few useful options that are worth going over:

- If you would like to do hybrid streaming and batch processing but process the data in multiple batches, you can use the following `trigger` option:

    ```
    .trigger(availableNow=True)
    ```

- If you want to control data that is ingested from overwriting data, you can use this option:

    CloudFiles.allowOverwrites

- This option is very useful for ignoring data that has been delivered before Autoloader has been started:

    CloudFiles.includeExistingFiles

- This option will set the maximum bytes that will be processed in a single trigger:

    CloudFiles.maxBytesPerTrigger

- This option can be useful with notification mode enabled; it will ensure that all files are processed:

    CloudFiles.backfillInterval

- This last option is used to set schema evolution. Schema evolution can be useful in some cases as it allows minor non-breaking changes to be accepted without the need for a DDL change. I don't feel this is a wise setting for all cases as schema enforcement is a basic principle of a data contract:

    cloudFiles.schemaEvolutionMode :

    Four modes are supported in schema evolution:

    - addNewColumns: In this mode, Autoloader will add new columns, but will fail on any other schema change
    - failOnNewColumns: In this mode, any columns that don't conform to the original schema will cause Autoloader to throw an error
    - Rescue: In this mode, a column is created to store columns that are different from the original column
    - None: In this mode, any columns that don't conform to the original schema are ignored and no error is thrown

With that, we have looked at dealing with incremental new changes to Delta tables using new files. This is a very common process that's used in almost every data lake and lake house. Next, we will look at managing several Spark jobs via Databricks Workflows.

Databricks Workflows

Now that we've gone through the YAML deployment of workflows in dbx, next, we will look at the web console. Here, we have the main page for workflows. We can create a new workflow by clicking the **Create job** button at the top left:

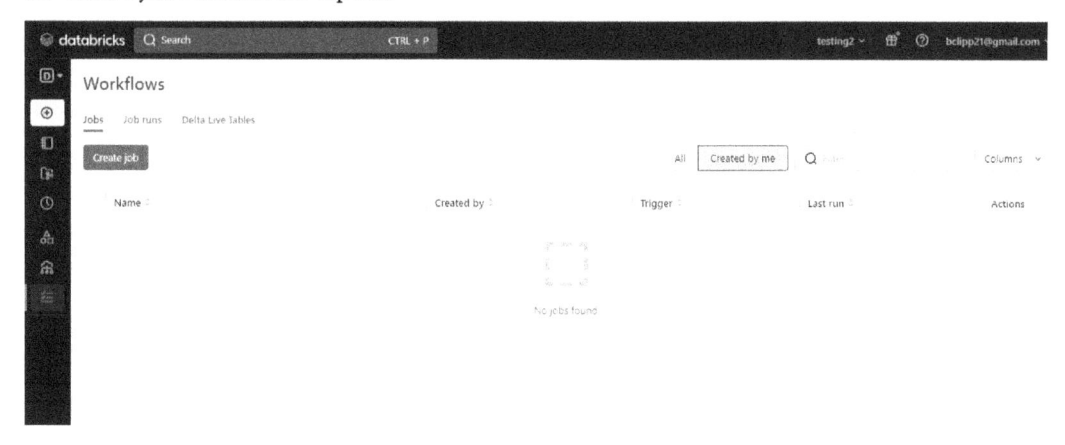

Figure 9.1: Create job

When you create a workflow, you will be presented with a diagram of the workflow and a menu for each step:

Figure 9.2: My_workflow

Be sure to match the package name and entry point with what is defined in `setup.py` if you're using a package:

Figure 9.3: Workflow diagram

When you run your workflow, you will see each instance run, its status, and its start time:

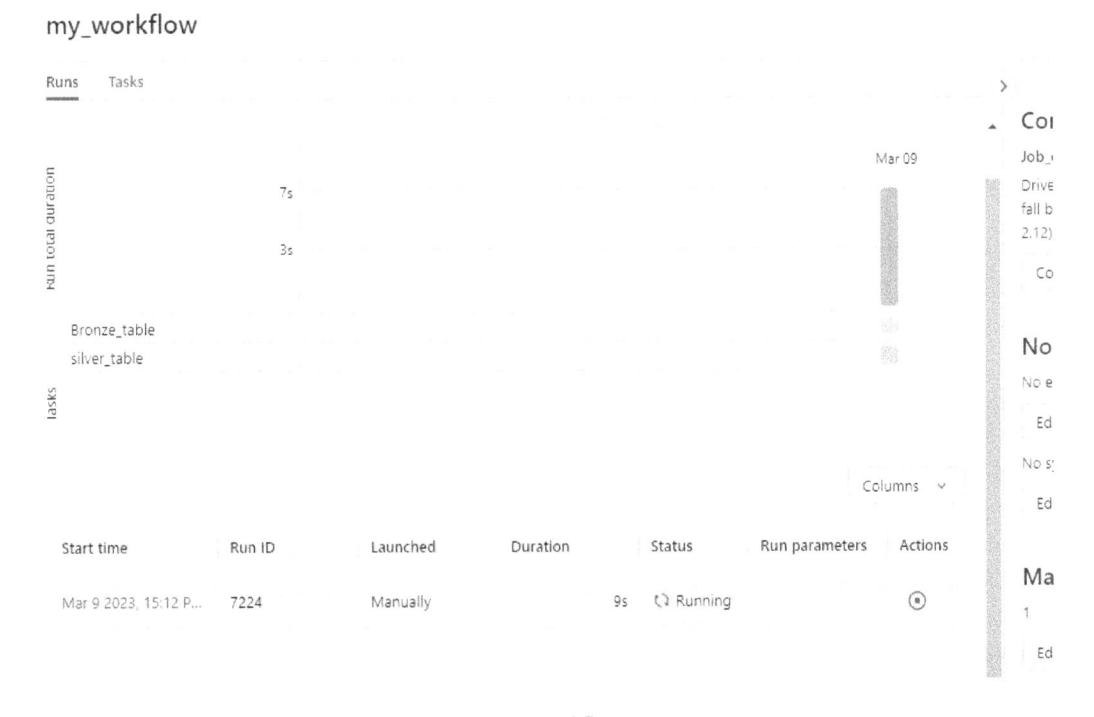

Figure 9.4: Workflow run

204　Orchestrating Your Data Workflows

Here is an example of a two-step workflow that has failed:

my_workflow run

Figure 9.5: Workflow flow

You can see your failed runs individually in the console:

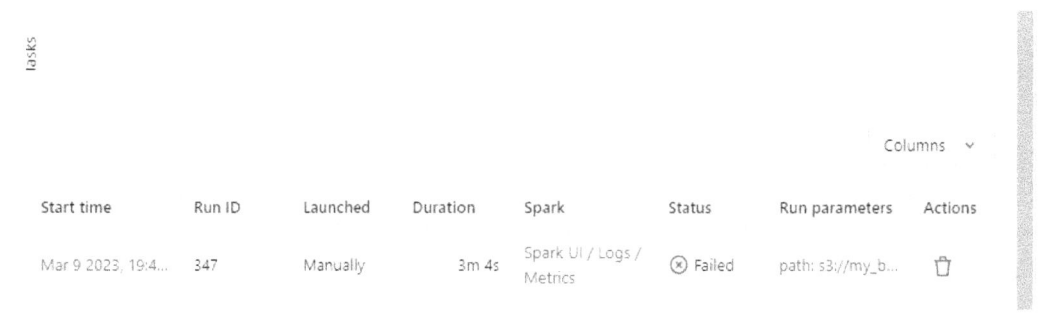

Start time	Run ID	Launched	Duration	Spark	Status	Run parameters	Actions
Mar 9 2023, 19:4...	347	Manually	3m 4s	Spark UI / Logs / Metrics	Failed	path: s3://my_b...	

Figure 9.6: Workflow run failed

You can pass runtime parameters in JSON format. By doing this, all the steps will have access to those parameters:

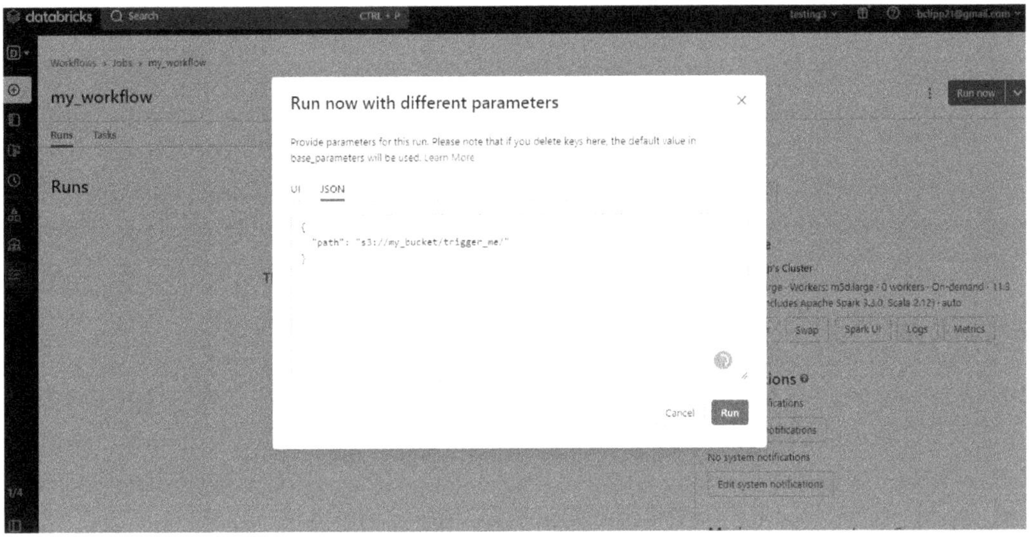

Figure 9.7: Run now with different parameters

When your job fails, you will want to look at the Spark logs for each step. These are organized separately:

Figure 9.8: Workflow output

Your workflows can have several types of steps. At the time of writing, Databricks supports the following:

- DBT
- Notebooks

- JAR files
- Scripts
- Delta Live Tables

With that, we have looked at the extremely powerful Databricks Workflows, which can in many ways go head-to-head with more specialized tools such as Airflow. Next, we will look at how Terraform can manage our workflow deployments.

Terraform

Databricks supports workflows in Terraform, and it's a very viable way to deploy and change your workflows.

Here is how you can define a workflow, also called a job in some interfaces. You must set your workflow name and the resource name. After that, you must define tasks within the workflow:

```
resource "databricks_job" "my_pipeline_1" {
 name = "my_awsome_pipeline"
   task {
....
       existing_cluster_id = <cluster-id>
   }
      task {
....
       existing_cluster_id = <cluster-id>
   }
}
```

Failed runs

When your workflows fail, you have the option to repair your run. You don't need to rerun the whole pipeline, and Workflows is smart enough to just run your failed steps. This brings up the important topic of creating idempotent steps in a workflow. In short, if you have an idempotent workflow, each step or task can be run multiple times or fail and restart but create the same output every time. In theory, this translates to workflows that do not create duplicate data but also know what data they're processing. You don't want to repair your workflow but then have new data from another process.

With that, we have looked at workflow management through Terraform, which can be very powerful and useful. Next, let's look at accessing the Databricks platform's REST APIs.

REST APIs

REST APIs are a way to access functionality and data over the network. Databricks, like many vendors, allows you to interact and change the platform through REST API interactions.

The Databricks API

Here are some useful endpoints you can interact:

- **Cluster API**: Manages clusters, including restart, create, and delete
- **Jobs API**: Manages jobs and workflows, including restart, create, and delete
- **Token API**: Creates and manages tokens in the workspace

Python code

Here, we have a basic client setup for a REST endpoint. In this example, it's `google.com`:

1. First, we must import the necessary libraries. Here, we are using the `requests` library exclusively:

    ```
    import requests
    from requests.adapters import HTTPAdapter, Retry
    ```

2. Next, we must set up a session and define our `Retry` pattern. We are using `Retry` because the nature of Network APIs can be finicky, so we want to make sure there is a wide range of time we can get our interaction through:

    ```
    session = requests.Session()
    restries = Retry(total=10,
                    backoff_factor=0.2,
                    status_forcelist=[500, 502])
    ```

3. Now, let's define `HTTPAdapter` by passing the retries in with `Max_retries`:

    ```
    adapter = HTTPAdapter(max_retries=restries)
    ```

4. Lastly, we will use our session and get the data at our endpoint:

    ```
    session.mount('http://', adapter)
    session.get("www.google.com")
    ```

Using the REST API can be a very effective way to manage the Databricks platform, but it is also extremely complex to scale and manage. Now, let's look at logging and how we can understand how our data workflows are run.

Logging

Logging is one of the core fundamental components when you're trying to scale your data platform. When your platform starts to grow, being able to centrally find related logs and correlate events becomes critical. That being said, it's not important to have a centralized logging system initially.

Databricks notebook logs

To access logs for a notebook in Databricks Workflows, click on the workflow you would like to inspect:

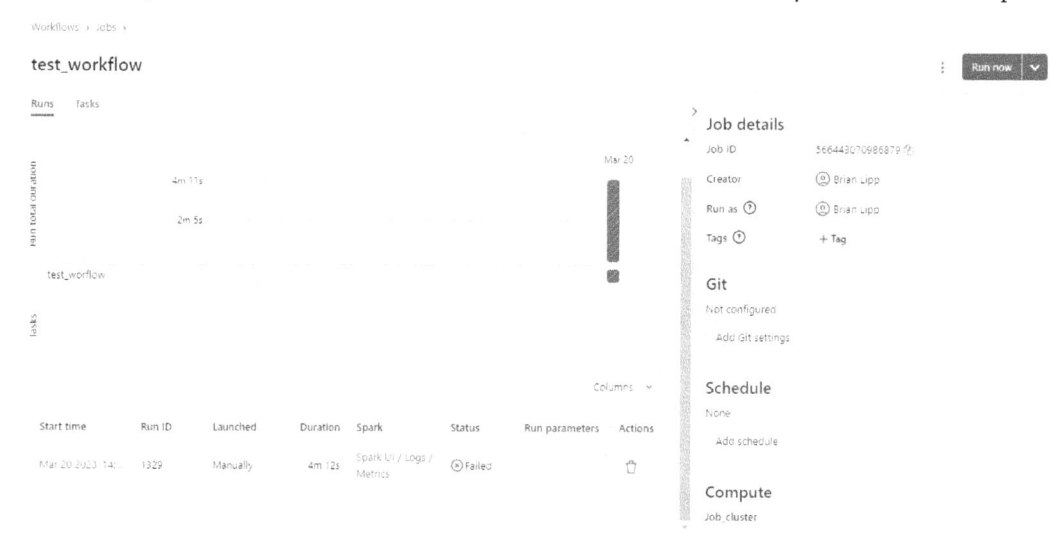

Figure 9.9: Workflow logging

Then, click on the notebook task. You will be presented with the cells that errored:

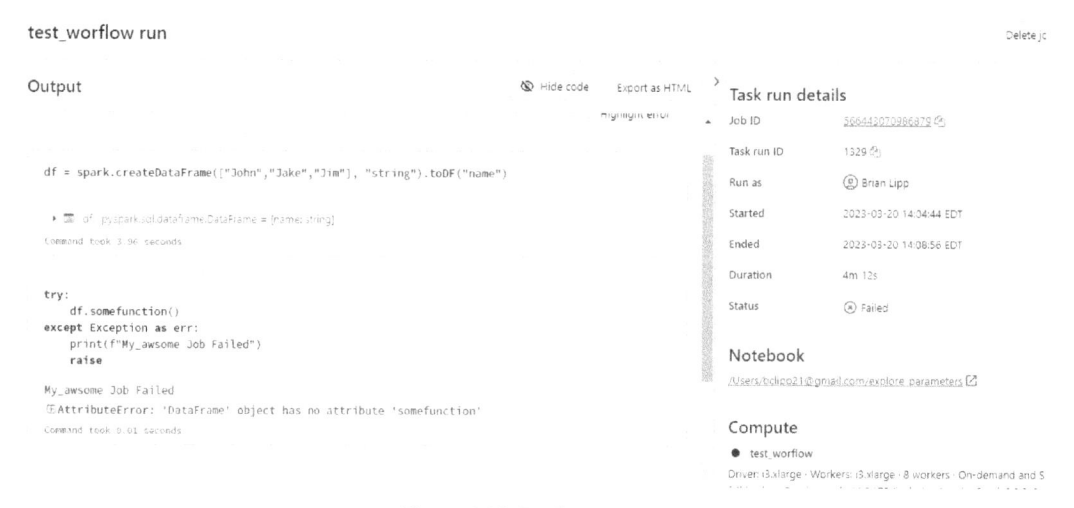

Figure 9.10: Further output

You also have access to the Spark log, as shown here:

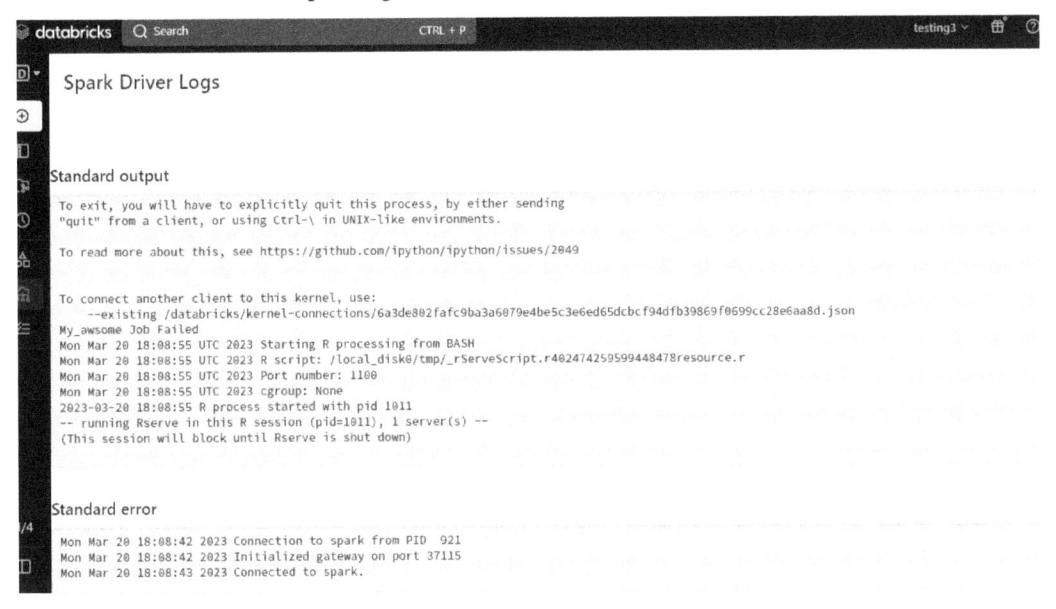

Figure 9.11: Workflow job error

Logging your code

When you test while writing code, it's important to log for debugs, tests, and errors. I'll go over a few options and directions you can take:

1. First, for our example, let's create a DataFrame that contains some example data:

    ```
    df = spark.createDataFrame(["John","Jake","Jim"], "string").
    toDF("name")
    ```

2. Now, let's create a class that will create our `logger` object:

    ```
    class MyLogger:
        def logger(self,spark, prefix = ""):
            log4j_logger = spark._jvm.org.apache.log4j
            return log4j_logger.LogManager.getLogger(prefix + self.__name__())
        def __name__(self):
            if self.__class__.__module__ == "__built-in__":
                return self.__class__.__name__
            return self.__class__.__module__ + "." + self.__class__.__name__
    ```

3. Now, we can instantiate our logger object and pass it to our Spark instance:

   ```
   logger = MyLogger().logger(spark)
   ```

4. Lastly, we can use our logger in a `try-catch` pattern:

   ```
   try:
       df.somefunction()
   except Exception as err:
       logger.fatal(f"my notebook failed!!!! with this error {err}")
       raise
   ```

   The output in the Spark logs will look something like this:

   ```
   XX/XX/XX 18:48:20 FATAL MyLogger: my notebook failed!!!! with this error 'DataFrame' object has no attribute 'somefunction'
   ```

Log4j

Log4j is a very popular logging tool for JVM languages. Spark in Databricks runs in a JVM and its core is written in Scala, a JVM language. It's always possible to change configurations on Log4j, but ideally, the best solution for log management is to take the logs produced by Log4j and ship them to a central logging platform such as Datadog. Many major log platforms have scripts and agents documented for working with Spark and Databricks.

Using a log mixin

Mixins are classes that are used to provide other classes with functionality, which is one useful way to give code access to a shared logger, among other functionalities. There are pros and cons to mix-ins, but for logging, I feel it's a very valid option for adding logging to your code:

```
class LoggingMixin:
    logger = MyLogger().logger(spark)
    def fatal_log(self, message):
        logger.fatal(f"{message}")
class MyClass(LoggingMixin):
    def my_etl(self):
        try:
            df.somefunction()
        except Exception as err:
            self.fatal_log(f"my notebook failed!!!! with this error {err}")
            Raise
```

As you can see, you can create a pipeline class and do some work and then log to the Spark logs in Databricks.

Logging can be one of the most useful tools in a data platform as it allows you to not only troubleshoot issues but also understand how processes are working or not working. Next, we'll look at managing information we don't want to share with other entities.

Secrets management

Secrets in our code and on our platform are bits of information that should not be shared or logged but can change over time. In an ideal world, secrets should be managed centrally in a companywide secrets manager such as HashiCorp Vault. That being said, it's often the case where companies just have not fully matured enough to reach this level. If your company doesn't have a central secrets manager, or your tool doesn't support accessing that secret, you're stuck with managing secrets for each tool.

Databricks secrets

To create a secret, first, you have to create a scope with Terraform:

```
resource "databricks_secret_scope" "secret-engineering" {
  name = "engineering-scope"
  initial_manage_principal = "users"
}
```

Then, you can create a secret in that scope:

```
databricks secrets put --scope "engineering-scope" --key <key-name>
databricks secrets list --scope <scope-name>
databricks secrets delete --scope <scope-name> --key <key-name>
dbutils.secrets.get(scope = "jdbc", key = "username")
```

Now that we have reached the end of the theoretical elements, let's put everything into practice.

Practical lab

Our cloud team will be triggering an AWS Lambda and passing the path to the data being delivered from our ingestion tool. They have asked for a Lambda that will pass that information to your workflow, which should be parameterized. This type of request is very common and allows Databricks to be interacted with using a variety of tooling, such as AWS Step Functions and Jenkins, among others.

Solution

In this solution, we will walk you through the Python code needed to complete the tasks. There are two ways to access Databricks via the REST API – using the `requests` package, as shown previously, and using the Python package provided by Databricks. In my solution, I am using the Databricks package to keep things simple. I have not come across a case where the package doesn't meet my needs, but if it's not good enough, you can always access the REST API directly.

Lambda code

Here, I am importing all my Python libraries. Take note of the `databricks_cli` pypi package. This will need to be installed:

```
from databricks_cli.sdk.api_client import ApiClient
from databricks_cli.jobs.api import JobsApi
import traceback
import logging
import json
import sys
```

Next, I am creating a function to trigger workflows that take the path of the file being delivered:

```
def run_workflow(path):
    api_client = ApiClient(
    host  = os.getenv("DATABRICKS_HOST"),
    token = os.getenv("DATABRICKS_TOKEN")
    )
    jobs_api = JobsApi(api_client)
    job_id = os.getenv("JOB_ID")
    jobs_api.run_now(job_id, notebook_params= f"{{ "path": {path} }}")
```

Now comes the meat of our Lambda code. Here, we will set up a `logger` instance, pull out the path from the Lambda trigger, and call our Lambda rubber function, handing it the path:

```
def lambda_handler(event, context):
    logger = logging.getLogger()
    logger.setLevel(logging.INFO)

    try:
        logger.info(f'event: {event}')
        path = event['path']
        run_workflow(path)
        logger.info(f'ran workflow with path: {path}')
        return {"status": "success", "message": None}

    except Exception as exp:
        exception_type, exception_value, exception_traceback = sys.exc_info()
        traceback_string = traceback.format_exception(exception_type, exception_value, exception_traceback)
        error_msg = json.dumps({
            "errorType": exception_type.__name__,
```

```
            "errorMessage": str(exception_value),
            "stackTrace": traceback_string
        })
        logger.error(error_msg)
```

Notebook code

Now, we need to create a notebook that will be in a workflow. First, we will access our path in the parameters by calling the workflow:

```
file_location = dbutils.widgets.get('path')
```

Next, we will define our schema. This is a very simplistic way to handle this, and having more structure around schema management is likely the way to go in production:

```
schema = StructType([ \
    StructField("name",StringType(),True), \
    StructField("id", StringType(), True), \
    StructField("salary", IntegerType(), True) \
  ])
```

Next, we will read our CSV file using the path given to us:

```
spark.readStream.format("cloudFiles") \
    .option("cloudFiles.format", "csv") \
    .option("delimiter", ",") \
    .schema(schema) \
    .load(file_location)
```

Finally, we will set the destination table and checkpoint, then append the data to our table:

```
checkpoint_location = /dbfs/tmp/my_check_point
egress_table_name =  "company_employees"
data_frame.writeStream.format("delta") \
    .outputMode("append") \
    .option("checkpointLocation", checkpoint_location) \
    .trigger(availableNow=True) \
    .toTable(egress_table_name)
```

Summary

We have covered a great deal of information in this chapter. To summarize, we have looked at loading incremental data efficiently, delved deeper into the Databricks Workflows API, dabbled with the REST API, and also worked with AWS Lambda.

In this next chapter, we'll go full steam ahead with data governance!

Part 4: Hands-on Project

In this part, you will get to build out the start of a data platform using popular tools like GitHub Actions Databricks, among others.

This part has the following chapters:

- *Chapter 10, Data Governance*
- *Chapter 11, Building out the GroundworkChapter 12, Completing our Project*
- *Chapter 12, Completing Our Project*

10
Data Governance

Data governance is one of the most complex topics in the data field. Data governance is the amalgamation of people, processes, and technology. It lays down the foundation for the creation, modification, usage, and decimation of data, and who owns what data and in what capacity. My approach will be to cover some fundamental ideas and go through how to apply some of them. Why is data governance important? When joining a project, I have often found that there are significant data governance issues. This can range from data quality to security or cataloging. Without data governance, you can see a wide variety of issues in your data. In this chapter, we're going to cover the following main topics:

- Databricks Unity Catalog
- Data governance
- Great Expectations

Technical requirements

The tooling used in this chapter is tied to the technology stack chosen for the book. All vendors should offer a free trial account.

I will be using the following:

- Databricks

Setting up your environment

Before we begin our chapter, let's take the time to set up our working environment.

Python, AWS, and Databricks

As we have with many others, this chapter assumes you have a working version of Python 3.6 or above installed in your development environment. We will also assume you have set up an AWS account and have set up Databricks with that AWS account.

The Databricks CLI

The first step is to install the `databricks-cli` tool using the `pip` Python package manager:

```
pip install databricks-cli
```

Let's validate that everything has been installed correctly. If this command produces the tool version, then everything is working correctly:

```
Databricks -v
```

Now, let's set up authentication. First, go into the Databricks UI and generate a personal access token. The following command will ask for the host created for your Databricks instance and the created token:

```
databricks configure --token
```

We can quickly determine whether the CLI is set up correctly by running the following command; if no error is returned, you have a working setup:

```
databricks fs ls
```

Lastly, let's set up our `workspace`, `clusters`, and `dbfs` folders:

```
databricks  fs mkdirs   dbfs:/chapter_9
databricks  workspace mkdirs   /chapter_9
databricks  clusters create -json-file    <file_path to tiny.json>
```

Here are the `tiny.json` file contents:

```
{   "num_workers":0, "cluster_name":"tiny",  "spark_version":"10.4.x-scala2.12",
   "spark_conf":{
      "spark.master":"local[*, 4]",    "spark.databricks.cluster.profile":"singleNode"
   }, "aws_attributes":{
      "first_on_demand":1,  "availability":"SPOT_WITH_FALLBACK",  "zone_id":"us-west-2b",
      "instance_profile_arn":null, "spot_bid_price_percent":100,
      "ebs_volume_type":"GENERAL_PURPOSE_SSD",
      "ebs_volume_count":3, "ebs_volume_size":100
   }, "node_type_id":"m4.large",   "driver_node_type_id":"m4.large",
   "ssh_public_keys":[ ],"custom_tags":{   "ResourceClass":"SingleNode"}, "spark_env_vars":{   "PYSPARK_PYTHON":"/databricks/python3/bin/python3"},
   "autotermination_minutes":10, "enable_elastic_disk":false,  "cluster_source":"UI",  "init_scripts":[ ], "data_security_mode":"NONE", "runtime_engine":"STANDARD"}
```

What is data governance?

Data governance is a buzzword that can have a very complex meaning. At its core, data governance is the processes and procedures that are in place around your data. Without data governance, you might see several data sources acting as a source of truth for the same key data items. This can cause data drift and inaccuracies in your data usage. To avoid this, the platform should identify the single source of truth for that specific data and define that source of truth for consumers to access. Another aspect of data governance is identifying the data owner, which ties back to some concepts in data mesh. Data owners are responsible for the quality of the data and resolving data issues. Data owners (or data stewards, as they are often called) are the point of contact for issues that users have with the data. Lastly, data governance can cover better metadata around your data, so that you can better understand, access, and secure your data. Metadata is data about data. It can be further classified as follows:

- Technical metadata
- Business metadata
- Operational metadata

Now that we have gone through the basic idea of data governance, let's explore data standards.

Data standards

Standards are one of the most important aspects of dealing with data issues. Simple examples are having phone numbers with and without the area code or having dates with or without the full year. Both cases are simple, but these types of issues can get more complicated. When working internationally, for example, you often must deal with currency conversion. It might be possible to pick a standard such as US currency, but this isn't always possible. Data standards cover the capture, replication, and maintenance of your data so that there is a consistent view of your data.

Standards are important so that our data is accurate across multiple perspectives, depending on the types of users accessing the data and the sources the data is coming from. One important tool for facilitating this type of user experience is the data catalog.

Data catalogs

A data catalog is a central hub for users to find and understand your data. In the data catalog, you will find the connection between your business metadata and technical metadata. Business metadata is about the data that pertains to business functions such as lines of business and business names. Technical metadata might be the schema of the data and the server and database. Sometimes, data catalogs can include data lineage information and data quality checks made on the data. Many products exist on the market that might give you some of these capabilities, such as Informatica. In many cases, I have seen companies build their own custom data catalog as well. At its root, users need a place to find certified datasets and understand what they specifically mean. *Why do we care so much about creating a central hub for metadata?* you might ask. When we open up this type of tooling to users, it changes how users interact with the data. A user can now explore and learn about the data, without needing to have multiple conversations to find out about a specific dataset.

Data catalogs hold metadata about data, but one source of metadata that data catalogs do not have is the lineage or the evolution of the data. Data lineage is extremely useful and helps create transparency.

Data lineage

When working with a published dataset, it's important to understand where that data came from and how it has evolved over time. There are regulations, depending on the industry that requires such documentation. This can also be very useful for troubleshooting data quality issues. The big issue with this type of documentation is that it isn't easily created, and is often attempted manually. There are some tools that can accomplish this but none are perfect. Databricks Unity Catalog now offers data lineage for tables. We will cover this feature and how to use it later in the chapter. In the following example, we will use our data lineage diagram from *Chapter 2*. Notice that we can see how each field in the sales table is created and what tables they come from.

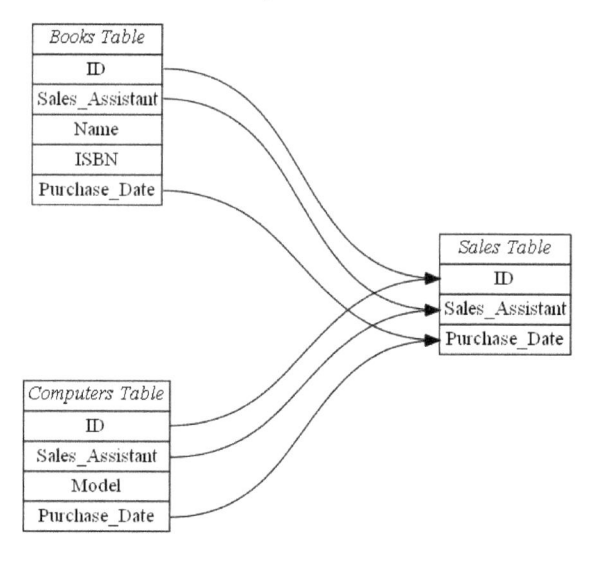

Figure 10.1: Simple data lineage

We have discussed recording lineage metadata and how useful it can be to users. Equally useful is the ability to secure data.

Data security and privacy

Often, the biggest concern with data usage is controlling access and dealing with sensitive data. This covers access to tables and databases. This can sometimes cover row-level access controls to datasets. This isn't the only area we must secure though; oftentimes, data is stored in a cloud storage service such as AWS S3. In those cases, you must secure the data and guarantee access controls on a per-file basis. Filtering out sensitive data can sometimes be critical for many organizations. It might seem trivial but, over the years, there have been several cases of large companies with data breaches that ended up costing significant amounts of money.

Data quality

Data quality is the level of usability of your data. This also translates into the amount of trust that business users can have in the data. It can cover a wide range of issues, including inconsistent formats, missing data, and bad data, among others. Sometimes, data quality issues can be solved by simply letting users look at the data, but often, this simplistic method will not work. Data quality is another one of those complex topics. It's difficult because there is no simple solution. There are a few approaches to attacking data quality, depending on where it is in the data pipeline and how we test for data issues.

One approach is to test the data in flight as the data is ingested using manually defined rules. You may find that your new data needs to be tested in context with other data in the table, so the table might need to be loaded into memory to test fully. In cases of complex modeling, you might need to test your ingested data by combining other datasets with the ingested data. This approach is very useful, but statically defining tests can be hard to scale across thousands of datasets, so there is a limit to static rules.

Another approach is to rule audits on tables at a schedule, which can be used in combination with other techniques. This allows business users to have guarantees that tables pass usability data quality checks. The downside to this approach is, again, if you are using static rules, then maintaining those rules when the table count grows can become impossible.

Lastly, there are ML- and AI-based tools that will monitor your data, learning from patterns and then alerting you when data quality is perceived. In many cases, these tools are very good but are unable to scale effectively without significant costs. We will now discuss using a Python tool called **Great Expectations** and how it can be used to do data quality checks.

Great Expectations

Great Expectations is one of many tools that can be used to run tests on your datasets. It is an open source tool that is very popular in the Python community. Great Expectations has a few useful features, the first being *Expectations* (data tests), which can be custom tests or tests provided by the library. The second is automated data profiling, which allows Great Expectations to scan a sample of your data to build tests for you. Data profiling is all about understanding the quality of data, baselining it, and then monitoring the quality over time. Finally, Great Expectations can create a data document that gives some background to the dataset based on the work Great Expectations has done.

First, let's install the needed Python library for the `great_expectations` package:

```
pip install great_expectations
```

Creating test data

Here, we use the `Faker` library to create fake data for our examples. We create the data in a pandas DataFrame, but we convert it into a Spark DataFrame.

First, we will import all of our needed packages:

```
from faker import Faker
import random
import pandas as pd
```

Now, we will create our `faker` object and create a function to produce fake data:

```
fake = Faker()
def create_rows(num=1):
    output = [{"name":fake.name(),
               "address":fake.address(),
               "email":fake.email(),
               "age":random.randint(1,100)} for x in range(num)]
    return output
```

Here, we call our function and turn it into a pandas dataframe. Then we convert the pandas dataframe into a PySpark DataFrame:

```
pandas_data_frame = pd.DataFrame(create_rows(10000))
data_frame = spark.createDataFrame(pandas_data_frame)
```

Data context

The data context is the configuration that Great Expectations will use. It can use a **YAML** or Python configuration file or even set this inline. Here, we create a data context configuration passing the `great_expectations` folder location:

```
data_context_config = DataContextConfig(
    store_backend_defaults=FilesystemStoreBackendDefaults(
        root_directory=ge_folder
    ),
)
```

Now, we pass that configuration to the `get_context` function and get a context back:

```
context = get_context(project_config=data_context_config)
```

Data source

Here, we set our configuration on our data. In the config, we define the data source name, connector name, and batch IDs. Note that we are using the Spark execution engine because we are using Spark DataFrames. There are other execution engines that you could use, such as pandas dataframes.

We now need to create a data source, but first, we need a data source config that tells Great Expectations about the data we will be using:

```
my_spark_datasource_config = {
    "name": "example_data",
    "class_name": "Datasource",
    "execution_engine": {"class_name": "SparkDFExecutionEngine"},
    "data_connectors": {
        "example_data_connector": {
            "module_name": "great_expectations.datasource.data_connector",
            "class_name": "RuntimeDataConnector",
            "batch_identifiers": [
                "pipeline_10",
                "run_id",
            ],
        }
    },
}
```

We will now use the `context` object and the `test_yaml_config` method to pass this config to the context and then add the data sources:

```
context.test_yaml_config(yaml.dump(my_spark_datasource_config))
context.add_datasource(**my_spark_datasource_config)
```

Batch request

Here, we are telling Great Expectations to run a batch request for the data we have defined. There are a variety of requests, but for our example, batch works best.

We are defining our batch request using key details. Here, I am using example data as the main characteristic:

```
batch_request = RuntimeBatchRequest(
    datasource_name="example_data",
    data_connector_name="example_data_connector",
    data_asset_name="initial_sample",
    batch_identifiers={
        "pipeline_10": "prod",
        "run_id": f"my_run_name_{datetime.date.today().strftime('%Y%m%d')}",
    },
    runtime_parameters={"batch_data": data_frame}, )
```

Validator

Now, we create a validator, which will take our Expectations suite or tests and run them against our batch request.

We will first name our suite:

```
expectation_suite_name = "example_data_suite"
```

Then, we will add the suite to the context we already created:

```
context.add_or_update_expectation_suite(expectation_suite_name=expectation_suite_name)
validator = context.get_validator(
    batch_request=batch_request,
    expectation_suite_name=expectation_suite_name,
)
```

Lastly, we will get a top output of the suite we are about to run:

```
print(validator.head())
```

Adding tests

Now, we will add some tests to create an Expectations suite. You add the tests to the validator.

Here, we add the rule that we expect no null values in the name column:

    validator.expect_column_values_to_not_be_null(column="name")

We then create a rule that says, in the age column, the values are from 0 to 100 only:

    validator.expect_column_values_to_be_between(
        column="age", min_value=0, max_value=100
)

Saving the suite

We now save our expectation suite:

    validator.save_expectation_suite(discard_failed_expectations=False)

Creating a checkpoint

Checkpoints are ways to organize and abstract the entire process to make testing your data easier. Here, we create a configuration, then we run our checkpoint.

First, we will create a name for our checkpoint:

    my_checkpoint_name = "version-0.15.50 insert_your_checkpoint_name_here"

Then, we will create the configuration for the checkpoint:

    checkpoint_config = {
        "name": my_checkpoint_name,
        "config_version": 1.0,
        "class_name": "SimpleCheckpoint",
        "run_name_template": "%Y%m%d-%H%M%S-my-run-name-template",
    }

Now, we will add the checkpoint to the context we already created:

    context.add_or_update_checkpoint(**checkpoint_config)

Lastly, we will run our checkpoint and see how our tests did:

```
checkpoint_result = context.run_checkpoint(
    checkpoint_name=my_checkpoint_name,
    validations=[
        {
            "batch_request": batch_request,
            "expectation_suite_name": expectation_suite_name,
        }
    ],
)
```

Datadocs

Datadocs are HTML documents that explain the expectation suite and the results of your tests. They can be very useful, and the following code will allow you to see the HTML page from your Databricks notebook:

```
html = ge_folder + f'uncommitted/data_docs/local_site/index.html'
with open(html, "r") as f:
    data = "".join([l for l in f])
displayHTML(data)
```

Testing new data

Now, we can reuse the same expectation suite against new data. Here, we create new data and then test it:

```
pandas_data_frame = pd.DataFrame(create_rows(10000))
data_frame = spark.createDataFrame(pandas_data_frame)
batch_request = RuntimeBatchRequest(
    datasource_name="example_data",
    data_connector_name="example_data_connector",
    data_asset_name="initial_sample",    batch_identifiers={
        "pipeline_10": "prod",
        "run_id": f"my_run_name_{datetime.date.today().strftime('%Y%m%d')}",
    },
    runtime_parameters={"batch_data": data_frame},
)
context.add_or_update_checkpoint(**checkpoint_config)
checkpoint_result = context.run_checkpoint(
    checkpoint_name=my_checkpoint_name,
    validations=[
        {
```

```
            "batch_request": batch_request,
            "expectation_suite_name": expectation_suite_name,
        }
    ],
)
```

Profiler

Can Great Expectations create tests for us? Yes, it can, by using a profiler. Here, we create a profiler using our validator:

```
from great_expectations.profile.user_configurable_profiler import
UserConfigurableProfiler
profiler = UserConfigurableProfiler(profile_dataset=validator)
```

If you would like to see what tests get created, you can with this method. Be careful as there can be very specific tests created that might not match your use case:

```
suite.get_column_expectations
```

Databricks Unity

When you start growing as an organization using Databricks, you run into the issue of having multiple workspaces with separate metastores. A metastore is really just a namespace that manages all the database objects in Databricks Spark. It can get complex dealing with multiple workspaces, and Unity's main focus was to solve those issues. Unity is a metastore that connects to all workspaces. Unity has a central governance layer that can handle object access across workspaces. Unity can also handle key management for cases where you need a key to access a storage layer. Unity also now creates data lineage on most pipeline-created tables. Oftentimes, people talk of self-service and discovery, with respect to a data catalog. Unity has many of the components for metadata but lacks some of the extra metadata features you might find in a data catalog, such as quality checks performed on the table.

Unity is a Hive metastore but on steroids, with some added custom code. Not all workspaces are connected to Unity; they must be configured to attach to Unity. The best practice for Unity currently as of writing this book is to group workspaces into cloud and region groups when attaching to Unity for cost savings.

Unity is designed to create an audit trail of all interactions with the metastore. This can be extremely useful when working with compliance agencies and when looking back to figure out what actions were taken and by whom. An example log event will have the following useful components: audit information (for example, account and timestamp), user information, workspace information, and the response, among other useful information.

Data lineage is created for all Unity registered tables, and all queries use Spark Dataframes. The lineage can't be captured if using Delta Live Tables or if the table has been renamed. Lastly, any lineage information older than 30 days is not displayed.

Unity allows for SQL to be used to define access controls on objects in the metastore. SQL is a common language in the data world for data object management, but there are many options in the Terraform API for Unity as well.

When a user is created, there is a default `deny all` on everything. As access is given for each object, the user will be able to interact with more resources. The metastore admin will be the user who defines access control for all objects in the metastore. Typically, it's best to have a group set as the metastore admin, which gets around the limitations of having a single user as the admin. Every object has an owner that is in charge of that object. It should be noted that access granted to an object that contains other objects will cause the objects in the container to have the same access granted; this also includes future objects as well.

There are a few objects that can hold other objects. I will explain each one:

- Metastore: The highest level of containment, which has a namespace organized by `catalog.database.table` with each section separated by a dot (period).
- Catalog: Catalog groups schemas or databases into logical organizational groups.
- Schema: Schemas or databases are used to organize tables.
- Table: Tables come in three types: managed, external, and views. Managed tables are tables in which the metastore manages both the location and the metadata. If you drop a managed table, it is deleted and its entry in the metastore is deleted. External tables are visible in the metastore, but dropping them only deletes the object in the metastore. Lastly, views (or global permanent views) are sets of transformations on tables that are used when accessing the view. Views are good for many different uses, such as access control, but care must be taken to avoid heavy processing costs. Views can be used to mask data and secure rows or columns with Unity based on the user's group.

The case statement with the following SQL can be used to connect your view to a group:

```
WHEN is_account_group_member('engineers') THEN TRUE
```

Access is given using the GRANT keyword. For example, the following will give analysts full access to sales:

```
GRANT ALL PRIVILEGES ON TABLE sales TO analysts;
```

Access is removed using the REVOKE keyword:

```
REVOKE ALL PRIVILEGES ON TABLE sales TO analysts;
```

Storage credentials can be set in Unity to create a clean user experience. This can be a huge game-changer for some cloud providers such as Azure, which basically allows Unity to handle all the details and lets users "magically" access data. These credentials are stored and managed using the UI or Terraform.

To view credentials in SQL, run the following:

```
SHOW STORAGE CREDENTIALS;
```

Creating a metastore

To set up Unity, you will need a S3 bucket and a role that allows access to the bucket. Unity will use this bucket for metastore-related data storage.

In your account, access the **Data** section and click **Create metastore**. You will be prompted for your bucket name and role ARN, among others. Also, note that you must be in the Premium tier to use Unity.

Figure 10.2: Metastore Unity

Now, once we click the name of our metastore, we can add our workspaces.

Figure 10.3: Unity configuration

First, let's create our schema:

```
CREATE SCHEMA chapter_10;
You can now create tables using normal SQL and grant access to those
tables.
CREATE TABLE chapter_10.chapter_10.sales
```

```
(
  id    INT,
  name STRING,
  location STRING
);
```

Delta Sharing

Let's enable Delta Sharing on our metastore.

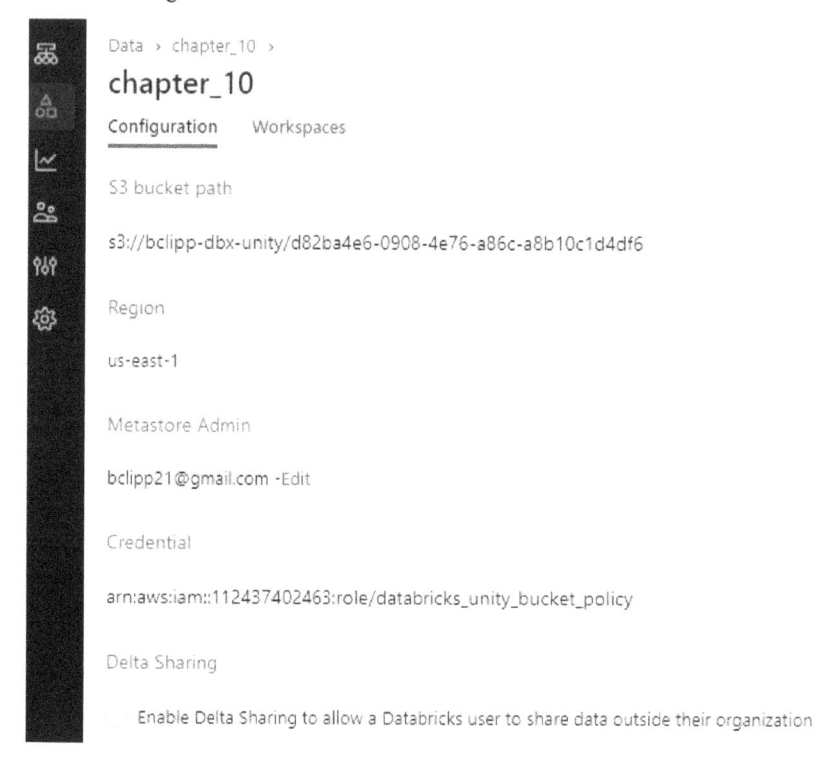

Figure 10.4: Unity Delta Sharing

Delta Sharing is an open protocol created by Databricks and is 100% open source. It allows datasets to be shared from cloud resources fully and securely. It can be used with a wide range of tools such as Excel, BI tools, Python, pandas, and Spark, to name a few. This might seem trivial, and you might think *let's just copy the data or open up access some other way*. Giving direct access is complex and often very risky from a security perspective. By using Unity, you can grant, track, and audit all Delta shares. There are limitations to Delta Sharing – the most important being that it requires the table to be a Delta Table. There are two main components of Delta Sharing: shares and recipients. A share is read-only access to a table that is registered in Delta Sharing. A recipient is a user with credentials and access to a Delta share. Another limitation of Delta Sharing is that it can't handle views.

Practical lab

Problem 1: Create a table and give access to a user through group ACL.

Create a user and group called `chapter_10_user` and `chapter_10_group`, respectively.

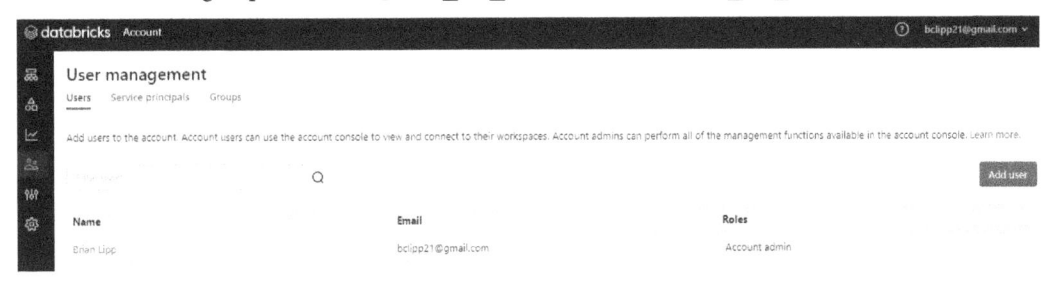

Figure 10.5: Managing users

Let's now create our user, `chapter_10_user`.

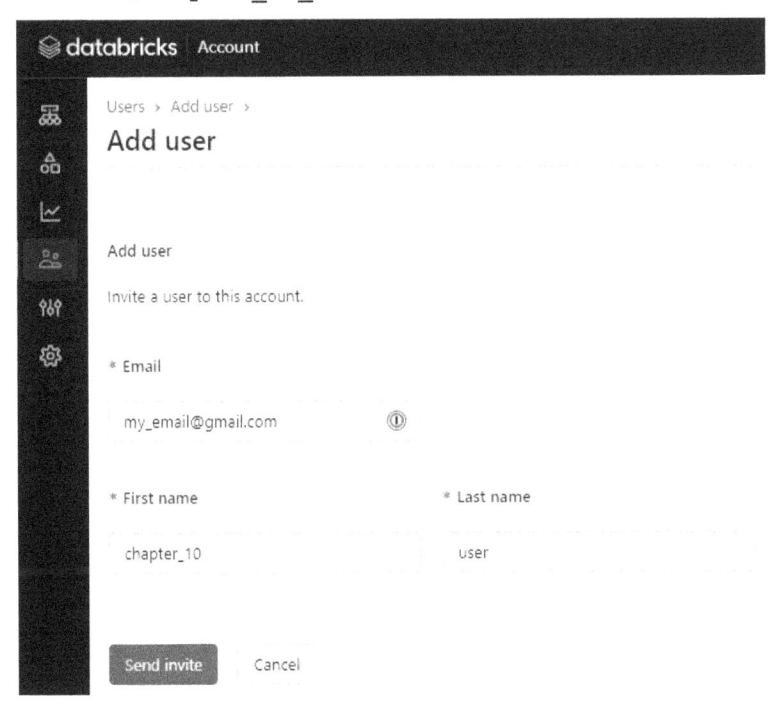

Figure 10.6: Configuring the user

Let's now create our group, `chapter_10_group`; we can click the **Groups** tab and then click **Add group**.

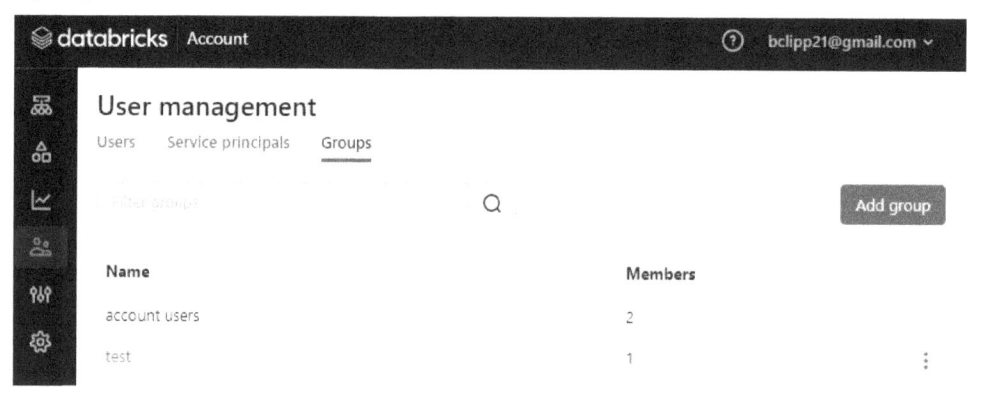

Figure 10.7: Group management

Once you type in the name, click **Save**.

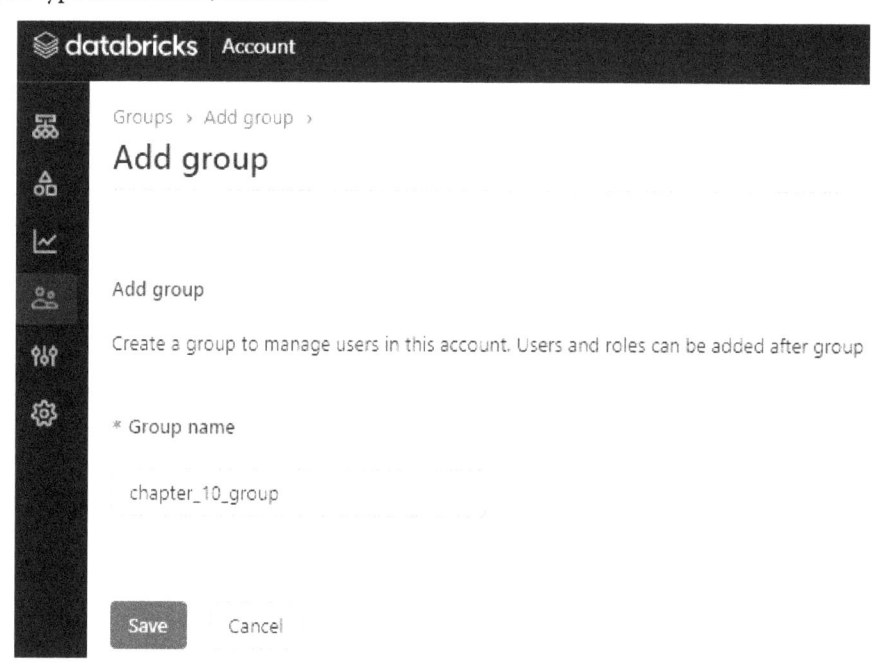

Figure 10.8: Adding a new group

Lastly, we need to add users to the group by clicking **Add members**.

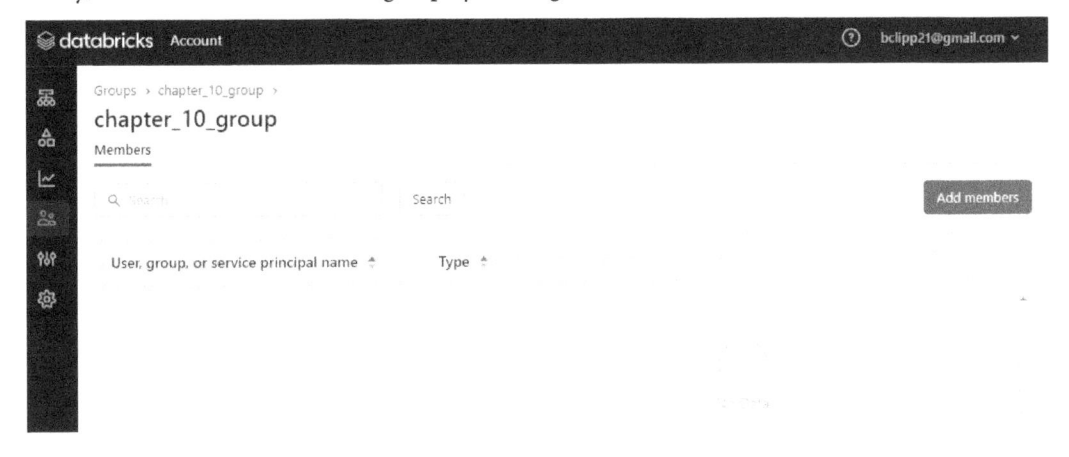

Figure 10.9: Group membership

Search for `chapter_10_user` and add the user to the group.

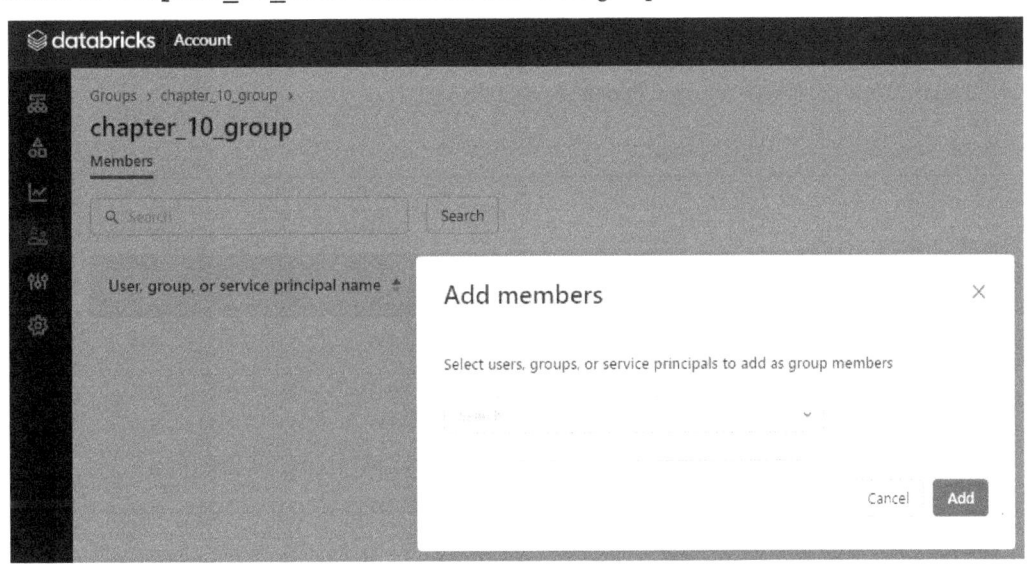

Figure 10.10: Group new user

We can now see our user is added to our group.

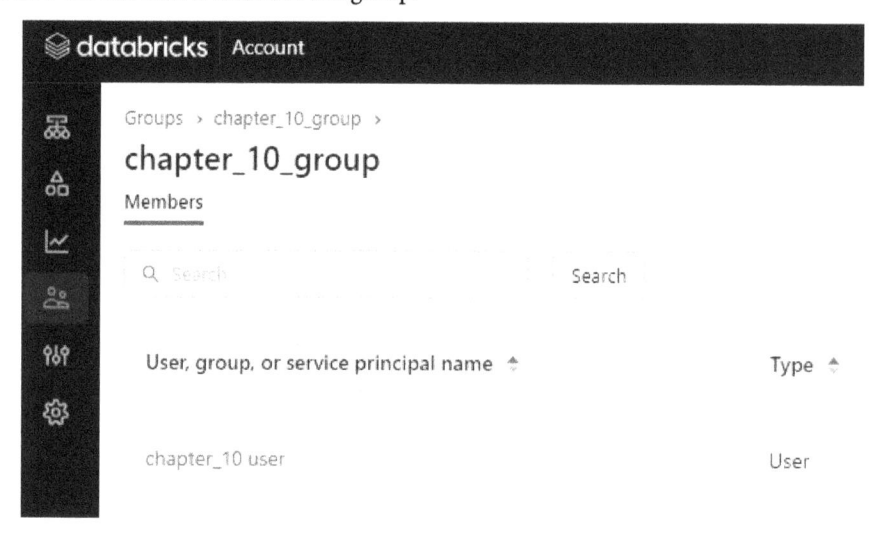

Figure 10.11: Group user management

Now, let's create a table called `engineering` and give `chapter_10_group` access to it. So here, we will run this in a notebook, which will define our table:

```
CREATE TABLE chapter_10.chapter_10.engineering
(
  ID INT,
  address STRING,
  name STRING,
  SSN INT
);
```

Now, let's run the following to give our user and group access:

```
GRANT ALL PRIVILEGES ON TABLE chapter_10.chapter_10.engineering  TO chapter_10_group;
```

Populate the table with test data.

We will first add the code to create fake data:

```
from faker import Faker
import random
import pandas as pd

fake = Faker()
```

```
def create_rows(num=1):
    output = [{"name":fake.name(),
               "address":fake.address(),
               "email":fake.email(),
               "age":random.randint(1,100)} for x in range(num)]
    return output

pandas_data_frame = pd.DataFrame(create_rows(10000))
data_frame = spark.createDataFrame(pandas_data_frame)
```

Create a suite of tests for our table.

Next, we will create our Great Expectations test suite.

First, let's import our libraries:

```
import datetime
import pandas as pd
from ruamel import yaml
from great_expectations.core.batch import RuntimeBatchRequest
from great_expectations.util import get_context
from great_expectations.data_context.types.base import (
    DataContextConfig,
    FilesystemStoreBackendDefaults,
)
```

Now, let's create our data context:

```
data_context_config = DataContextConfig(
    store_backend_defaults=FilesystemStoreBackendDefaults(
        root_directory=ge_folder
    ),
)
context = get_context(project_config=data_context_config)
```

We will now define our data source:

```
my_spark_datasource_config = {
    "name": "chapter_10_problem",
    "class_name": "Datasource",
    "execution_engine": {"class_name": "SparkDFExecutionEngine"},
    "data_connectors": {
        "example_data_connector": {
            "module_name": "great_expectations.datasource.data_connector",
            "class_name": "RuntimeDataConnector",
```

```
                "batch_identifiers": [
                    "pipeline_10",
                    "run_id",
                ],
            }
        },
    }
    context.test_yaml_config(yaml.dump(my_spark_datasource_config))
    context.add_datasource(**my_spark_datasource_config)
```

Next, we set up the batch run request:

```
batch_request = RuntimeBatchRequest(
    datasource_name=" chapter_10_problem",
    data_connector_name="example_data_connector",
    data_asset_name="initial_sample",
    batch_identifiers={
        "pipeline_10": "prod",
        "run_id": f"my_run_name_{datetime.date.today().
strftime('%Y%m%d')}",
    },
    runtime_parameters={"batch_data": data_frame},
)
```

Lastly, we will create our test suite and validate our data:

```
expectation_suite_name = " chapter_10_problem_suite"
context.add_or_update_expectation_suite(expectation_suite_
name=expectation_suite_name)
validator = context.get_validator(
    batch_request=batch_request,
    expectation_suite_name=expectation_suite_name,
)
validator.expect_column_values_to_not_be_null(column="name")
validator.expect_column_values_to_be_between(
    column="age", min_value=0, max_value=100
)
validator.save_expectation_suite(discard_failed_expectations=False)
```

Summary

We have climbed through many techniques for our data platform. Let's take some time to review those ideas as we close this chapter. We discussed the ins and outs of data governance basics. We transitioned into data catalogs and the importance of having a metadata catalog. With data catalogs, we also discussed data lineage or the evolutionary path of each column in our data. We next covered basic security in a Databricks platform using grants. We then tackled data quality and testing for quality using the Great Expectations Python package. Data quality is a complex topic, and this approach addresses one direction. Other directions include allowing users to report errors or using complex AI systems. Finally, we delved into Databricks Unity Catalog, an enhanced Hive metastore-based product offering metastore capability across many workspaces, among many other growing features.

We have yet to cover all the theory chapters and will look at a comprehensive lab across two chapters. We will also cover new technologies to keep things interesting.

11
Building out the Groundwork

In this chapter, we will set up our environment and build the template for all the hard work we will do in the final chapter on our project. Some of the tooling we will use might be new and we will introduce it with explanations. The main tooling introduction is to GitHub Actions, which is a CI tool used to automate code-related tasks. We will be using this to run code checks in all of our repos. Poetry will be used to manage our Python code and package it into a PyPI repo. Organizing our code like this helps in many ways and allows us to share the code across systems. Lastly, we will be working with the PyPi public system to deploy and manage our Python packages. This isn't the normal process, but to avoid creating a private server, this public service was used. In production, typically, you normally use a hosted PyPI service or hosts your own server. Those tools were chosen simply to introduce something new in the final project. As mentioned before, all the tools are very generic and can be replaced with alternatives if desired. By the end, you will have a **Continuous Integration** (**CI**)-enabled environment for both your Python and Terraform code. The goal at the end of the chapter will be to have a working template, with which we can build the rest of our projects.

Technical requirements

The tooling used in this chapter is tied to the tech stack chosen for the book. All vendors should offer a free trial account.

I will be using the following:

- Databricks
- GitHub
- Terraform
- PyPI

Setting up your environment

Before we begin our chapter, let's take the time to set up our working environment.

The Databricks CLI

The first step is to install the `databricks-cli` tool using the `pip` Python package manager:

```
pip install databricks-cli
```

Let's validate that everything has been installed correctly. If this command produces the tool version, then everything is working correctly:

```
Databricks -v
```

Now let's set up authentication. First, go into the Databricks UI and generate a **personal access token** (**PAT**). The following command will ask for the host created for your Databricks instance and the created token:

```
databricks configure --token
```

We can quickly determine whether the CLI is set up correctly by running the following command, and if no error is returned, you have a working setup:

```
databricks fs ls
```

Git

Git will be used in this chapter and there are many ways to install it. I would recommend using https://git-scm.com/download/ for Git.

When you run `git version`, you should see a message explaining your Git version.

I also prefer to set the color of the output when using the Git CLI:

```
git config --global color.ui auto
```

Once installed, you should set up authentication with your GitHub account. If you do not have one, you will need one for this chapter:

```
git config --global user.name <>
git config --global user.email <>
```

If you prefer to set the username for a specific repo, first, browse the repo and run the following:

```
git config color.ui auto
git config user.email <>
```

GitHub

I will be using GitHub and its CLI in this chapter. First, let's create a PAT. You have a few options to choose from when authenticating with GitHub. Ideally, SSH is the best choice I believe, because SSH is more secure. For simplicity purposes, we will be using a PAT. Now, let's set up the GitHub CLI from `https://cli.github.com/` and follow the directions to install it.

You should see a help menu when you now run the gh command.

Let's now set up the authentication for the GitHub CLI:

```
gh auth login
```

You will get the following set of questions:

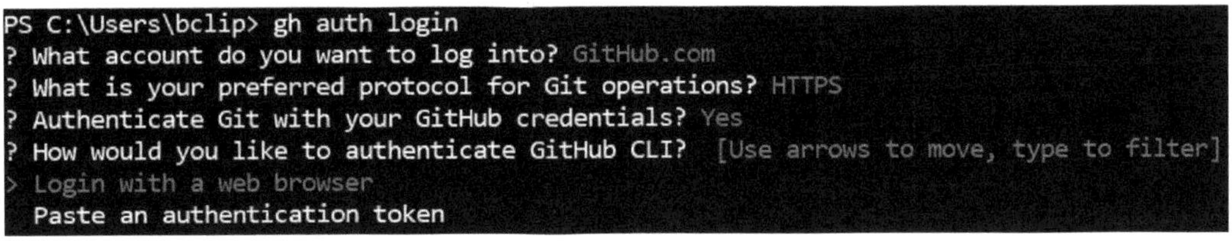

```
PS C:\Users\bclip> gh auth login
? What account do you want to log into? GitHub.com
? What is your preferred protocol for Git operations? HTTPS
? Authenticate Git with your GitHub credentials? Yes
? How would you like to authenticate GitHub CLI?  [Use arrows to move, type to filter]
> Login with a web browser
  Paste an authentication token
```

Figure 11.1: GitHub authentication

The CLI will give you an access code. When your browser opens up, type that code into the browser. You will then be presented with the following screen:

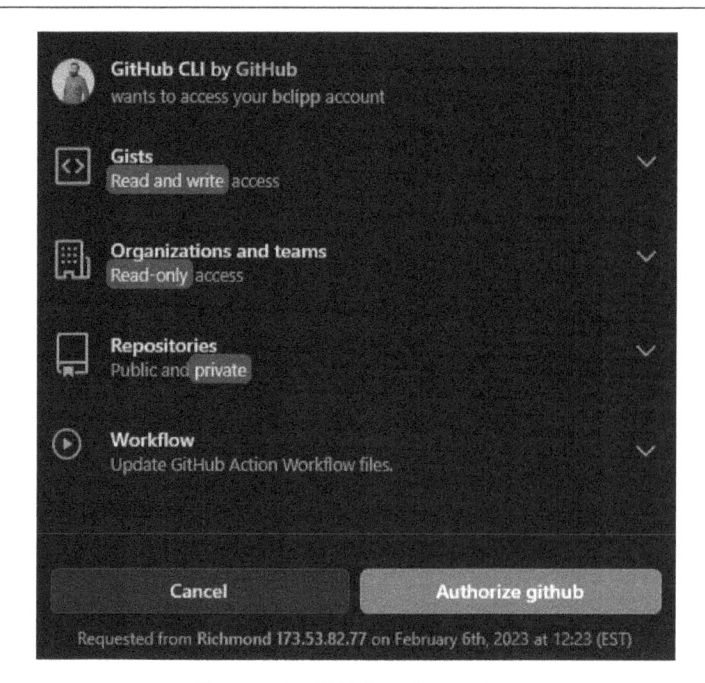

Figure 11.2: GitHub authorization

You are now set up with the GitHub CLI.

Let's create our repo using the GitHub CLI:

Figure 11.3: GitHub repo create

Now, we have run the `gh repo create` command and we have answered the questions using the example screenshot provided.

pre-commit

We will be using `pre-commit` to run basic quality checks on our code before committing it to GitHub.

Let's install `pre-commit` and our code quality tools using `pip`:

```
poetry add black flake8 pre-commit pylint --dev
```

Notice we are setting these tools to be in the dev group. It will not be used by the application itself.

Terraform

We will be using Terraform Cloud and the Terraform CLI. Let's first set up the Terraform CLI by following the instructions at this link: https://developer.hashicorp.com/terraform/tutorials/aws-get-started/install-cli.

Next, we will need to create a Terraform Cloud account at https://app.terraform.io/session.

Next, let's connect the CLI to our Cloud account and run `terraform login`. You will see the following screenshot:

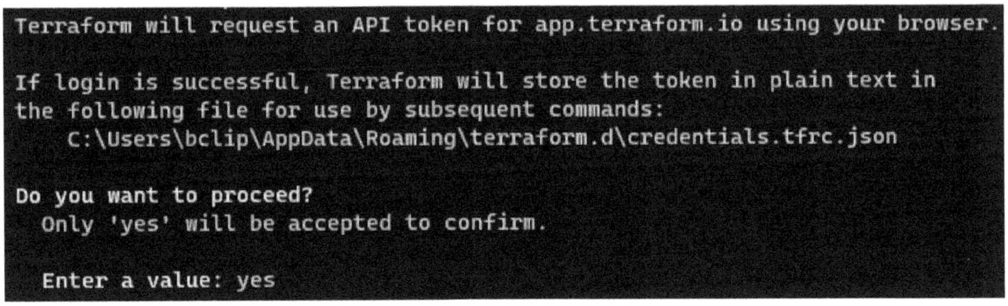

```
Terraform will request an API token for app.terraform.io using your browser.

If login is successful, Terraform will store the token in plain text in
the following file for use by subsequent commands:
    C:\Users\bclip\AppData\Roaming\terraform.d\credentials.tfrc.json

Do you want to proceed?
  Only 'yes' will be accepted to confirm.

  Enter a value: yes
```

Figure 11.4: Terraform CLI token request

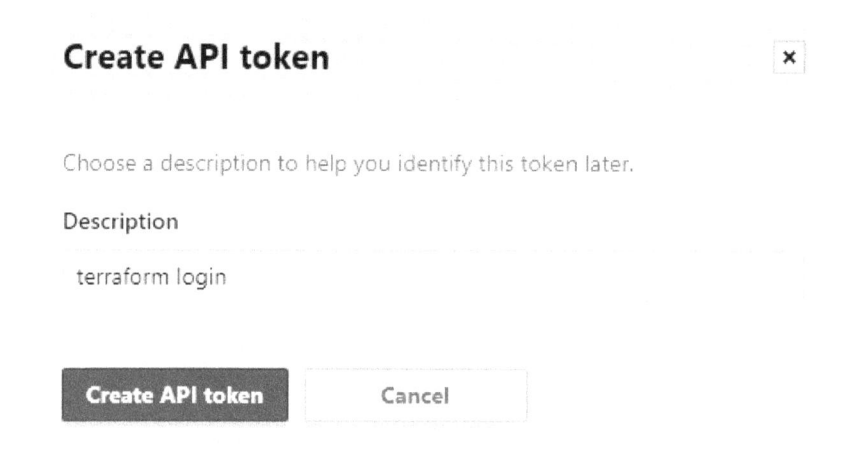

Figure 11.5: Terraform CLI token creation

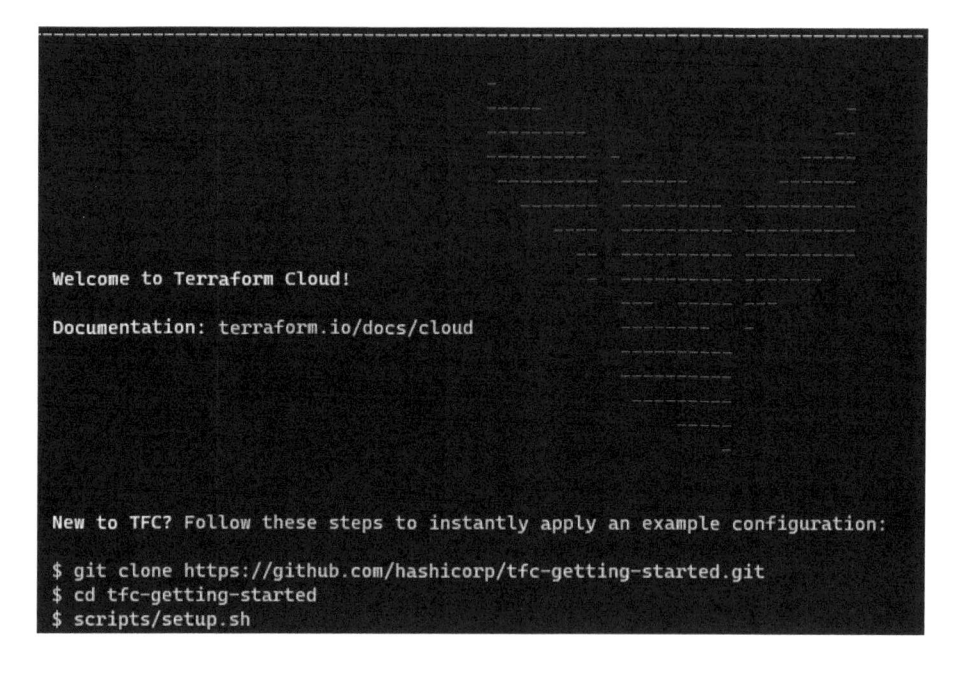

Figure 11.6: Terraform CLI token setup complete

PyPI

So, we won't set up a private Python PyPI server. Instead, we will opt for simplicity and just use the public PyPI infrastructure. This obviously would not be the path to go down in production, but it makes learning very simple.

All you will need is a user registered at `https://pypi.org/account/register/`.

The only real requirement you will need on the PyPI website will be an API token. To create an API token, just navigate to **Account settings**.

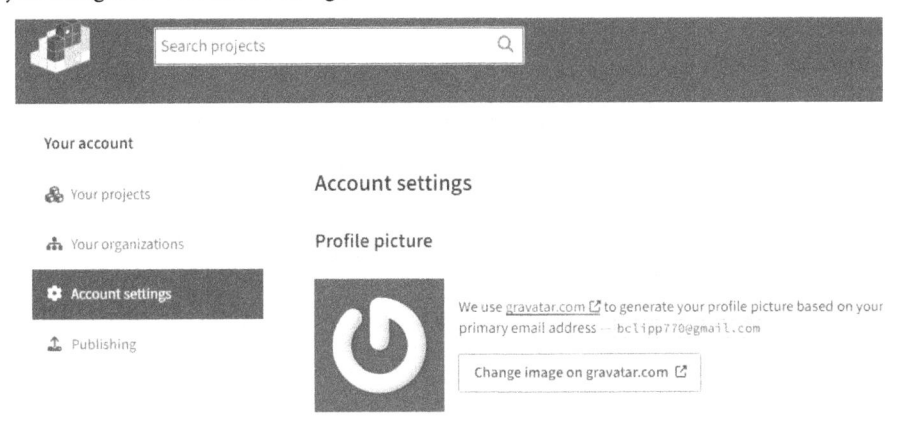

Figure 11.7: PyPI login

Then, click **Add API token** and it will present you with a new token, which you must securely copy (do not commit to Git!).

Figure 11.8: PyPI token setup

Creating GitHub repos

So, we are going to set up our GitHub infrastructure and use GitHub Actions. First things first, let's create our repositories. They will have empty README files. I am going to create five repositories, one for infrastructure as code, one for docs, one for an ML application, one for an ETL application, and one to manage DDL:

- `infra`: `gh repo create infra-project --public --add-readme`
- `docs`: `gh repo create docs-project --public --add-readme`
- `ML-Job`: `gh repo create ML-Jobs-project --public --add-readme`
- `ETL-Jobs`: `gh repo create ETL-Jobs-project --public --add-readme`
- `SCHEMA-Jobs`: `gh repo create SCHEMA-Jobs-project --public --add-readme`

Now that every repo is created, let's introduce a new tool we will use on all the Python repositories. We will use Poetry to manage our projects, which is a very easy-to-use package management system. It will also allow you to deploy Python applications very easily to PyPI. To install Poetry currently, you run a script. Poetry doesn't manage your Python version, so that's something you will need to manage yourself. The safest thing to always do is navigate to Poetry's website and follow the directions there: https://python-poetry.org/docs/

Currently, I run `curl -sSL https://install.python-poetry.org | python3 -`.

After that, clone each repository as follows:

```
git clone <repo url>
```

Then, one by one, navigate into each repository and set up your new Poetry project:

```
poetry new ml-jobs
poetry new schema-jobs
poetry new etl-jobs
```

Once we have our `pre-commit` YAML set to install all the needed components, run the following. Notice we are running everything within our Poetry managed environment:

```
poetry run pre-commit install
```

You can make `pre-commit` test your whole repo by using the following command:

```
poetry run pre-commit run --all-files
```

Let's set up our token now so we don't need to do it later. It will need to be done in each repo using Poetry, and, within each repo, the Poetry-created folder (created by the new command we ran before):

```
poetry config pypi-token.pypi your-api-token-from-pypi
```

Later, we will use the following commands to manually deploy our PyPI packages.

`build` just creates our wheels locally. They will be in the `dist` folder, ready for deployment to `pypi`:

```
poetry build
```

We can publish and build in one step using the following command:

```
poetry publish --build
```

Terraform setup

We will be using the infrastructure repo to store our infrastructure as code. I will go through the Terraform code in a little bit, but keep in mind we are using `pre-commit` on this repo also. It will reformat, lint, and syntax check your Terraform code. I can't stress enough how useful this is, and I wish more teams followed this approach.

Initial file setup

I'm going to shy away from repeating the exact same setup for each Python repo given, in this chapter, we will only have the base template created. Instead, I will walk through one repo and the infrastructure repo and explain the key files.

I create a visible tree of the folder structure I used in Windows. The majority of the work is done in Linux but here and there, I am switching to Windows:

```
tree /f
```

Schema repository

Here, we can see the basic folder structure. I have removed anything not committed or not useful to explain. One example might be `pytest` cache folders. I will show each Python repository to reinforce and make everything clear:

```
    .gitignore
    │   .pre-commit-config.yaml
    │   mypy.ini
    │   README.md
    │
    ├───.github
```

```
│   └──workflows
│           python-app.yml
│
└──schema-jobs
    │   poetry.lock
    │   pyproject.toml
    │   README.md
    │
    ├──dist
    │       schema_jobs-0.1.0-py3-none-any.whl
    │       schema_jobs-0.1.0.tar.gz
    │
    ├──schema_jobs
    │       __init__.py
    │
    └──tests
            __init__.py
```

Schema repository

Here, I added a few wheels, which are stored in the `dist` folder:

```
│   poetry.lock
│   pyproject.toml
│   README.md
│   __init__.py
│
├──dist
│       etl_jobs-0.1.0-py3-none-any.whl
│       etl_jobs-0.1.0.tar.gz
│       etl_jobs-0.1.1-py3-none-any.whl
│       etl_jobs-0.1.1.tar.gz
│
├──etl_jobs
│       main.py
│       __init__.py
│
└──tests
        __init__.py
```

ML repository

Finally, our ML repo will look basically the same as the others:

```
│   .gitignore
│   .pre-commit-config.yaml
│   mypy.ini
│   README.md
│
├───.github
│   └───workflows
│           python-app.yml
│
│
└───ml-jobs
    │   poetry.lock
    │   pyproject.toml
    │   README.md
    │
    │
    ├───dist
    │       ml_jobs-0.1.0-py3-none-any.whl
    │       ml_jobs-0.1.0.tar.gz
    │
    ├───ml_jobs
    │       .pylintrc
    │       __init__.py
    │
    └───tests
            __init__.py
```

Here are a few key files we are creating. They will be almost identical in each repository so I will only share them once generally.

mypy is a very useful type-enforcement tool for Python. Here, we are telling mypy basic defaults and to ignore errors in any libraries we use since we just want to check the code we write:

```
mypy.ini
[mypy]
warn_redundant_casts = True
warn_unused_ignores = True
[mypy-*]
ignore_missing_imports = True
```

Next, we will look at our `pre-commit` YAML for Python repositories. Note that we are using `mypi`, `black`, `pylint`, `isort`, and `flake8`. Ideally, you want to format your code first and then lint it. Also, we have passed useful arguments such as for `black` compatibility, among others. Another useful option that I didn't include was to run your unity tests in `pre-commit`. This should be pretty fast and will also really reduce the amount of failing unit tests in your CI:

```yaml
.pre-commit-config.yaml
repos:
-   repo: https://github.com/pre-commit/pre-commit-hooks
    rev: v2.3.0
    hooks:
    -   id: check-yaml
    -   id: end-of-file-fixer
    -   id: trailing-whitespace
-   repo: https://github.com/psf/black
    rev: 22.10.0
    hooks:
    -   id: black
        exclude: notebooks/
-   repo: https://github.com/pycqa/isort
    rev: 5.12.0
    hooks:
        - id: isort
          args: ["--profile", "black"]
-   repo:   https://github.com/pycqa/flake8
    rev: 4.0.1
    hooks:
        - id: flake8
-   repo: https://github.com/PyCQA/pylint
    rev: v2.15.9
    hooks:
    -   id: pylint
        args:
            ["ml-jobs"]
-   repo: https://github.com/pre-commit/mirrors-mypy
    rev: v0.961
    hooks:
    -   id: mypy
```

Poetry is managed by a project TOML file. I would note the name, version, and packages laid out in this file, as well as the dependencies we have set up in the development group:

```
pyproject.toml
[tool.poetry]
name = "etl-jobs"
version = "0.1.1"
description = ""
authors = ["Brian L <XXXXXXXXX>"]
readme = "README.md"
packages = [{include = "etl_jobs"}]
[tool.poetry.dependencies]
python = "^3.9"
[tool.poetry.group.dev.dependencies]
black = "^23.3.0"
flake8 = "^6.0.0"
pre-commit = "^3.3.1"
pylint = "^2.17.4"
[build-system]
requires = ["poetry-core"]
build-backend = "poetry.core.masonry.api"
```

python repository python-app.yml

Each Python repository will have a CI YAML file created that uses GitHub Actions. Important things to note are that the action is run only on pull requests and that we are walking through setting up `pre-commit` and then testing our full repository to make sure everything attempting to be merged passes:

```
name: Python application
on:
  push:
    branches: [ "main" ]
  pull_request:
    branches: [ "main" ]
permissions:
  contents: read
jobs:
  build:
    runs-on: ubuntu-latest
    steps:
    - uses: actions/checkout@v3
    - name: Set up Python 3.11
      uses: actions/setup-python@v3
      with:
```

```
        python-version: "3.11"
    - name: Install Poetry
      uses: snok/install-poetry@v1
    - name: Install dependencies
      working-directory: ./etl-jobs
      run: |
        poetry install
    - name: Run Pre-commit
      working-directory: ./etl-jobs
      run: |
        poetry run pre-commit install
        poetry run pre-commit run --all-files
    - name: Test with pytest
      working-directory: ./etl-jobs
      run: |
        # poetry run poetry run pytest
```

Infrastructure repository

Let's finally take a look at our Terraform repository. Here, we will look at files that are unique to our infrastructure-as-code work:

```
    |   .gitignore
    |   .pre-commit-config.yaml
    |   main.tf
    |   README.md
    |
    ├───.github
    |   └───workflows
    |           python-app.yml
    main.tf
```

`main.tf` is a very generic way to set things up. It would be more pragmatic to create modules and separate state files for groupings of infrastructure. This would be to complex for this book, so please be sure to follow the best practices when managing your code grouping in production.

Initially, we will set up our hosted Terraform Cloud config. I love Terraform Cloud. It takes all the headaches out of Terraform. Without it, you will need to manage a state file (and when it gets corrupt, you need to deal with that ball of wax). You will need to also manage locking so that multiple users are not deploying at the same time:

```
terraform {
  required_version = ">= 1.3.9"
  cloud {
```

```
    organization = "brians_stuff"
    workspaces {
      name = "cli"
    }
  }
```

Next, we will set up our provider, Databricks. You can always look up the provider documentation to better understand its API. Honestly, this provider can be a little confusing sometimes, but looking through the docs and then testing it out always is a clear path:

```
  required_providers {
    databricks = {
      source  = "databricks/databricks"
      version = "1.0.0"
    }
  }
}
```

Now, we will set up our HOST and TOKEN variables that will allow us to talk to Databricks. The host again is the URL used to access the Databricks workspace and the token is created for API access. We set this all up in *Chapter 8* and provided those variables to Terraform:

```
variable "HOST" {
  type = string
}
variable "TOKEN" {
  type = string
}
provider "databricks" {
  host  = var.HOST
  token = var.TOKEN
}
```

The next group of code is to set up our shared clusters. You could as an alternative create ephemeral job clusters, but the API at the time of writing this didn't support those options. So, if that's required, you will need to manually modify your workflows after deployment. Hopefully, this will be added very shortly:

```
data "databricks_spark_version" "latest_lts" {
  long_term_support = true
}
data "databricks_spark_version" "gpu_ml" {
  ml = true
}
resource "databricks_library" "jobs_cluster_lib_etl" {
```

```
    cluster_id = databricks_cluster.tiny-packt.id
    pypi {
      package = "etl-jobs==0.1.1"
    }
  }
  resource "databricks_library" "jobs_cluster_lib_schema" {
    cluster_id = databricks_cluster.tiny-packt.id
    pypi {
      package = "schema-jobs==0.1.0"
    }
  }
  resource "databricks_library" "jobs_cluster_lib_ml" {
    cluster_id = databricks_cluster.tiny-packt-ml.id
    pypi {
      package = "ml-jobs==0.1.0"
    }
  }
  resource "databricks_cluster" "tiny-packt" {
    cluster_name            = "tiny-packt-etl"
    spark_version           = data.databricks_spark_version.latest_lts.id
    node_type_id            = "m5.large"
    autotermination_minutes = 10
    autoscale {
      min_workers = 1
      max_workers = 2
    }
    aws_attributes {
      first_on_demand         = 1
      availability            = "SPOT_WITH_FALLBACK"
      zone_id                 = "us-west-2b"
      spot_bid_price_percent  = 100
      ebs_volume_type         = "GENERAL_PURPOSE_SSD"
      ebs_volume_count        = 3
      ebs_volume_size         = 100
    }
  }
  resource "databricks_cluster" "tiny-packt-ml" {
    cluster_name            = "tiny-packt-ml"
    node_type_id            = "g4dn.xlarge"
    autotermination_minutes = 10
    spark_version           = data.databricks_spark_version.gpu_ml.id
    autoscale {
      min_workers = 1
```

```
    max_workers = 2
  }
  aws_attributes {
    first_on_demand        = 1
    availability           = "SPOT_WITH_FALLBACK"
    zone_id                = "us-west-2b"
    spot_bid_price_percent = 100
    ebs_volume_type        = "GENERAL_PURPOSE_SSD"
    ebs_volume_count       = 3
    ebs_volume_size        = 100
  }
}
```

Next, we have our workflows, or, as the API currently calls them, multi-task jobs.

The jobs are pretty basic. Note that you can add a schedule, an email notification on a status, where the wheel will be pulled from, and the entry point of the job:

```
resource "databricks_job" "etl" {
  name                = "etl"
  max_concurrent_runs = 1
  email_notifications {
    on_success = ["XXXX@gmail.com", "XXXX@gmail.com"]
    on_start   = ["XXXX@gmail.com"]
    on_failure = ["XXXX@gmail.com"]
  }
  task {
    task_key            = "a_extract"
    existing_cluster_id = databricks_cluster.tiny-packt.id
    python_wheel_task {
      package_name = "etl_jobs"
      entry_point  = "main"
    }
    timeout_seconds           = 1000
    min_retry_interval_millis = 900000
    max_retries               = 1
  }
  task {
    task_key            = "b_ransform_and_Load"
    existing_cluster_id = databricks_cluster.tiny-packt.id
    depends_on {
      task_key = "a_extract"
    }
    python_wheel_task {
```

```
          package_name = "etl_jobs"
          entry_point  = "main"
        }
        timeout_seconds            = 1000
        min_retry_interval_millis  = 900000
        max_retries                = 1
      }
    }
```

This job will look very similar to the first. If you know HCL, then you could reduce the duplicate code, but to keep things simple, let's just manually create the job code:

```
resource "databricks_job" "schema-jobs" {
  name                 = "schema-jobs"
  max_concurrent_runs  = 1
  # job schedule
  #schedule {
  #  quartz_cron_expression = "0 0 0 ? 1/1 * *" # cron schedule of job
  #  timezone_id = "UTC"
  # }
  email_notifications {
    on_success = ["XXXXX@gmail.com", "XXXXX@gmail.com"]
    on_start   = ["XXXXX@gmail.com"]
    on_failure = ["XXXXX@gmail.com"]
  }
  task {
    task_key            = "schema-jobs"
    existing_cluster_id = databricks_cluster.tiny-packt.id
    python_wheel_task {
      package_name = "schema_jobs"
      entry_point  = "main"
    }
    timeout_seconds            = 1000
    min_retry_interval_millis  = 900000
    max_retries                = 1
  }
}
resource "databricks_job" "ml-jobs" {
  name                 = "ml-jobs"
  max_concurrent_runs  = 1
  # job schedule
  #schedule {
  #  quartz_cron_expression = "0 0 0 ? 1/1 * *" # cron schedule of job
  #  timezone_id = "UTC"
```

```
  # }
  email_notifications {
    on_success = ["XXXXX@gmail.com", "XXXXX@gmail.com"]
    on_start   = ["XXXXX@gmail.com"]
    on_failure = ["XXXXX@gmail.com"]
  }
  task {
    task_key           = "ml-jobs"
    existing_cluster_id = databricks_cluster.tiny-packt.id
    python_wheel_task {
      package_name = "ml_jobs"
      entry_point  = "main"
    }
    timeout_seconds           = 1000
    min_retry_interval_millis = 900000
    max_retries               = 1
  }
}
pre-commit-config.yaml
```

Next, let's look at our `pre-commit` YAML file; it differs from the Python versions simply because we are calling Terraform commands to format, lint, and check for any known issues in our code:

```
repos:
  - repo: https://github.com/antonbabenko/pre-commit-terraform
    rev: "v1.79.1"
    hooks:
      - id: terraform_fmt
      - id: terraform_tflint
      - id: terraform_validate
      - id: terraform_tfsec
python-app.yaml
```

Lastly, let's take a look at our GitHub Actions YAML. This action will run on pull requests like the Python project versions. It differs in that it installs some useful added components that `pre-commit` is calling:

```
name: Python application
on:
  push:
    branches: [ "main" ]
  pull_request:
    branches: [ "main" ]
permissions:
```

```
      contents: read
jobs:
  build:
    runs-on: ubuntu-latest
    steps:
    - uses: actions/checkout@v3
    - name: Set up Python 3.11
      uses: actions/setup-python@v3
      with:
        python-version: "3.11"
    - run: pip install pre-commit
    - name: Run Pre-commit
      run: |
        curl -s https://raw.githubusercontent.com/terraform-linters/tflint/master/install_linux.sh | bash
        curl -s https://raw.githubusercontent.com/aquasecurity/tfsec/master/scripts/install_linux.sh | bash
        pre-commit install
        pre-commit run --all-files
```

Summary

We wrapped up a very fun chapter deep-diving into several tools to set up our new project. We set up GitHub, Git, Terraform, `pre-commit`, and a PyPI project. We also started the code scaffolding for all our apps. It might not be clear at first, but these initial steps are some of the most important in any project. In the next chapter, we will look at the Python code for each app and how the users will interact with our data.

12
Completing Our Project

So, we are at the end of the project, and we now need to add meat to our work. We have built the scaffold of our project, but we don't really have anything else at the moment. We still need to create code for all of our apps. When we have done this, we will deploy the code to the public PyPI servers. This will be critical because we are now going to pull our pipeline code from a code repository, which is the ideal scenario. We will also set up CI for our code, which will do the checking and scanning of our code. Given the limited space, we will not be covering deployment using the CI of pipeline code, but this is the next step in that process. We will also cover schema management and some limited data governance. The goal is to have a working example of a data pipeline that is in line with something you would see in production.

This chapter covers the following topics:

- Documentation
- Faking data with Mockaroo
- Managing our schemas with code
- Building our data pipeline application
- Creating our machine learning application
- Displaying our data with dashboards

Technical requirements

The tooling used in this chapter is tied to the technology stack chosen for the book. All vendors should offer a free trial account.

I will be using the following:

- Databricks
- GitHub

- Terraform
- PyPI

Documentation

When starting out on a project, it's good to catch up on the basics of what the project is about and how it will be interacted with. Here, we will lay out our schemas and high-level C4 System Context diagrams. For these diagrams, I used PlantUML code, which is another simple language for creating diagrams. PyCharm will display them and check your syntax so it is very easy to work with.

Schema diagram

Schema diagrams are very useful for users who want to get a basic understanding of the data and how they might use it. Normally, in a schema diagram, you will find the field names, the types, and sometimes sample data. This type of diagram works well for structured data with few columns. If your data is semi-structured or has a significant number of columns, I would avoid using this diagram and use something in JSON format instead.

Here we have 3 tables in our Bronze layer: `sales`, `machine_raw`, and `sap_BSEG`.

N8j2:float	42mj:float	6tk3:binary
11.329	13.523	1
74.375	24.277	1
71.942	55.736	0

Figure 12.1: Bronze layer 1

MANDT:string	BUKRS:string	BELNR:string	GJAHR:float	BUZEI:float
sdfs	guyu5t	1.5	4.3	1.6
weth	fghe	1.1	4.2	14.3
fdghdf	dfger	12.4	4.8	1.9

Figure 12.2: Bronze layer 2

ORDERNUMBER:int	SALE:float	ORDERDATE:int	STATUS:binary	CUSTOMERNAME:string	PHONE:string	ADDRESSLINE:
2	55.736	1684115918	1	John Smith	8348552345	123 anystreet

Figure 12.3: Bronze layer 3

ADDRESSLINE:string	CITY:string	STATE:string	STORE:string
123 anystreet	New York	NY	234

Figure 12.4: Bronze layer 4

As stated earlier, to create these diagrams, I used PlantUML, which is very simple to read and should be stored in a GitHub repository. The advantage of using PlantUML or similar tools over GUI-based tools is that this can be done in a CI process, with pull requests and automated deployments:

```
@startuml
<style>
class {
    BackgroundColor transparent
    linecolor transparent
}
</style>


hide empty members
hide circle

class "<#lightblue,#black>|=
N8j2:float   |=  42mj:float   |=   6tk3:binary   |\n\
<#white>|    11.329   |    13.523    |  1  |\n\
<#white>|    74.375   |    24.277    |  1  |\n\
<#white>|    71.942   |    55.736    |  0  |" as machine_raw {
}


class "<#lightblue,#black>|=  MANDT:string   |=  BUKRS:string   |=
BELNR:string   |= GJAHR:float  |=  BUZEI:float   |\n\
<#white>|   sdfs   |   guyu5t   |  1.5  |  4.3| 1.6 |\n\
<#white>|   weth   |   fghe    |  1.1  |  4.2| 14.3 |\n\
<#white>|   fdghdf  |   dfger   |  12.4  |  4.8| 1.9 |" as sap_BSEG {
}


class "<#lightblue,#black>|= ORDERNUMBER:int  |=SALE:float  |=
ORDERDATE:int  |=STATUS:binary  |= CUSTOMERNAME:string  |= PHONE:string
|=ADDRESSLINE:string  |= CITY:string  |= STATE:string  |= STORE:string
|\n\
<#white>|   2   |   55.736   |   1684115918 |  1  | John Smith  | 8348552345 |
123 anystreet  | New York  | NY| 234|" as sales {
}


@enduml
```

262　Completing Our Project

Next, we have our Gold sales table and the PlantUML code, but first, let's see our diagram:

CUSTOMERNAME:string	AVG: float	TOTAL:float
2	55.736	1684115918

Figure 12.5: Gold layer

Our PlantUML code here should look very similar; we are adding some HTML for added visual improvements:

```
@startuml
<style>
class {
    BackgroundColor transparent
    linecolor transparent
}
</style>
hide empty members
hide circle
class "<#lightblue,#black>|= CUSTOMERNAME:string  |= AVG:
float|=TOTAL:float  |\n\
<#white>|   2   |   55.736   |   1684115918  |" as sales {
}
@enduml
```

Finally, we have our Silver `machine_raw` table with PlantUML.

Here, we have our final schema diagram created by PlantUML:

N8j2:float	42mj:float	6tk3:binary	engine type
11.329	13.523	1	153-1
74.375	24.277	1	1805-1
71.942	55.736	0	4,009-1

Figure 12.6: Silver layer

Here is the PlantUML code for this schema diagram:

```
@startuml
<style>
class {
    BackgroundColor transparent
    linecolor transparent
}
</style>
hide empty members
```

```
hide circle

class
"<#lightblue,#black>|=  N8j2:float   |=  42mj:float   |=  6tk3:binary  |=
engine_type|\n\
<#white>|    11.329   |   13.523    | 1 |153-1  |\n\
<#white>|    74.375   |   24.277    | 1 |1805-1|\n\
<#white>|    71.942   |   55.736    | 0 |4,009-1|" as machine_raw {
}
@enduml
```

The PlantUML code we are using can be divided into two groups. The first is HTML for the background, borders, and similar components. Feel free to adjust these as needed for your preference. The second group is simple PlantUML. We are using fake values for clarity for those who might be learning about the tables for the first time. Be sure to update the data that you are using if the types change.

C4 System Context diagram

Here we have our basic C4 System Context diagram. C4 is a universal architecture diagramming model. There are many diagrams you can use in a project and I recommend exploring all of them for your projects. To save space, I will only show the System Context diagram. In this diagram, we are concerned with external entities and how they interact with our app, as well as any tools that get used. In our case, we have three types of users and a data delivery tool that all interact with our data platform:

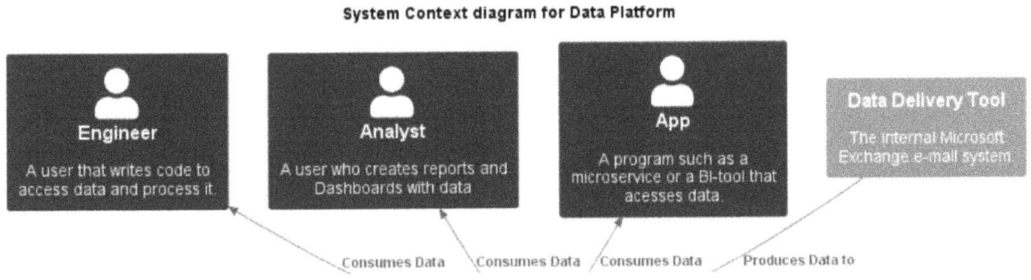

Figure 12.7: C4 System Context A

264　Completing Our Project

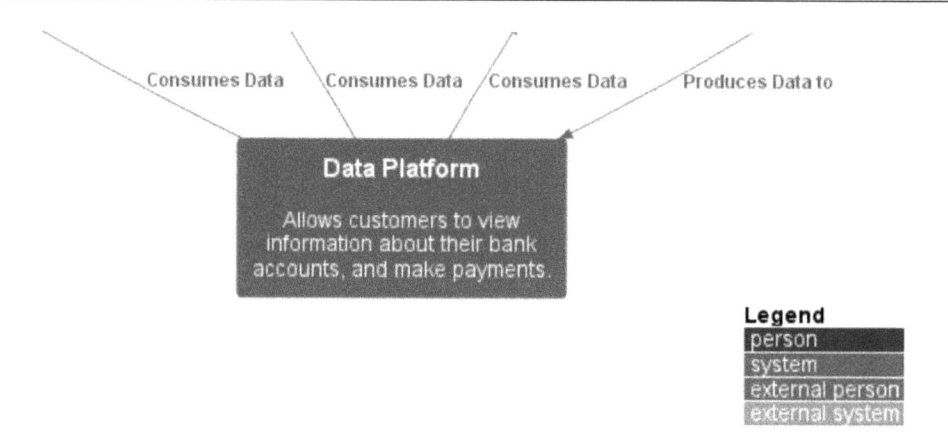

Figure 12.8: C4 System Context B

We'll plot these using the following code:

```
@startuml
!include https://raw.githubusercontent.com/plantuml-stdlib/C4-PlantUML/master/C4_Context.puml
' uncomment the following line and comment the first to use locally
' !include C4_Context.puml

LAYOUT_WITH_LEGEND()

title System Context diagram for Data Platform

Person(SE, "Engineer", "A user that writes code to access data and process it.")
Person(Analyst, "Analyst", "A user who creates reports and Dashboards with data")
Person(App, "App", "A program such as a microservice or a BI-tool that accesses data.")

System(platform, "Data Platform", "Allows customers to view information about their bank accounts, and make payments.")
System_Ext(API, "Data Delivery Tool", "The internal Microsoft Exchange e-mail system.")


Rel_Back(SE, platform, "Consumes Data")
Rel_Back(Analyst, platform, "Consumes Data")
Rel_Back(App, platform, "Consumes Data")
```

```
Rel(API, platform, "Produces Data to")

@enduml
```

Now we have two useful groups of documents that could be the start of our technical documentation. I would also suggest documentation for the cloud setup, networking information, and use cases for your project. Lastly, it is important to outline the SLAs and who to contact for further information. We will discuss faking data for our project next.

Faking data with Mockaroo

Faking data is a very important topic for anyone working with data pipelines. You are not always able to use real data. This could be for many reasons, including legal and company policies. In fact, this has often been the case for me. Faking data can also be problematic because does the fake data fully resemble your real data? Probably not. I think for this purpose we are mimicking real data, so it's perfectly fine.

Mockaroo is a free hosted data service that can also be used to create simple REST APIs. Here, I created our three raw data schemas and then clicked on the button that says **CREATE API**.

Here, we are creating a schema for our `machine` API. We are using two **Number** and one **Binomial Distribution** column types. When done, you can click **CREATE API**.

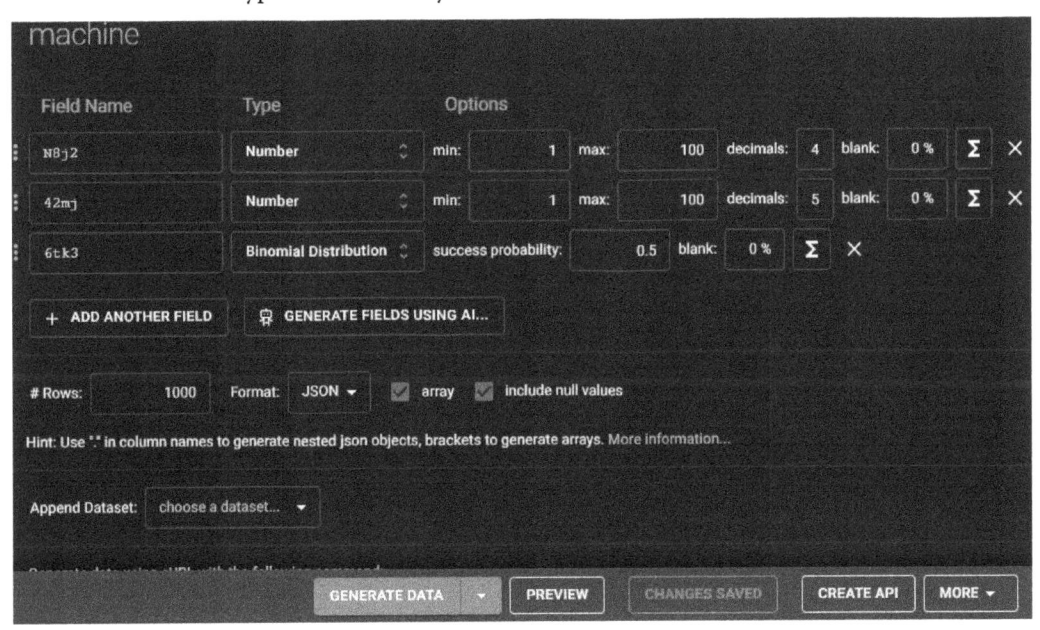

Figure 12.9: Mockaroo machine schema

266   Completing Our Project

Next, we are creating a schema for our `sales` API. We are using several columns, as outlined in the following figure. When done, you can click **CREATE API**.

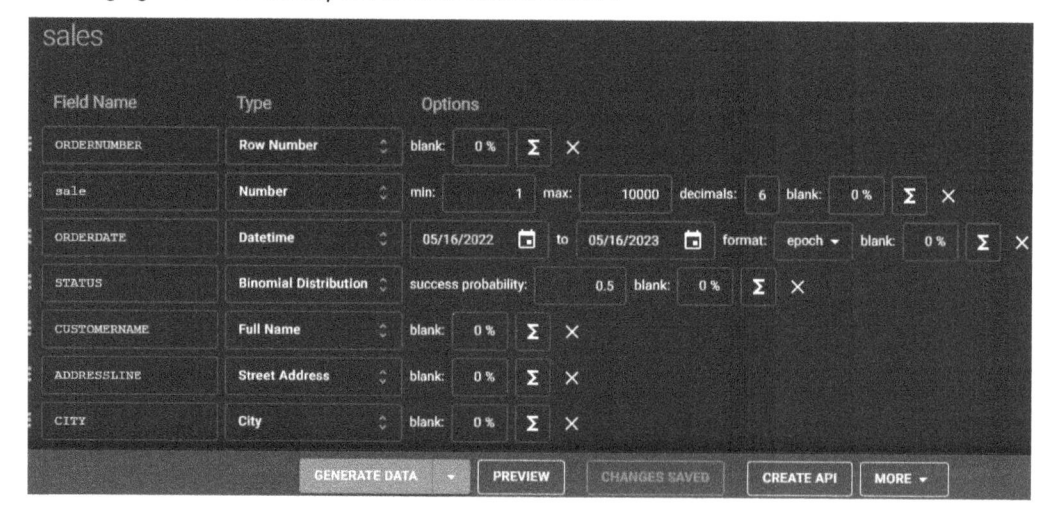

Figure 12.10: Mockaroo sales schema

Finally, we are creating a schema for our `SAP_BSEG` API. Our columns are much smaller than the previous schema. When done, you can click **CREATE API**.

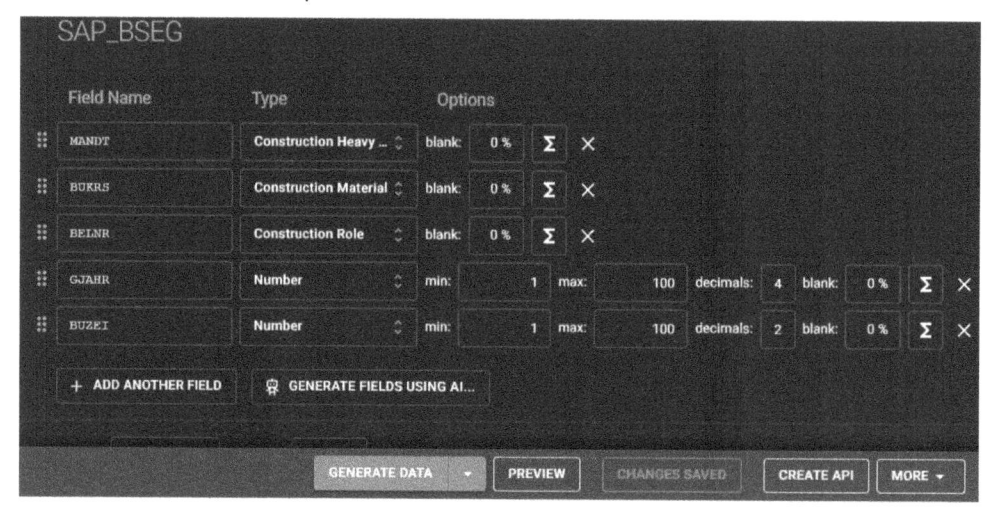

Figure 12.11: Mockaroo SAP schema

In each API, Mockaroo will give you a sample `curl` command to run:

    curl -H "X-API-Key: **xxxx**" https://my.api.mockaroo.com/sap_bseg.json

Take note of your key as the code connecting to the REST API will use it.

We now have usable REST APIs providing us with the fake data that we outlined. Next, we will dive into writing the code for managing our schemas.

Managing our schemas with code

Our schema app will manage setting up and updating any schema changes we have to Databricks. It's important to have a mechanism to manage schemas. Data swamps quickly form when the schema is not managed correctly. In this project, we are not referencing the schema app to have a central view of the schema. This might be a good idea for your project but creates the added overhead of dealing with package versioning.

In our configuration folder, we will keep data classes that define how we want our database and tables configured from a high level:

```
schema-jobs/schema_jobs/jobs/configuration/database_configuration.py
"""
fill in

"""
import abc
from dataclasses import dataclass


class DatabaseConfig(abc.ABC):
    """
    fill in

    """

    database_name = "dev"


@dataclass
class DatabaseConfiguration(DatabaseConfig):
    """
    fill in
    """

    database_name = "dev"
```

Like our database, we are defining our table configuration. Each table has a name, a database, and a schema function that produces the current schema:

schema-jobs/schema_jobs/jobs/configuration/table_configs.py

First, let's import the required libraries:

```
import abc
from dataclasses import dataclass

from schema_jobs.jobs.utility.schema.schemas import (
    bronze_machine_raw,
    bronze_sales,
    bronze_sap_bseg,
    gold_sales, silver_machine_raw,
)
```

Now, we are going to create base classes to work with. By creating a base class, we define what our table configuration will look like:

```
class TableConfig(abc.ABC):
    """
    fill in

    """

    table_name = ""
    database_name = ""
    schema = ""
```

We will now inherit from it and add some information to our table configuration. We do this for each table:

```
@dataclass
class TableConfigBronzeMachineRaw(TableConfig):
    """
    fill in

    """

    table_name = "bronze_machine_raw"
    database_name = "dev"
    schema = bronze_machine_raw()
```

```python
class TableConfigSilverMachineRaw(TableConfig):
    """
    fill in

    """

    table_name = "silver_machine_raw"
    database_name = "dev"
    schema = silver_machine_raw()
```

We will add two more Bronze table configurations:

```python
@dataclass
class TableConfigBronzSapBseg(TableConfig):
    """
    fill in

    """

    table_name = "bronze_sap_bseg"
    database_name = "dev"
    schema = bronze_sap_bseg()


@dataclass
class TableConfigBronzeSales(TableConfig):
    """
    fill in

    """

    table_name = "bronze_sales"
    database_name = "dev"
    schema = bronze_sales()
```

Completing Our Project

We now end with our Gold table and we add all the tables to a list for easy access:

```
@dataclass
class TableConfigGoldSales(TableConfig):
    """
    fill in

    """

    table_name = "gold_sales"
    database_name = "dev"
    schema = gold_sales()


tables = [
    TableConfigBronzeMachineRaw,
    TableConfigBronzSapBseg,
    TableConfigBronzeSales,
    TableConfigSilverMachineRaw,
    TableConfigGoldSales,
]
```

Here is the main function that will be run with our workflow. It will create the database and then create all tables currently defined:

```
schema-jobs/schema_jobs/jobs/deploy/deploy_database_tables.py
"""
fill in

"""

from schema_jobs.jobs.configuration.database_configuration import
DatabaseConfiguration
from schema_jobs.jobs.configuration.table_configs import tables
from schema_jobs.jobs.utility.schema.database import deploy_database
from schema_jobs.jobs.utility.schema.table import deploy_table


def deploy_database_tables():
    """
    fill in
    """
    spark = SparkSession \
        .builder \
```

```
        .appName("Schema App") \
        .getOrCreate()
    deploy_database(DatabaseConfiguration)
    for table in tables:
        deploy_table(table)


if __name__ == "__main__":
    deploy_database_tables()
```

Here, we have helper functions that build out some of our database objects:

```
schema-jobs/schema_jobs/jobs/utility/schema/database.py
"""
fill in
"""

from pyspark.sql import SparkSession
from schema_jobs.jobs.configuration.database_configuration import
DatabaseConfig


def deploy_database(config: DatabaseConfig):
    """
    fill in
    """
    SparkSession.getActiveSession()
    SparkSession.getActiveSession().sql(
        f"CREATE DATABASE IF NOT EXISTS {config.database_name};"
    )
```

One important file is the schema file, which will define all the functions that produce our schema:

```
schema-jobs/schema_jobs/jobs/utility/schema/schemas.py
"""
fill in
"""
```

Let's get all the required imports for our application:

```
from pyspark.sql.types import (
    BooleanType,
    BooleanType,
    DoubleType,
```

```
    IntegerType,
    StringType,
    StructField,
    StructType,
)
```

Now, we will define the schema for each table in code format to use later. We are using Spark Schema APIs, which will be shared across all of our pipeline applications and used to create our tables. The goal is to have a central place for schemas and not to repeat code in several places.

We will go through the Bronze tables first:

```
def bronze_machine_raw():
    """
    fill in
    """
    schema = StructType(
        [
            StructField("N8j2", DoubleType(), True),
            StructField("42mj", DoubleType(), True),
            StructField("6tk3", BooleanType(), True),
        ]
    )
    return schema
```

Now we will add the Silver tables:

```
def silver_machine_raw():
    """
    fill in
    """
    schema = StructType(
        [
            StructField("N8j2", DoubleType(), True),
            StructField("42mj", DoubleType(), True),
            StructField("6tk3", BooleanType(), True),
            StructField("engine_type", StringType(), True),
        ]
    )
    return schema
```

Here, we are adding the `bronze_sap_bseg` table. One thing to note is that we are allowing `Null` values, but this doesn't always need to be the case. In cases where you want a `Null` value to return an error when trying to use `insert`, change `True` to `False`:

```
def bronze_sap_bseg():
    """
    fill in
    """
    schema = StructType(
        [
            StructField("MANDT", StringType(), True),
            StructField("BUKRS", StringType(), True),
            StructField("BELNR", StringType(), True),
            StructField("GJAHR", DoubleType(), True),
            StructField("BUZEI", DoubleType(), True),
        ]
    )
    return schema


def bronze_sales():
    """
    fill in
    """
    schema = StructType(
        [
            StructField("ORDERNUMBER", IntegerType(), True),
            StructField("SALE", DoubleType(), True),
            StructField("ORDERDATE", StringType(), True),
            StructField("STATUS", BooleanType(), True),
            StructField("CUSTOMERNAME", StringType(), True),
            StructField("ADDRESSLINE", StringType(), True),
            StructField("CITY", StringType(), True),
            StructField("STATE", StringType(), True),
            StructField("STORE", StringType(), True),
        ]
    )
    return schema
```

Now, the final table (the Gold table) is completed. We didn't keep the tables in any order, which might not be the best approach. Also, we could have separated this code into smaller files organized by layers to make it easier to manage:

```
def gold_sales():
    """
    fill in
    """
    schema = StructType(
        [
            StructField("CUSTOMERNAME", StringType(), True),
            StructField("AVG", DoubleType(), True),
            StructField("TOTAL", DoubleType(), True),
        ]
    )
    return schema
```

Now that we are done with the schema application, we will start looking at our pipeline application.

Building our data pipeline application

We now have our ETL app. Configuring it is more complex than the schema app but basically works the same.

Here, we define our REST APIs; each API has a name that matches the table name and a URL:

```
etl-jobs/etl_jobs/configuration/api_raw_data/apis.py
"""
fill in
"""
```

We have a tiny `import` section but let's start here first:

```
import abc
from dataclasses import dataclass
```

Here we follow the same base configuration pattern. First, we create a base class and then we inherit that class, adding information. This pattern allows us to create uniformity and control the look of each class:

```
class restConfig(abc.ABC):
    """
    fill in
```

```
"""
name = ""
url = ""
```

We will now inherit from the base class and add information to our configuration:

```
@dataclass
class MachineRestConfiguration(restConfig):
    """
    fill in
    """
    name = "bronze_machine_raw"
    url = "https://my.api.mockaroo.com/machine.json"


class SalesRestConfiguration(restConfig):
    """
    fill in
    """
    name = "bronze_sales"
    url = "https://my.api.mockaroo.com/sales.json"


class BronzeSapBsegRestConfiguration(restConfig):
    """
    fill in
    """
    name = "bronze_sap_bseg"
    url = "https://my.api.mockaroo.com/sap_bseg.json"


Apis = [
    MachineRestConfiguration,
    BronzeSapBsegRestConfiguration,
    SalesRestConfiguration,
]
```

Next, we have the main function to run our ETL job. The function calls all the APIs and runs through extracting, transforming, and loading the new data:

```
etl-jobs/etl_jobs/jobs/extract/elt_data_api.py
"""
fill in

"""
from etl_jobs.configuration.api_raw_data.apis import Apis
from etl_jobs.util.extract.api import get_api_data
from etl_jobs.util.load.delta_spark import append_table, to_spark_data_frame
from etl_jobs.util.transform.gold_sales import transform_gold_sales
from etl_jobs.util.transform.polar_bear import transform_machine_bronze
```

Here we have a function that parses through our list of APIs, which comes from our previous imports. Then, it takes the data and transforms it using the predefined transformations we imported previously. Finally, we save the new table with the correct table name:

```
def etl_data_api():
    """
    fill in
    """
    spark = SparkSession \
        .builder \
        .appName("Schema App") \
        .getOrCreate()
    for api in Apis:
        raw = get_api_data(api.url, "XXXX")
        if api.name == "bronze_machine_raw":
            append_table(to_spark_data_frame(raw), "bronze_machine_raw", "dev")
            transformed = transform_machine_bronze(raw)
            append_table(to_spark_data_frame(transformed), "silver_machine_raw", "dev")
        if api.name == "bronze_sales":
            append_table(to_spark_data_frame(raw), "bronze_sales", "dev")
            transformed = transform_gold_sales(raw)
            append_table(to_spark_data_frame(transformed), "gold_sales", "dev")
        else:
```

```
            append_table(to_spark_data_frame(raw), api.name, "dev")


if __name__ == "__main__":
    etl_data_api()
```

In this function, we are calling our API and using the `polars` library to hold the data (`polars` is a Rust library that is very fast for non-cluster usage):

```
etl-jobs/etl_jobs/util/extract/api.py
"""
fill in
"""

import pandas as pd
import polars as pl
import requests


def get_api_data(url: str, key: str):
    """
    fill in
    :param url:
    :param key:
    :return:
    """
    headers = {"x-api-key": key}
    response = requests.get(url, headers=headers)
    json = response.json()
    return pl.from_pandas(pd.DataFrame(json))
```

Next in our Load process, we have a Spark function that takes a Spark dataframe and appends it to the given table:

```
etl-jobs/etl_jobs/util/load/delta_spark.py
"""
fill in
"""
from pyspark.sql import SparkSession
from pyspark.sql.types import BooleanType, IntegerType
from pyspark.sql.functions import col


def to_spark_data_frame(data_frame):
```

```
        pd_data_frame = data_frame.to_pandas()
        return SparkSession.getActiveSession().getActiveSession().
createDataFrame(pd_data_frame)


def append_table(data_frame, table_name, database_name):
    """
    fill in
    """
    if "machine_raw" in table_name:
        cast_data_frame = data_frame.withColumn("6tk3_new",
col("6tk3").cast(BooleanType())).drop(
            "6tk3").withColumnRenamed("6tk3_new", "6tk3")
        cast_data_frame.write.mode("append").format("delta").
saveAsTable(database_name + "." + table_name)
    elif "bronze_sales" in table_name:
        cast_data_frame = data_frame.withColumn("ORDERNUMBER_new",
col("ORDERNUMBER").cast(IntegerType())).drop(
            "ORDERNUMBER").withColumnRenamed("ORDERNUMBER_new",
"ORDERNUMBER").withColumn("STATUS_new",

                            col("STATUS").cast(

                                BooleanType())).drop(
            "STATUS").withColumnRenamed("STATUS_new", "STATUS")
        cast_data_frame.write.mode("append").format("delta").
saveAsTable(database_name + "." + table_name)
    else:
        data_frame.write.mode("append").format("delta").
saveAsTable(database_name + "." + table_name)
```

Our `sales` table needs some summary statistics, and we are creating them here with this function:

```
etl-jobs/etl_jobs/util/transform/gold_sales.py
"""
fill in
"""

from pyspark.sql.functions import avg, sum

from etl_jobs.util.load.delta_spark import to_spark_data_frame

def transform_gold_sales(data_frame):
    return to_spark_data_frame(data_frame).groupBy("CUSTOMERNAME").
agg(avg("SALE").alias("AVG"), sum("SALE").alias("TOTAL"))
```

To make things interesting, I added a transformation while extracting the machine data, using the `polars` library:

```
etl-jobs/etl_jobs/util/transform/polar_bear.py
"""
fill in
"""

import polars as pl

def transform_machine_bronze(data_frame: pl.dataframe):
    """
    fill in
    :param data_frame:
    :return:
    """
    return data_frame.with_columns(
        (
            (pl.col("N8j2").round(0) * pl.col("N8j2").round(0))
            .cast(pl.Int64)
            .cast(pl.Utf8)
            + "_"
            + pl.col("6tk3").cast(pl.Utf8)
        ).alias("engine_type")
    )
```

So, we have our pipeline application done, and it was a big one, I will say! Lots of useful code and a variety of ideas to try out. Polars is a new tool that many people are testing out to see whether it's useful. I suggest you give it a try on your next project. Next, we will look at our ML pipeline code.

Creating our machine learning application

Here is the main ML function. It will call functions to load data, create modeling data, and train our model:

```
ml-jobs/ml_jobs/jobs/build_sales_model.py
from ml_jobs.utils.data_prep.get_train_test_split import get_train_test_split
from ml_jobs.utils.extract.get_table import get_table
from ml_jobs.utils.management.setup_experiment import setup_experiment
from ml_jobs.utils.model.train_sales import train_sales


def build_sales_model():
```

Completing Our Project

```
    """
    fill in
    """
    spark = SparkSession \
        .builder \
        .appName("Schema App") \
        .getOrCreate()

    gold_sales = get_table("sales")
    model_data = get_train_test_split(gold_sales)
    experiment = setup_experiment("/Users/bclipp21@gmail.com/",
"chapter_12", "1.2")
    train_sales(model_data)


if __name__ == "__main__":
    build_sales_model()
```

Next, we have the function that handles creating our training and testing data. It will return a dictionary with all of our useful data:

```
ml-jobs/ml_jobs/utils/data_prep/get_train_test_split.py
"""
fill me in
"""
import pandas as pd
from sklearn.model_selection import train_test_split


def get_train_test_split(sales):
    """
    fill me in
    """
    pd_sales = pd.DataFrame(sales)
    y = pd_sales["AVG"]
    X = pd_sales.drop("AVG", axis=1)
    X_train, X_test, y_train, y_test = train_test_split(
        X, y, test_size=0.34, random_state=613
    )
    return {"X_train": X_train, "X_test": X_test, "y_train": y_train,
"y_test": y_test}
```

Here, I created a helper function that will return the needed dataframe form of a table:

```
ml-jobs/ml_jobs/utils/extract/get_table.py
"""
fill me in
"""

from pyspark.sql import SparkSession


def get_table(table_name):
    """
    fill me in
    """

    SparkSession.getActiveSession().read.table(table_name)
```

Our next module is a helper function that sets up everything for our experiment:

```
ml-jobs/ml_jobs/utils/management/setup_experiment.py
"""
fill me in
"""


def setup_experiment(base, name, version):
    """
    fill me in
    """
    experiment = mlflow.create_experiment(
        f"{base}/{name}/experiments/", tags={"version": "1.0", "env": "DEV"}
    )
    model_path = f"{base}/{name}/experiments/model"
```

Lastly, we have a module that will train our new model for us and log everything in `mlflow`:

```
ml-jobs/ml_jobs/utils/model/train_sales.py
"""
fill me in
"""
import mlflow
import numpy as np
from sklearn import metrics
from sklearn.ensemble import RandomForestRegressor
```

```python
def train_sales(model_data, experiment, model_path):
    """
    fill me in
    """

    max_depth = 2
    n_estimators = 100
    with mlflow.start_run(experiment_id=experiment):
        rf = RandomForestRegressor(
            max_depth=max_depth, n_estimators=n_estimators, random_state=0
        )
        rf.fit(model_data["X_train"], model_data["y_train"])
        y_pred = rf.predict(model_data["X_test"])
        rmse = np.sqrt(
            metrics.mean_squared_error(model_data["y_test"], model_data["y_pred"])
        )
        mlflow.log_param("max_depth", max_depth)
        mlflow.log_param("n_estimators", n_estimators)
        mlflow.log_metric("rmse", rmse)
        mlflow.sklearn.log_model(rf, "model")
        mlflow.sklearn.save_model(rf, model_path)
```

We now have a working code that produces an ML model, which is our main goal. You can fine-tune that model as needed to get whatever use case you have working. Whatever algorithm or hyperparameters aside, this should be the first step you take normally. Let's build some dashboards to better understand our data.

Displaying our data with dashboards

There are many ways to create dashboards; more often than not, I find simple notebooks with useful metrics are the more common dashboards. Here, I created a SQL-only notebook, which looks at the Gold sales table and creates a scatter plot of the data. This could be scheduled to update at any cadence needed using the `schedule` option at the top left.

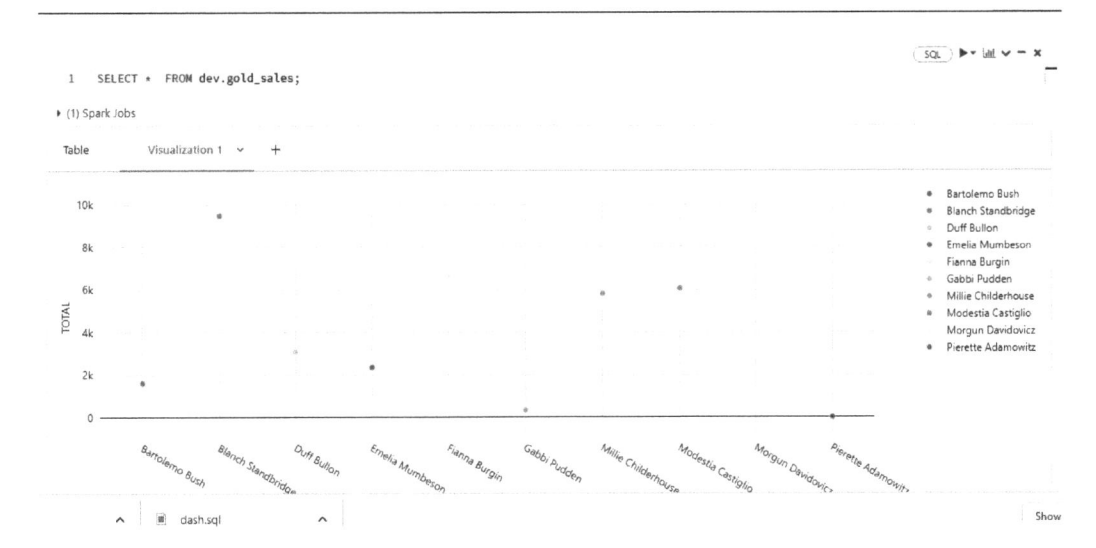

Figure 12.12: Databricks chart 1

Next, we will run a SQL command to do a count of failed engine data and passed engine data. Simple queries such as these are very common in dashboard notebooks.

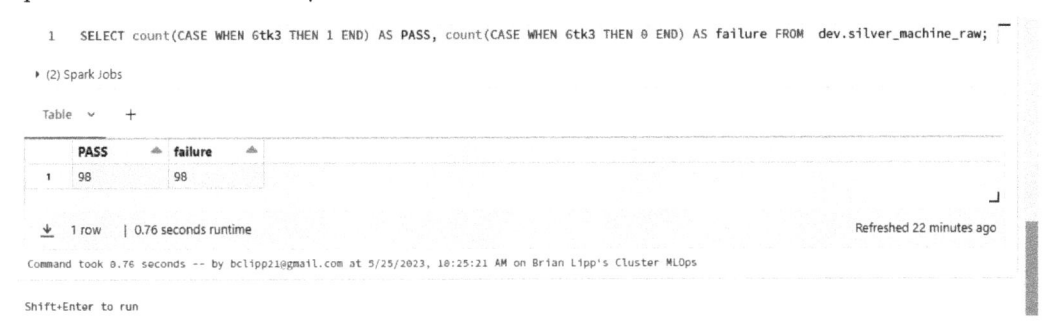

Figure 12.13: Databricks chart 2

Summary

So, here we are at the end of our project and data platform architecture journey. We covered topics including Spark, Delta Lake, Lambda architecture, Kafka, and MLOps. We also looked at how to build pipelines, package those pipelines, and deploy them centrally. Also, we delved into governance and platform design. This chapter and *Chapter 11* built the initial beginnings of production-ready data pipelines. These pipelines can be used as the foundation of your data platform.

It's my hope that you can take this project as a starting point for your next data platform project and build off it. I have presented many ideas and kernels of best practices. It's up to you to continue the journey in your own projects. It doesn't matter whether you choose the same tools or replace them with other tools that you prefer, the fundamental ideas should stay the same.

Index

A

access
  setting up, from Databricks to DBT Cloud 159-161
Adaptive Query Engine (AQE) 50
alerts 152
analytics layer 9
Apache Spark 48
  architecture 48
  broadcasting 51
  caching 50
  components 48, 49
  interacting, with Kafka 106, 107
  job creation pipeline 51, 52
  partitions, shuffling 49
  partitions, working with 49
  practical exercises 62-65
  working environment, setting up 45
atomicity, consistency, isolation, duration (ACID) 4
Autoloader 199
  streaming DataFrame, creating 199
Autoloader, ways to detect new files
  directory listing mode 200
  file notification mode 200

AutoML 124
  reference link 124
Avro format 7
AWS account 68
  setting up 88, 217

B

bagging 123
bar charts 140-142
basic client setup
  for REST endpoint 207
batch processing 69
  data, reading 71
  data skew 70, 71
  in stream 80
  partitioning 70
batch request 224
batch stream hybrid 80
BI tools
  connecting 154-157
bloom filter 62
  using 62
boosting 124
bootstrap aggregation 123
broadcasting 51

brokers 93
bubble charts 141, 144
business intelligence (BI) 9

C

C4 System Context diagram 263-265
caching 50
   memory only 50
   memory-only sterilized 50
   memory with two other nodes 50
change data capture (CDC) 60
change data feed (CFD) 60
checkpoint
   creating 225, 226
CI tooling 176
   Git 176, 177
   GitHub 176, 177
   pre-commit 177, 178
cloud data storage 47
   NoSQL 47
   object storage 47
   relational data storage 47
Cluster API 207
code
   schemas, managing with 267-274
   testing 180
comma-separated values (CSV) files 6
Confluent Kafka 89
   reference link 89
   signing up 89-91
Confluent Schema Registry 96-101
consumer 95, 96
consumption layer 9
create, read, update, delete (CRUD) 4, 92
cross-validation 121
   performing 121-123

D

dashboards
   creating, to handle factory errors 161-165
   data, displaying with 282
data
   cleaning and preparing 23
   displaying with dashboards 282
   practical lab 40
   problem data, loading 40
   problem data, solution 41
   testing 226
databases 4
Databricks 68, 168, 198
   setting up 88, 217
Databricks API 207
Databricks CLI 68, 88, 168, 169, 198, 218, 240
Databricks Filesystem (DBFS) 190
Databricks notebook logs 208, 209
Databricks notebooks, tips and tricks
   filesystem magic 148
   language magic 148
   magic 147
   Markdown 147
   running, other notebooks 148
   terminal 148
   Widgets 148
Databricks secrets 211
Databricks SQL analytics 149
   accessing 149
   alerts 152
   dashboard 152
   queries 151
   query history 153
   SQL editor 150, 151
   SQL warehouse 149, 150

Databricks Unity 227, 228
  Delta Sharing 230
  metastore, creating 229
Databricks Workflows 202-206
  failed runs 206
  in Terraform 206
data catalog 219, 220
  batch request 224
  checkpoint, creating 225
  data context 223
  Data Doc 226
  data lineage 220
  data quality 221
  data security and privacy 221
  data source 223
  data, testing 226
  Great Expectations 222
  profiler 227
  suite, saving 225
  test data, creating 222
  tests, adding 225
  validator 224
data documentation 32
  data lineage graphs 33-35
  diagrams library 32, 33
data faking 265
  with Mockaroo 265-267
data governance 219
data governance layer 9
data lake 4, 5
data mesh
  principles 18
  terms, defining 18
  theory and practice 16, 17
data mesh, principles
  data, as product 18
  data governance 19

  data is available 19
  data ownership 18
data modeling patterns 35
  relational modeling 35-38
data pipeline application
  building 274-279
data platform architecture, at high level 8, 9
  analytics layer 9
  consumption layer 9
  data governance layer 9
  ingestion layer 9
  processing layer 9
  semantic view 10
  serving layer 9
  storage layer 9
data processing
  column names, fixing 29
  columns, casting 28
  complex data types 29-32
  duplicate values 23, 24
  outlier identification 27
  RegEx, using 26, 27
  working, with nulls 24-26
data security and privacy 221
data skew 70, 71
data standards 219
data types, ML
  qualitative data 120
  quantitative data 120
data visualization
  data, validating 140
  principles 139
  user, understanding 139
data visualization, with notebooks 140
  bar charts 140, 142
  bubble charts 141, 144
  GUI data visualizations 145-147
  histograms 140, 144

288 Index

line charts 140
  multiple line chart 142
  pie charts 140
  scatter plots 140, 143
  single line chart 141
data warehouses 4
data workloads
  orchestrating 199
dbx 179
  commands 179, 180
  used, for creating pipeline 190-195
DBX CLI 169, 199
Delta architecture 14, 15
Delta Lake 52
  current database, setting 54
  default location database 53
  helper database utilities 54
  specified location database 54
  tables, grouping with databases 53
  transaction log 52
Delta Lake table 54
  change data feed (CFD) 60
  cloning 59, 60
  data, deleting 58
  data, updating 58
  example 55
  files, managing 61
  managed table 55, 56
  merging 58, 59
  reading 57
  schema, updating 57
  time travel 60
  unmanaged table 56
Delta Sharing 230
Delta streaming 80
Delta tables
  incremental new changes, handling 200

dimensional modeling 38
  key terms, using 38, 39
directed acyclic graph (DAG) 52
directory listing mode 200
Docker 169
  commands 173
Docker Desktop
  installation link 169
documentation
  C4 System Context diagram 263-265
  schema diagram 260-263

E

environment
  Python, installing 22
  setting up 22
  workflow initialization 22
events 92
event stores 6
Extract, Transform, and Load (ETL) 38

F

fake data
  creating 81
  creating, problem 81
  creating, with Python 81
  problems, solutions 82-84
fake data, with Python
  folders, setting up 81
feature engineering 120
feature store 127, 128
file formats 6
  Avro format 7
  CSV file 6
  JSON 6
  Parquet 8

Index

file notification mode 200
filesystem magic 148

G

Git 170, 176, 177, 240
  download link 170
GitHub 170, 171, 176, 177, 241
  authentication 241
  authorization 241
GitHub CLI
  repo, creating with 242
GitHub repos
  creating 246, 247
Graphviz
  installing 22
Great Expectations 222
group
  creating 231-236
GUI data visualizations 145-147

H

histograms 140, 144
Hyperopt 129, 130
hyperparameters 123
  example 123
  model, training 123

I

Infrastructure as Code (IaC) 167
ingestion layer 9
integration test 181

J

JavaScript Object Notation (JSON) format 6
Jenkins 183
  console 174
  plugins, customizing 175
  user, creating 175
  working with 175
Jenkinsfile 184-186
job creation pipeline 51
  analyzed logical plan 51
  analyzed logical plan, with cache 51
  optimized logical plan 52
  selected physical plan 52
  Spark plan 52
  unresolved logic plan 51
Jobs API 207

K

Kafka 87, 91
  Spark, interacting with 106, 107
Kafka and Spark
  integrating, to build Delta tables 107-114
Kafka architecture
  brokers 93
  consumer 95, 96
  partitions 92
  producers 93-95
  topics 92
Kafka Connect 101-106
Kappa architecture 11, 12
  versus Lambda architecture 10

L

lakehouse 13
lakehouse, seven central tenets 13
   ACID transactions 14
   data diversity 13
   language-agnostic 13
   openness principle 13
   processing diversity 13
   storage and compute, decoupling 14
   workflow diversity 13
Lambda architecture 10, 11
   versus Kappa architecture 10
language magic 148
line charts 140
Log4j 210
logging 208, 211
   code 209, 210
log mixin
   using 210

M

machine learning 119
   cross-validation 121-123
   data 119
   data, fitting 121
   data, splitting up 120, 121
   data types 120
machine learning application
   creating 279-282
magic 147
Markdown 147
medallion data pattern 15
   bronze data 15
   gold data 16
   silver data 15
mixins 210

MLflow 125
   features 125-127
   feature store 127
MLflow project
   creating 132-134
MLOps 117
   benefits 125
   practical lab 130, 131
   working environment, setting up 117
Mockaroo 265
   data, faking with 265-267
   URL 130
multiple line chart 142

N

NoSQL 47
   data models and technologies 37, 38
notebooks
   running, in makeshift chain 148

O

object storage 47
offset 92
One Big Table (OBT) approach 40
online analytical processing (OLAP) 4
online transaction processing (OLTP) 4

P

parameters 123
Parquet format 8
partitions 49, 92
   shuffling 49
   working with 49
personal access token (PAT) 170, 240
pie charts 140

Poetry 251
practical lab 211
  Lambda code 212
  Notebook code 213
  problem data, loading 158, 159
  solution 211
pre-commit 172, 177, 178, 243
processing layer 9
producer 93-95
profiler 227
pull request 176
PyPI 244
  token setup 245
Python 68
  installing 22
  packages 178, 179
  setting up 88, 217
  used, for creating fake data 81
Python wheels
  building 178

Q

qualitative data 120
quantitative data 120
queries 151
query history 153

R

relational database management
    systems (RDBMSs) 4
relational data storage 47
relational modeling 35
resilient distributed dataset (RDD) 49
REST APIs 207

S

scatter plots 140, 143
schema diagram 260-263
schema evolution 201
  supported modes 201
schemas
  managing, with code 267-274
secrets management 211
semantic view 10
serving layer 9
shuffling 49
single line chart 141
software development life cycle 176
Spark schemas 72, 73
  decisions, making 74
  unwanted columns, removing 74
  working, with data in groups 74, 75
Spark Streaming 199
SQL editor 150, 151
SQL warehouses 149, 150
stacking 124
storage layer 9
streaming DataFrame
  creating, with Autoloader 199
stream processing 77
  batch processing in 80
  batch stream hybrid 80
  debugging 79
  Delta streaming 80
  reading, from disk 78
  transformations 78
  writing, to disk 79
suite
  saving 225

T

terminal 148
Terraform 172, 173, 181, 206, 243
  CLI, commands 182
  HCL 182, 183
  IaC 181
  installation link 172
  repo, creating 186-190
  using, to create cluster 186-190
Terraform CLI
  token setup 243
  URL 243
Terraform Cloud account
  URL 172, 243
Terraform setup
  infrastructure repository 252-257
  initial file setup 247
  ML repository 249-251
  schema repository 247, 248
test data
  creating 222
tests
  adding 225
Token API 207
topics 92

U

unit test 180
user
  creating 231-236
User Defined Function (UDF) 75-77

V

validator 224
virtual environment
  setting up 22

W

Widgets 148
working environment, Apache Spark
  AWS setup 46
  Databricks CLI, installing 46
  Python setup 45, 46
working environment, MLOps
  AWS setup 118
  Databricks CLI, installing 118
  Python setup 118
  setting up 117

Y

YAML 223

Z

Z-ordering 62
  bloom filter, using 62
  speed, adding 62

⟨packt⟩

Packtpub.com

Subscribe to our online digital library for full access to over 7,000 books and videos, as well as industry leading tools to help you plan your personal development and advance your career. For more information, please visit our website.

Why subscribe?

- Spend less time learning and more time coding with practical eBooks and Videos from over 4,000 industry professionals
- Improve your learning with Skill Plans built especially for you
- Get a free eBook or video every month
- Fully searchable for easy access to vital information
- Copy and paste, print, and bookmark content

Did you know that Packt offers eBook versions of every book published, with PDF and ePub files available? You can upgrade to the eBook version at Packtpub.com and as a print book customer, you are entitled to a discount on the eBook copy. Get in touch with us at customercare@packtpub.com for more details.

At www.packtpub.com, you can also read a collection of free technical articles, sign up for a range of free newsletters, and receive exclusive discounts and offers on Packt books and eBooks.

Other Books You May Enjoy

If you enjoyed this book, you may be interested in these other books by Packt:

Hands-On Graph Neural Networks Using Python

Maxime Labonne

ISBN: 978-1-80461-752-6

- Understand the fundamental concepts of graph neural networks
- Implement graph neural networks using Python and PyTorch Geometric
- Classify nodes, graphs, and edges using millions of samples
- Predict and generate realistic graph topologies
- Combine heterogeneous sources to improve performance
- Forecast future events using topological information
- Apply graph neural networks to solve real-world problems

Data Engineering with Python

Paul Crickard

ISBN: 978-1-83921-418-9

- Understand how data engineering supports data science workflows
- Discover how to extract data from files and databases and then clean, transform, and enrich it
- Configure processors for handling different file formats as well as both relational and NoSQL databases
- Find out how to implement a data pipeline and dashboard to visualize results
- Use staging and validation to check data before landing in the warehouse
- Build real-time pipelines with staging areas that perform validation and handle failures
- Get to grips with deploying pipelines in the production environment

Packt is searching for authors like you

If you're interested in becoming an author for Packt, please visit `authors.packtpub.com` and apply today. We have worked with thousands of developers and tech professionals, just like you, to help them share their insight with the global tech community. You can make a general application, apply for a specific hot topic that we are recruiting an author for, or submit your own idea.

Share Your Thoughts

Now you've finished *Modern Data Architectures with Python*, we'd love to hear your thoughts! Scan the QR code below to go straight to the Amazon review page for this book and share your feedback or leave a review on the site that you purchased it from.

`https://packt.link/r/1-801-07049-0`

Your review is important to us and the tech community and will help us make sure we're delivering excellent quality content.

Download a free PDF copy of this book

Thanks for purchasing this book!

Do you like to read on the go but are unable to carry your print books everywhere?

Is your eBook purchase not compatible with the device of your choice?

Don't worry, now with every Packt book you get a DRM-free PDF version of that book at no cost.

Read anywhere, any place, on any device. Search, copy, and paste code from your favorite technical books directly into your application.

The perks don't stop there, you can get exclusive access to discounts, newsletters, and great free content in your inbox daily

Follow these simple steps to get the benefits:

1. Scan the QR code or visit the link below

   https://packt.link/free-ebook/9781801070492

2. Submit your proof of purchase
3. That's it! We'll send your free PDF and other benefits to your email directly

www.ingramcontent.com/pod-product-compliance
Ingram Content Group UK Ltd.
Pitfield, Milton Keynes, MK11 3LW, UK
UKHW051447030325
4835UKWH00037B/530

9 781801 070492